*Ex Libris
Jack Keilty*

CHARLES I

To Francis,
in gratitude for his generous support.

CHARLES I

by

Hilaire Belloc

"I came, I saw, God conquered." —KING JOHN III, 1683

Norfolk, VA
2003

Charles I.

Copyright © 2003 IHS Press.

Charles I copyright the Estate of Hilaire Belloc.

Preface, typesetting, layout, and cover design
copyright IHS Press.
All rights reserved.

Charles I was originally published in Philadelphia and London by J.B. Lippincott Co., in 1933. The present edition is based upon the third edition of the work, published in 1936 by Cassell and Co., Ltd., of London. The spelling, punctuation, and formatting of the Cassell edition of 1936 have been largely preserved. Minor corrections to the text have been made in light of earlier editions.

ISBN: 0-9718286-3-6

Library of Congress Cataloging-in-Publication Data

Belloc, Hilaire, 1870-1953.
  [Charles the First, King of England]
  Charles I / Hilaire Belloc.
     p. cm.
Originally published: Charles the First, King of England. London : Cassell, 1933.
  ISBN 0-9718286-3-6 (alk. paper)
  1. Charles I, King of England, 1600-1649. 2. Great Britain--History--Charles I, 1625-1649. 3. Great Britain--Kings and rulers--Biography. I. Title.
  DA396.A2B4 2003
  942.06'2'092--dc21

                                                  2003009211

Printed in the United States of America.

Gates of Vienna Books is an imprint of IHS Press.
For more information, write to:

Gates of Vienna Books
222 W. 21st St., Suite F-122
Norfolk, VA 23517

TABLE OF CONTENTS

	PAGE
FOREWORD..7	
by Dr. Clyde Wilson	
INTRODUCTION..11	
by Michael Hennessy	

CHARLES I

THE PROBLEM..23	
THE CIRCUMSTANCE..27	
STUART..52	
THE FORMATIVE YEARS...63	
BUCKINGHAM	
I. THE SPANISH MATCH...77	
II. THE ATTACK BEGINS..91	
III. THE BLOW..107	
MATURITY..123	
SCOTLAND..144	
THE EFFORT FOR UNITY	
I. THE CENTRAL EFFORT...153	
II. THE EFFORT IN THE CHURCH..................................164	
III. THE EFFORT IN IRELAND.....................................168	
IV. THE ABORTIVE EFFORT IN SCOTLAND....................174	
THE MENACE..177	
THE CRISIS..194	
THE GREAT REBELLION..216	
THE TRIUMPH OF THE GREAT REBELLION.........234	
THE HOSTAGE	
I. HOSTAGE OF THE SCOTCH......................................246	
II. HOSTAGE OF THE PARLIAMENT.............................250	
THE KILLING OF THE KING...270	

Charles I, King of England
An oil painting after Van Dyck, 1636

FOREWORD

WARNING. Belloc's writings are highly addictive. Fortunately, the craving they create can be readily satisfied. He wrote so much and so well that the supply never runs out, and the best of his works can be reread endlessly.

Belloc was one of the very best writers of nonfiction English prose in the twentieth century, which is simply another way of saying that he had a virile, independent mind which expressed itself – archaically – through the written word.

I like Belloc most when he is retelling, in inimitable fashion, his own experiences, as in *Hills and the Sea, The Cruise of the "Nona," The Four Men,* or *The Path to Rome*. His verse, which I suppose would be classified by the misleading label "light," is always a delight:

> When I am dead, I hope it may be said
> His sins were scarlet, but his books were read.

Belloc was also one of the few courageous souls who was able to view his own times without the facile optimism that characterizes most contemporary thinkers, especially in the English-speaking world. In *The Servile State* (1912) and many other works, he warned that vaunted modern "progress" was undermining the Western spirit and conditions of freedom, and leading the masses of us back into serfdom. Not much has happened since to contradict his foreboding.

The West that Belloc admired was not the West of great cities, immense accumulations of capital, ignorant and hysterical mass media, and "democratic" politicians with oil on the tongue and both hands in the till. It was rather the once (and future?) West of a gentry and yeomanry free and independent in mind and property, presided over by personally responsible rulers and informed by the true Faith. In this respect he and his few but dauntless comrades-in-arms found allies in the Southern Agrarians and a few other thinkers on the western side of the great water.

Given this view of the world, Belloc's numerous biographies and histories are guaranteed to irritate pedants, positivists, Whigs, and other enemies of the human race. The fact that Belloc can think, write lucid narrative, portray historical personalities convincingly, and reach conclusions that have not been pre-digested by others opens an immense gap between his histories and the writings of the great bulk of bureaucratized, "professional" historians that flourished in his time and since.

Historical writing for more than a century has been dominated by Whigs. People who assume that the history of mankind is a tale of "progress." The latest point in time is the highest and best point in time, and all has been tending toward this, our moment. Such has been the implicit assumption of our times, even on the part of those who were not aware that such an assumption controlled their thinking. Such mindsets have made history very dull by removing from it the drama of contingency and human choice. In Whig history, Evil is no longer a permanent force in the world, and human nature does not remain the same in all times. Rather, enlightened policies and proper education will eradicate evils and mould the plastic human world into proper shape. One would think that the twentieth century would have disabused even the most sanguine publicists of the Whig philosophy of history, but not so. The most rabid of its current practitioners are even proclaiming "the end of history" in a perfected world of "democratic capitalism."

In Belloc's own time and place, the Whig philosophy carried specific implications: Protestantism is better than Catholicism; capitalism is better than what went before; "science" is better than "superstition." Proponents of this historical trajectory usually believed, though they did not always avow, that what was inevitably to come, socialism and "rationalism," would be even better.

In such an intellectual milieu Belloc wrote very iconoclastic history. His biographies concentrate in the late-Middle-Ages and Reformation eras of the European past. This was the germinating time for Whiggery, and Belloc portrays the downsides of "progress" powerfully. Today, for those of us occupationally doomed to function as

FOREWORD

historians, dipping into Belloc's biographies is like a refreshing swim after a long, hot day plowing through desert sand. Here is real grappling with important human experience, instead of what flourishes today – largely a weird combination of deterministic "social science" and uncritical, romantic endorsement of favored causes.

In his life of *Charles I*, Belloc comments that the duty of a historian is to help us understand ourselves and our situation, and that the true method of the historian calls for examination of Circumstance and Character. If that be so, Belloc does his duty in the highest degree.

                              Dr. Clyde Wilson
                              University of South Carolina
                              August 14, 2003
                              Feast of St. Eusebius

Charles I, Henrietta Maria, and Two Children
FROM AN ENGRAVING AFTER VAN DYCK CA. 1632

INTRODUCTION

"THE only institution ever devised by men for mastering the Money Power in the State is monarchy." Belloc? Not quite. But the statement is one with which the older Belloc was in substantial agreement. The comment belongs to Napoleon, and in 1932, the year before Belloc wrote *Charles I*, his book of the same name was published. It is therefore perhaps not surprising that Belloc's study of Charles I is an amplification of this idea. For his book on the first Charles is, amongst other things, a study of the attempt by the monarchy in England to oppose the Money Power: it was the failure of this attempt which led to the temporary extinction and permanent emasculation of the British Crown. This was a disaster from which not even the energies of Charles II and James II could rescue it; and the principal factor in this collapse was the supremacy of the Rich and the accompanying privatisation of power.

In 1933, Belloc, a man of 63, was still in full flood as an author. In 1927, an American publisher asked him to write a book on Cardinal Richelieu; Belloc consented on the condition that he could first write a book on James II, a monarch whose character and fate had always held a fascination for him. *James the Second* was famously written over ten days in the Saharan foothills, and published in 1928. Belloc had a fascination with Monarchy – and a fascination with the challenges it encountered following the break-up of Christendom. It seemed to him inevitable that once the unity in Faith of the nations of Europe had broken down, then within these nations unity would again be threatened.

Robert Speaight, in his biography of Belloc, argues that his immersion in history during the mid-1920s and throughout the 1930s converted him from Republicanism to Monarchy. This is an unfortunate simplification, not just of Belloc's ideas but of the supposed contradictions between those two concepts. No doubt Belloc imbibed deeply of republicanism as a young man. It was perhaps inevitable, given both his French nationality – he was not naturalized as British until 1902 – and the enormous influence on him of his time with the French artillery, that he recognise the comparative decrepitude of the French monarchy. And he did carry his admiration of Danton to the grave with him.

On the other hand, Belloc emerged much wiser from the wilderness of his parliamentary years, into which his youthful political idealism had led him. That parliamentary experience, fermented under the influences of Cecil Chesterton and Father Vincent McNabb, resulted in some of his greatest works: *The Servile State*, *The Party System*, and *The House of Commons and Monarchy*. And even as a youthful republican he had venerated the memory of Napoleon, a memory undamaged by that great general's imperial pretension.

It is therefore difficult to read any of Belloc's later works that touch upon the struggle between Monarchy and Parliament and not smell the sulphurous anger of the author at some point. Belloc knew what Parliament was and he loathed it. He knew that for a monarchy to be a good government it required that one man be good; he knew that for a democracy to be a good government it required a massive majority of parliamentarians to be good; and he knew that electioneering and the stranglehold of the political parties made this a practical impossibility.

Before discussing Belloc's *Charles I* in some detail, it may be sensible to touch upon his "mixed" reputation as an historian. Belloc certainly had the intellectual apparatus to write what even moderns would currently accept as competent and accurate history. A first class Honours degree from Oxford University was not given for oratorical abilities or prose skills alone. The fact that Belloc often did write what moderns would not accept as competent or accurate history is something that redounds to the discredit of the moderns, not of Belloc. His sights were set very much higher, and there can be no doubt that Belloc was one of the greatest animators of the historical past in the English language. Macaulay could write beautifully – but Belloc could write just as well, and most historians, even modern ones, would have to concede that Belloc was in general terms more accurate.

The truth is that historians are wary of Belloc. Many easily disparage him; a good number airily admit his talents but would not

INTRODUCTION

admit him to the reading list for their students; few will risk praise. Guedella, a historian who preceded Belloc by about a generation and who remains of good standing even today, actually sought Belloc's advice and research skills on occasion; and Norman Stone said in a comparatively recent newspaper interview that "in the end, I shall go to Trevelyan's enemies, Hilaire Belloc and Lord Acton, both Catholics, for an understanding of modern England." No doubt, on a purely academic level, even his greatest advocates would advise some caution. On the verge of my departure to Oxford to read Modern History I was warned off him by one tutor, only to find him on the reading list of another: "Read him first," I was told approvingly. "He is largely right in his conclusions, somewhat over-selective in his facts; most of what you will then read thereafter you will find happily fits into his analysis, which is as it should be, because, as I said, he is indeed largely right."

The reasons for Belloc's uncertain reputation are these: he (they say) wrote history as propaganda, history that reflected his own desire to exalt Catholicism; he (they say) made many simple and glaring errors in his books and was lackadaisical about correcting them in subsequent editions; he (they say) did not reference his sources and therefore *a priori* has to be treated as untrustworthy.

Firstly, it has to be understood that no history is objective or unbiased. The golden ideal – as some moderns would have it – of "perfect history" is unattainable by man. It is impossible for any historian not to be *selective* in his facts and evidence. All historians attempt to reach conclusions, and in so doing can logically be accused of bias and selectivity in the attempt.

Secondly, Belloc acknowledged his inability to get every fact right all the time, and remarked frequently upon other historians' failure ever to get anything fundamentally right. Quite how so many "more accurate" historians could count every single tree and list them by species and size and *never see the wood* was something that often caused Belloc great mirth. Belloc was often slapdash – except with regard to his "set-pieces," rarely checked his facts once written down, and almost never checked his publishers' galley proofs. In writing his study of James II, he relied upon a small book of notes and his voluminous but not infallible memory. What was remarkable about Belloc was the fact that any errors he committed in no way impaired his ability to discern the Truth, or seriously undermined the strength of his conclusions.

Thirdly, Belloc *loathed* the systematic and frequent use of footnotes. The prime cause of this loathing was Edward Gibbon who, in his *Decline and Fall of the Roman Empire*, showed rare mastery of the black art of deceitful footnoting. Belloc's loathing was also a reaction against the growing paralysis hindering historical writing, with historians often writing only for other historians and consequently keen to devote to each line of their text at least six lines of self-important footnotes. He believed most footnotes to be unnecessary; frequently, they only referenced other secondary sources which themselves then did likewise. Often, when followed up, the source referred to was found to contradict the text, or to be entirely without relevance.

Belloc understood the importance of the primary sources more than most of today's historians. Indeed he was, more than other historians, forced to rely upon the original evidence since so much of the historical commentary that had been written in English was Whig, Protestant bunk. Thus is Belloc also a deliberately and strenuously didactic historian. This is a great heresy these days, and is an even greater heresy on account of what Belloc was being didactic about. In our universities, history is now written as a bare, turgid stream of data capped with a pleading codicil from the author that the facts are so complicated that he can see no pattern but the hope remains that some pattern may be discerned in the future. When opinion surfaces at all, it is tentatively held and robustly restrained from being presented as fact. Belloc's history was certain, decisive, trenchant – the very qualities that weak-willed prevaricators loathe in the Faith.

For this reason there is a touch of peculiar hybridity about Belloc's biographical studies. In each case Belloc was interested in the *person*, and was often sympathetic, across religious boundaries, to at least some parts of his subject; but that subject was also a tool for facilitating an exposition of the political, economic, cultural, and theological facts that were the all-embracing context for the life of that subject. Belloc is recording his understanding of history by means of these subjects, whose lives have in fact helped him develop this understanding. So in these biographical studies, we often get a great deal of incisive preliminary contextualization – and then we

INTRODUCTION

get psychological study, biographical detail, and Belloc's justly famous "set-pieces." For Belloc, History must serve Truth, for all history was the record of conflict of one kind or another, and all conflict was ultimately theological, residing within the frame of the great truths of the Faith.

It would be unwise to minimize the importance to Belloc's historical works of their "set-pieces." The accompanying analysis was invaluable, of course, but Belloc knew that true history has to raise the dead no less than to tell the Truth. Belloc had this in common with Michelet and Macaulay – that he could breathe life into the past. Belloc's *The Eye Witness* and his *Miniatures of French History* consist wholly of short "set-pieces." All of his biographical studies carry at least one "set-piece" worthy of immortality; in *Charles I*, the trial and execution of the King of course dominate the text, but more minor episodes, such as the attempted relief of La Rochelle, also seize the imagination. Belloc takes great care over these vignettes: the narrative pace slows, analysis gives way to description, the whole vocabulary and syntax shifts, and before our eyes, in painstaking accuracy, a great event is summoned up. Belloc knew that in the accurate invocation of the past lay as much Truth as in analysis; and, curiously, his ability to summon up the past belies to some extent the sceptic in him. He felt this history as he felt his Faith.

***

It is for a good reason that this book on Charles Stuart opens with a chapter entitled "The Problem." Nor is this unconnected to the fact that Belloc progressed no further than 1612 in his multi-volume *History of England*. The welter of biographical studies that issued from his pen around the time of the publication of the last volume of this *History*, and those which followed, cover a variety of periods and countries, but most are of English figures and most deal with "The Problem" as it developed up to 1612 or as it approached its *denouement* thereafter.

What is "The Problem"? Belloc puts it thus: "How and why did the English kingship so fail in the person of its last possessor, Charles Stuart?" More generally Belloc saw it as why the full power of the

CHARLES I

monarchy decreased over the years following the Reformation until it was extinguished on a cold January afternoon in 1649, when Charles Stuart lost his head. Thereafter a King was a king not "by the grace of God" but thanks to Parliament. The nature of this problem was not unique to England; a similar problem afflicted France, and Belloc's later studies of Louis XIV and Richelieu were attempts to manifest the differences between the English and French problems, and to explain why France's course was different. The French Revolution was, of course, one of Belloc's few blind spots: he consistently refused to see the Revolution as an unmitigated disaster. In essence he felt that it had to a good degree saved the French polity from a catastrophe similar to that which befell England by Cromwell's hand.

Belloc at the outset makes it clear that the catastrophic uncrowning of England was no inevitability, however strong were the forces arrayed against the monarchy. In making this statement he has in his sights two enemies of Truth. The influence of deterministic, quasi-Marxist history was growing steadily in his time, and he wished to expose its principal error: its failure to take into account Personality, and the free will of the major protagonists. Likewise, the Protestant, Whig version of history still held a good proportion of the masses in thrall with its mesmerising and self-congratulatory account of the inevitable rise of "democratic" England to world dominance. Both parties believed in Progress, albeit of different sorts. Belloc believed in Sin and Grace and the often-constrained but still free will of man to choose between them.

The second chapter, "The Circumstance," sets out with superb concision the development of this tragedy up to the birth of Charles Stuart. In his thorough exposition it is possible to see all the factors that would weigh so heavily on Charles's reign as to make it almost insupportable. The point is made with great force that, to all external observers, the power of the monarchy appeared to be growing following the Reformation. Early modern Kingship perhaps reached its apogee under the bloody rule of Elizabeth I, though the elaborate ceremonial surrounding monarchy continued to intensify thereafter. By the time Charles I was on the throne, the degree of deference he was shown, and the manner in which he was dressed, served his food and all the rest, was striking even by the later standards of Louis XIV, *Le Roi Soleil.*

INTRODUCTION

Beneath this veneer the solidity of monarchical power was shrinking and being undermined. As Belloc puts it: "The old Elizabeth believed in her own power; as the century ended, her great subjects believed in it, though it was already flickering out." What threw the monarchy into crisis? Belloc cites firstly the troubled reigns of preceding monarchs, in which vacillations of policy, principally over the religious question, led to the undignified scrambling around for power-bases outside the monarchy. By Elizabeth's death, the actual exercise of royal power required, more than it ever had before, external support from interested, thus *rich*, parties. Secondly, he cites the financial decay of the Crown. This was both relative and absolute. There was tremendous inflation over the period; the King's greater subjects grew relatively richer while the King's own financial resources shrank. There were many and complex reasons for this, but it has to be noted again that many of them hinged upon the handing over of ecclesiastical properties and endowments to supporters during the reigns of Henry VIII and Edward VI. Thirdly, there was an increasing reliance – principally for financial reasons – upon Parliament, a Parliament which had itself gained greater prominence by the compliant part it had played in the Reformation, and in which the key players were now men of greater substance and wealth than they had been in the past. Fourthly, monarchical power was undermined by the growth of power of the judiciary, by their increasing independence of the monarchy, and by their alliance with the new Rich. Again, this development was largely a consequence of the reliance upon the judiciary by the monarchy during the turbulent Reformation years. They were now truly a power to be reckoned with.

This is the context, the background, from which Belloc, with great clarity and with vivid touches, follows the tragedy of Charles's life along its momentous course. As Belloc traces the ebb and flow of events, and of the forces which were to have such a tremendous influence on Charles's life, he never surrenders to the idea that the vanquishing of the King was inevitable. Catholicism has always fought against the madness of determinism in all its forms, and in history Belloc does likewise: time and time again, Belloc stresses the incalculable potency of personality, of character, in figures such as George Villiers, the first Duke of Buckingham, and Thomas Wentworth, the Earl of Strafford, in the heady mix of affairs and events. And time and time again he comes back to the personality of Charles, a man formed from a sickly infancy through an adolescence in a febrile and often vicious court: "His nature, trained in isolation, was fluid against the first onset of attack: then there came a moment when the attack reached something quite different from the first fluid resistance – a stone wall. It was thus that he came to his death. Men were led to think him pliable; when they came unexpectedly on rigidity, they were infuriated."

As Belloc makes clear, Charles was no passive victim of events. Although buffeted by forces that at the onset of his reign already held in many ways the upper hand, he attempted to restore power and dignity to the monarchy. Belloc refers to these attempts as "the effort for unity"; and in so describing them, again he knowingly strikes a crucial note in the analysis of this turbulent part of British history. After all, when True Religion broke down, Christendom broke down across Europe; and when Christendom broke down, so too did national unity – not just in the age-old terms of perennial dynastic dispute, but in terms of something more catastrophic: the sundering of the people from their rulers, and from each other. The chronic heresy of individualism unleashed by the Renaissance no longer beat against the walls of the Church but flooded Europe, and it was every man for himself. The absurd totem of the Treaty of Augsburg (1555), "*cuius regio eius religio*," a fig leaf for unity behind which arbitrary tyranny must either coerce a disparate people in spiritual matters or loose anarchy upon the land, was the most clear sign that the Truth must now kneel before State Power. This inversion, a direct consequence of the revolts of Luther and Calvin (the former freeing rulers from authority, the latter from responsibility), led as often to war within a nation as war between nations, as a consequence of the struggle of religious factions for power. The principle of unity was replaced by the arbitrary religious persuasion and political strength of whichever ruler currently happened to hold sway over his lands.

Charles I, despite his deep love for his Catholic wife, and notwithstanding his own religious leanings which were towards a more "catholic" form of Anglicanism, could only operate in this new context. There being now no Christendom, the highest political ideal was national unity, which was only achievable through political force; and

INTRODUCTION

as the obstacles in the path of such unity became more difficult to pass, the political force wielded to deal with them had to grow correspondingly. In this straining against the current lies the main reason for the growth in absolutism seen in this period – most notable in France, but also discernable in the activities of Charles. And it was easily discerned and criticized by those who eventually caused his death. It was an effort to prevent the disintegration of the national polity.

In some respects, Charles succeeded – at least temporarily. Some of the anarchy and rot of the his father's reign was undone until powers within Parliament had their day and the country fell under the tyranny of Oliver Cromwell. Despite his loathing for Parliament, Belloc took great pains to show how the forces we casually label "parliamentary" were not representative of a majority of the parliamentarians of the time. It is important to stress, however (despite the fact, which Belloc points out, that religion was *not* the prime factor in the rebellion against the Crown), that Charles's effort for unity in the matter of religion was the principal cause of hostilities breaking out when they did, and in the form they did. The religious settlement that Charles inherited was not to his liking, nor was it settled. Puritanism, which Elizabeth had had some success in suppressing in England, was rampant in Scotland. Charles's attempt to impose a variant of the quasi-sacramental, ritualist, hierarchical, and Arminian form of Protestantism that he favored led to open rebellion in Scotland, aided and abetted by those who nevertheless had little concern for the things of God: for Charles was also seeking to restore to the Crown some of the revenues and lands of the Church pilfered since the days of Edward VI.

War with Scotland led to the need to summon Parliament (which Charles had dissolved in acrimony eleven years earlier) to raise monies for the defence of England. That Parliament once summoned was manipulated by the enemies of the Crown within it to demand, in return for limited fiscal support for Charles, a permanent hold over the revenues and other areas of the Crown's power. Charles would not stoop to blackmail, although he stooped lower than he should have, and sacrificed his close friend and adviser Thomas Wentworth to the scaffold. The war that followed of course led directly – although not inevitably – to Charles's own death.

CHARLES I

I will not trace the sequence of events that led from Charles's raising of his Standard in 1642 to the lowering of his head over the block less than seven years later. These are years filled with war and political negotiations and skulduggery; and Belloc is expert in describing and analysing both. In particular, Belloc always felt very much at home when writing about war and matters military; and the passages on the wars and campaigns are concise and decisively written. On the painfully complicated political events that led to Charles's execution, he is appropriately painstaking. The desperate convolutions seem endless, but Belloc follows their path to the execution with panache and dignity, much as did Charles.

Today, when historians summon up the courage to venture an opinion, there tend to be two extreme views of Charles's reign and his tragic end. One is that no monarch, however gifted or talented, however politically able and conciliatory, could have avoided the headsman's axe. The other is that Charles was a bad king who essentially died by his own hand, the victim of his own reckless incompetence and stupidity, who brought the monarchy to shipwreck when it could have been steered into the peaceful harbour of some negotiated constitutional settlement. I have even read historians who have posited both theories simultaneously, albeit in some amended form, perhaps without being aware of their radical inconsistency, or – more probably – as a result of a sheer sense of hopelessness. Belloc would not have been surprised. If he were today available on prescription, he should without hesitation be recommended to every History Faculty as an antidote to wretched agnosticism and relativism, and to the ignorant slavery that still ties most historians to the one or two "facts" of contemporary thought that still prevail – the supremacy of democracy, the progressive effects of capitalism, and the abhorrent nature of the old Catholic order.

Belloc taught history as *fact* in his books, fact unsullied by the smugness of the historians of his day who worshipped the Money Power at the altar of secular, liberal democracy. He understood that a true understanding of fact required a true understanding of reality, an understanding almost uniquely preserved within the Faith. He considered it easier for a camel to pass through the eye of a needle than for a man with no understanding of the Faith to write true his-

INTRODUCTION

tory. In our age, when reality as understood by the vast majority of our peers seems even further from the teachings of Christ and His Church, who can say that he was wrong?

>Michael Hennessy
>August 15, 2003
>Feast of the Assumption of the
>Blessed Virgin Mary

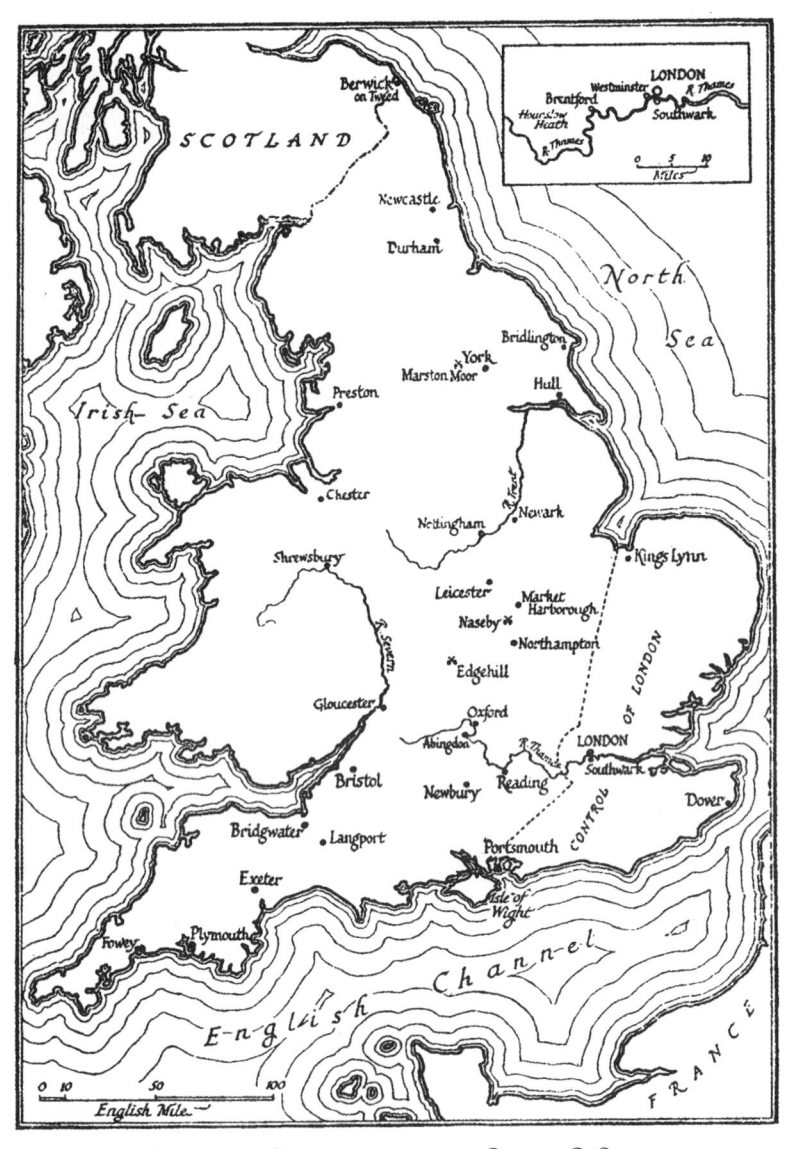

Main Sites of the Civil War

THE PROBLEM

THERE IS AN INSTITUTION AS OLD AS THE WORLD: MONARCHY—Kingship. In most places and in most times men have agreed to be governed by Kings, having found in such government something consonant to their nature.

In one man there seemed to stand incarnate all the men of the community and to be concentrated in him their common weal. He was the visible symbol of their unity.

Today all Christendom is hungry for monarchy. In the United States, partly by the provision of the Constitution, more by its development in the nineteenth century, the principle of an executive in the hands of one man was preserved. But in Europe it was gradually lost, and replaced by the rule of a few; in practice, of the rich, under the guise of representatives. That experiment is breaking down before our eyes, and monarchy is returning.

Why and how was it lost? The first great western country to lose it was England. In England a rebellion three hundred years ago deposed and killed the King. Thenceforward the wealthier classes who had raised that rebellion gradually ousted the Crown and took over its power. How and why did English kingship so fail in the person of its last possessor, Charles Stuart? That is the problem approached in this book.

From before the beginning of all record, for centuries upon centuries, the people of Britain had known no other rule. When they had been divided into warring tribes, each tribe or city had its King; when they had formed part of the high Roman civilisation they looked to one mighty monarch above them in the person of the Emperor; when they fell back again, during the Dark Ages, into half a hundred clans or groups of various tongue and religion, yet each unit among them had its King. When the greater part of the island slowly reunited under the term "England," a common monarchy re-arose and there was a King of England in whom communal authority and action was vested; he reigned in the south, from Winchester or Westminster, unquestioned for eight hundred years. The dynasty would change, by marriage or by force of arms; the territory over which it ruled would expand or diminish, the office was held by weak hands and by strong – imperilled when it passed to a child or when powerful subjects rebelled against it, yet always surviving and taken for granted as the air which men breathed.

During the Christian centuries after the conversion of the Pagan Roman Empire kingship began in each province of Christendom to take on a mien still more exalted and, as it were, sacramental. It had inherited from Rome the sense of majesty, the awe and worship of that authority by which men lived, and already in the last of the Pagan Imperial Courts the Emperor was something divine. But with the triumph of the Christian system in the Dark and Middle Ages something more intimately religious entered into that central idea; the King was anointed as well as crowned; he was sacred through these symbols, which were endowed with an effective power.

It was in France that this majesty of kingship took on its colours and began to shine, and from the crownings and anointings at Rheims the spirit spread throughout the west. Over England that spirit lay with as profound an effect as over any princedom among Christian men. It must be the first priest in England – the Archbishop of Canterbury – who should anoint and crown the King claimant; only after that stamp of religion had been set was he King indeed. From him proceeded all acts of government and control; in his name was the peace preserved; he was the framer of national policy; he appointed to every national office; by him alone could be created a special title of nobility, and by him were the armies summoned and led.

All Europe and particularly England was in this mood, because England was upon a scale which helped her to be singularly united. The King of France held a double power direct over his own lands but shadowy over his great vassals; the little realms that were growing up beyond the Pyrenees, as the land of Spain was slowly reconquered from the Mohammedan, had each their King but were each for centuries too small to weigh heavily in the balance of Europe. For a time there had been a King vaguely over the Germans, but long

THE PROBLEM

since, almost from the end of the Dark Ages, the chieftains of the various German districts had alone really ruled. In Italy the cities and principalities and the territory of the Papal monarchy were similarly divided. But in England kingship was firmly welded, after a model suited to it, having a territory not too large for central rule yet of an extent wide enough to make the realm a principal factor in the business of Europe.

So things had been in the minds of men for centuries; kingship went back long beyond all tradition.

A child born in the turn of the sixteenth and seventeenth centuries, at the end of the year 1600, was to inherit this hitherto unquestioned office, and apparently to inherit it undiminished in reputation or effect. He was to come to the kingship of his fathers in true descent of the Blood Royal, and, destined as it would seem, to administer as those before him had administered and to hand on this same power and majesty to his posterity. Yet in the lifetime of that child – and it was not a long one – monarchy in England crumbled, or rather was destroyed. He himself acted that tragedy and took the tragic part therein. First he was thwarted by his more powerful subjects through his early years, from the day when as a young man of twenty-five he came to his own after his father's death. Next they took arms against him, when he had not long passed his fortieth year. They gradually destroyed his national forces, they triumphed over him, they belittled him by one humiliation after another, and at last, before he had reached his fiftieth year, they put him to death. With him died the English monarchy – he was the last ruling King of England, the last who governed as Kings had governed for untold years.

This child so born in 1600, and so destined to see the tragic close of all for which he had stood, was Charles Stuart.

Why did so mighty a change come upon him and upon his office, and in his time? How did a revolution so complete, and, as it would seem, so improbable and unprepared, come to so rapid a conclusion with himself for the victim?

Two elements combine in all such problems: Circumstance; and the Character of the Man. The Circumstance, when we shall have probed it to its depth and comprehended it in full, exhibits a process apparently inevitable. Men are tempted to say when they know what forces have been at work to produce some astonishing historical thing, "I now see that it could not have been avoided, and that no matter who had been there he would have suffered the same fate." But this is a mechanical illusion, for there is also present the factor of personality.

It is not conceivable that another character seated on Charles Stuart's throne would have lived to see the monarchy at his death what it had been at his birth; but it is true that there were those qualities in the man which by their temper, rather than their proportion, of strength and weakness, not only rendered the evil more certain but gave it the shape it took.

It was not only fate, it was also something in Charles Stuart himself – his virtues mainly – which destroyed the Crown of England and the power thereof.

It behoves us then as we approach this great story first to see as clearly as may be what the Circumstance was – how monarchy and its society stood in that year 1600 in England, and why there lay within the structure of the community, as it then was, the forces that would bring down the Throne. Only when we have thus understood the Circumstance can we proceed to the Character and its development in life; only then can we observe how that Character reacted to such Circumstance, how the Circumstance thwarted and constrained the Character, and led it down the paths to sudden death.

THE CIRCUMSTANCE

When that boy was born in the year 1600, the boy in whose person the English monarchy was to fail, how stood that monarchy, the matter of the whole affair?

The aged Elizabeth sat on the Throne of England. She had still three more years to live. About her there still shone – but falsely – the splendour which had illumined the English Crown in its highest days. But her long reign had been imperilled, tortuous and unhappy, with a declining population and wealth and with a people divided among themselves not only on her own her right to rule (for she was a bastard in the eyes of Europe and in the eyes of many of her subjects) but also on the right or wrong of that new society which a group of political and religious adventurers had established in her name.

Yet when old Elizabeth died, more than forty mortal years after her crowning, the monarchy of England was still in all outward appearance what it had been – wholly master of the State and that from which emanated all government.

The person of the monarch was as sacred as ever, spoken of with the same awe; the office that person held was still higher than all other human estate and was thought to be responsible only to God. There was still an impassable moral gulf between the holder of that office and the greatest subject. Even in the unhappy old Queen's absence, the men who brought in the dishes to her table genuflected to the empty chair wherein she would have sat; she was treated with as much pomp as you could find in any court of Europe, even in the new and glorious court of Spain itself.

But there was between the appearance of all this and the real thing beneath, a threatening contrast. It is often so with institutions already undermined; they are at their most splendid external phase when they are ripe for downfall. For power was passing from the Crown, though power seemed wholly to proceed therefrom, and though the rich men who were themselves the agents of the decline in kingship, did not realise that they were themselves stepping into its place. The old Elizabeth believed in her own power, as the century entered, her great subjects believed in it, though it was already flickering out.

What were the reasons for this? Why was the English monarchy in especial suffering decline, while monarchy elsewhere in Christendom was growing stronger than ever? Why was English kingship standing prepared for replacement by the power of the wealthier classes?

These were the reasons:—

For the last fifty years and more first, a child (a weak and diseased child), then an elderly woman also diseased, isolated and out of touch with her time, then this third, this woman Elizabeth, abnormal in physique, repeatedly sickening, had been in turn called sovereign. Where everything was so personal, such a succession had progressively weakened the power of the Crown, for there had been no King. The forms of awe, of dread, of worship, which were proffered – and were sincerely proffered – could not make up for the lack of real strength. The office required a man, and for over fifty years there had been no man.

In the opening phase when the diseased child was nominally monarch for a little space of six years, power was openly exercised by a few very wealthy men, most of them quite newly enriched, who relying on a group of violent religious revolutionaries, imposed a new, detested worship, and under the cover of it had looted the royal fortune at will. This was the so-called "reign" of little half-brother, Edward, the sixth of that name, who died exhausted before he was seventeen.

Mary, the elderly woman who succeeded, certainly legitimate, in her youth the idol of London and the populace, had been kept away from public eyes for many years; she had lived secluded. She restored the ancient popular religion, but she violently inflamed the small but intense, determined and growing minority who were bent upon achieving the religious revolution. Under her acceptance and in her name, the Council persecuted all dissidents; they burnt heretics for four years and did but exasperate division.

THE CIRCUMSTANCE

Elizabeth herself had come to the Throne, though of a birth the legitimacy of which was doubtfully admitted, she had been put upon the Throne not as of right, but by the support of two men – William Cecil and her brother-in-law, the King of Spain. She was the candidate of the Spaniards, against the French who favoured the candidature of the legitimate heiress, Mary, the young Queen of Scotland. By this inception all her reign was coloured. The genius of William Cecil moulded it. He was the chief and the presiding genius among a clique of men all bent on enriching themselves; Elizabeth for their figurehead and their symbol – and it was William Cecil who governed England, not the Queen. It was he who chose agents of high ability (such as the master of his spy-system, Walsingham), he who, with the rest, carried out a fixed policy, foreign and domestic.

That policy was directed to avoiding disturbance in England over the religious quarrel which had everywhere bred war and was in process of ruining the strength of France, close at hand. He set up a newly established Church, meeting the intense religious revolution half-way and confirming its principal demands – the abolition of the Mass, the marriage of clergy, the liturgy in English, and the repudiation of the unity of Christendom through the repudiation of the authority of the Papacy. William Cecil more than any other one man by his individual genius began to make the worship of the nation replace the old idea of Catholic Europe. It was through him and his that the quarrel with Spain, his original supporter and ally was fomented and most successfully brought to its fruit by long and subtle intrigue, until at the very end of the effort he could defy the Spanish power. It was through him and his that Elizabeth's cousin, the unfortunate Queen of Scotland and rightful Queen of England, taking refuge in England from a rebellion at home, was more and more strictly imprisoned and finally put to death – with the responsibility for that killing thrown upon the exceedingly reluctant Elizabeth. She had never intended it, it was done in spite of her, although she would have been glad to see her rival put out of the way so only that she had not the blame of overtly ordering the death.

This work of the great Cecil was continued by his second son, Robert, the big-headed humpback dwarf, of a genius almost equal to his father's.

CHARLES I

There had thus been more than half a century by the time this boy, Charles Stuart was born in 1600 – he who was to inherit the Throne of England as grandson of the murdered Queen of Scotland – a passing of real rule from the hands of the monarch to the hands of others.

This progressive decline might have been arrested by the coming to the Throne of some strong and masculine personality, had the long weakness of monarchs been the only form of decay in the royal power; but there was present another form of decay, more continuous, even less apparent but more profound and of increasing effect. The Crown was decaying financially.

Power may not be created by wealth: it may come first and seize wealth; but it is not compatible with lack of wealth; and the wealth of the English Crown, the secure income of it, and the sufficiency of that income to purchase the things and services whereby the Crown must maintain its government, was getting less and less. This process of financial decline had also been growing for much more than half a century – that is, for all the active lifetime of a man: during the whole of that period a public frame of mind was established and habits of thought and procedure in public affairs became rooted: an unconscious taking-for-granted the impoverishment of the government and the habit – or right – of subjects to resist new claims for supply. This financial decay of the Crown of England, continuous and unchecked, might be compared to the process of anaemia in a human body. It was a loss of blood going on all the time.

Producing this impoverishment there were three causes at work; but to understand how those causes had their effect we must first grasp what it is difficult for the modern mind to grasp – something quite contrary to our daily experience as it has been formed by centuries of political habit: *the income of the government was based by immemorial tradition upon endowment and not upon taxes.*

Men had thought for centuries past of the Crown as something with an income of its own like the income of a private man (though very much larger), and derived, like the income of a private man, from the administration of its own sources of revenue. There was no distinction between the money which a King spent upon his private trinkets and what he spent upon his ships and the salaries of his of-

THE CIRCUMSTANCE

ficials, his embassies, the whole conduct of his control over society. Today we can only think of the income of the government in terms of money supplied to it out of the private incomes of the governed – what we call "taxes." This idea of regular taxes did not, in 1600, exist. It had never hitherto existed. The King paid for what he regularly needed, however public the service, out of what he privately owned – his control of the forest and waste lands, his ownership of manors, his feudal dues paid to him personally as an owner of feudal rights over his direct tenants, through wardships, and the proceeds of his courts of justice. And the very word "tax" meant in those days almost the opposite of what it means today. It did not mean a regular recurrent levy; it meant a special payment made to meet a particular crisis, and not to be repeated.

Now that being the way in which men thought of public affairs and the revenue necessary for their conduct, three things, I say, had continued to ruin the financial power of kingship in England.

The first was a steady and great rise in prices. The things for which the monarch had to pay cost more and more with every decade in terms of the currency. What an English pound would buy seventy years before had become by this time, towards the end of Elizabeth's reign, less than half what they had been before. Horses, the living of a labourer, salaries, and all the rest of it, were more than twice as dear as they had been a lifetime before and were becoming dearer. In half a lifetime after Elizabeth's death – when this child now just born, Charles Stuart, himself became King in 1625 – prices had nearly doubled again. The pound in 1625 would buy but a quarter of what it had bought less than a century before. To meet this rise in prices (which was due in the main to the influx of the precious metals from the newly discovered Spanish colonies in America into Europe) the English government had been pushed to every shift. They had played with the currency just as we play with it today, calling that a pound which was not really a pound, paying their salaries in depreciated currency, and the rest of it. But that trickery could not last – it never does. Half-way through the process sound money was restored, and prices continued to rise. They rose, and rose, and still rose.

But the income of the Crown under the child Edward VI, under his half-sister Mary, and under Elizabeth, did not rise as prices rose, for it was in the main customary. The feudal dues and most other forms of royal revenue, were fixed payments in pounds; and the pound would buy less and less and less as the years went on. That was the first cause of financial decay in the Crown.

The second cause was the growth of the modern State. Those sixty or seventy years corresponded to the effects of the Renaissance. A more developed society, greater and more splendid buildings, greater and more expensive fortifications, artillery, ships – an increase everywhere in the claims which the Crown had to meet; all the progress of a new world demanding more and more costly administration was at work. While the monarchy was getting progressively poorer the calls upon it were getting progressively greater as the modern state grew.

And the third cause was this: the three successive weak controls, a control hardly existent in the case of the diseased boy who had begun the series, somewhat strengthened but still declining his sister Mary, still declining under the long reign of his sister Elizabeth, laid open the royal revenue to filching by powerful subjects, weak control permitted the capital (as we should call it today) which produced the royal revenue to be looted and raided and consequently diminished by private interests. Nearly all the great new endowment which the Crown should have had from its seizure of the monasteries and hospitals and colleges under Henry VIII had passed to private hands. The very wealthy nobles, old and new, took to themselves by grant, and even by usurpation, great blocks of what had been Crown property. Notably the boundaries of the royal forests shrank – to the advantage of the greater landlords.

You have a typical case in the family of Wriothesley, who (under the title of Southampton) added to their enormous fortune by encroachment upon Crown land. You have another typical case, a small one but most significant, in what was done in one instance out of a hundred by Hatton – the handsome young fellow who had been picked out by Elizabeth at a dance and given the Chancellorship (of all posts!), and enriched himself immoderately. That small instance was Hatton's capture of rents belonging to the Church, part of the endowment of the Bishopric of Ely. He had them handed over to him by force without a shadow of right, and hence Hatton Garden

THE CIRCUMSTANCE

in London today. That sort of thing was going on wholesale with all public endowment during all the half-century from 1540 to the end of Elizabeth's reign in 1603. Crown lands were given away, encroached on, sold at specially low prices to the favoured. Crown dues were alienated and Crown rents transferred.

These three causes of impoverishment, all at work together, threatened soon to make impossible the carrying on of the government by the monarch, but for a certain precarious avenue of escape. And it was through the working of that avenue of escape that the great change from monarchy to aristocracy was to come, and the final breakdown of the Crown.

From of old, for many hundreds of years, when there had been especial needs, something outside the regular annual needs of the government, when for instance there had come the strain of a war (and that was the most usual occasion) the King would ask for a grant from his subjects; most of it of course from his wealthier subjects, though there had been many examples of a grant falling upon all possessors of wealth and even (very rarely, by a Poll tax) upon the whole population. But these were not what we mean today by regular taxes, they were *grants;* they were and remained exceptional. Even when they had to be frequently begged for by the King because war was prolonged (the most usual reason) they were always thought of as exceptional; they were not felt to be part of the regular revenue. They were grudged, they were jealously watched, every care was taken that they should not be permanent.

New these exceptional and voluntary grants were made through the medium of an institution called "Parliament," an institution common to all Western Europe and one which had risen early in the Middle Ages, spreading from the first examples in the Pyrenees to Spain in the south, throughout the French states, and to England in the north.

We must not be confused by the similarity of name, the word "Parliament." What we mean by this word today is very different from what it meant then. "Parliament" meant then the old national council of very wealthy men surrounding the Crown, the Bishops and the greater Lords, supplemented in rare and especial fashion by a group of delegates – clerical and lay – which delegates were thus especially and occasionally and exceptionally summoned for the purpose of making especial, occasional and exceptional gifts, not as of right but as of grace, to the King. Suppose the King was attacked, for instance, and could not defend his realm upon his regular revenue, his subjects (however reluctantly) would help him with a grant. The delegates of the clergy would debate among themselves, bargain with the officers of the King or with the King himself, and consent to a levy from their members, that is, from the endowments of the Bishoprics and the parish priests, and, in another fashion, from the great monasteries. The squires of land, the men who were lords of one village or more, and the greater lords above them, and all who were freeholders in the counties, might help, when these occasional and exceptional Parliaments were summoned, to choose delegates of their own – two for each county – and in the Chartered Towns there was choice of the same kind made in all sorts of varying fashions – sometimes by the corporations alone, sometimes by all those who had burgess rights, sometimes (much more rarely) by the inhabitants of the place at large. But there was never regular voting on a large scale. A small group gathered, of such freeholders as were at hand; by these or on these – delegates were chosen or imposed. These delegates were nearly all of them, and naturally, of the wealthier classes and especially local lords of manors – with a few rich merchants and a sprinkling of lawyers.

The delegates met the permanent Council of great men, the "Lords," but sat separately from them, and were called "The Commons" – a term which does not mean common people but the spokesmen for owners of land in general, as distinguished from specially great owners. These, after debate and bargaining, just as in the case of the clergy, could allow a grant and authorise it to be levied upon those for whom they spoke. But such grants were never thought of as regular revenue – it was the difference between a tip and a salary, between a present you make and a sum of money you pay because you owe it. The grants thus made in such Parliaments as were summoned were gifts, *not* permanent in character, and with every safeguard taken to prevent their becoming so.

If there had been no other source of revenue but these two – the regular income of the Crown upon which it was supposed to

THE CIRCUMSTANCE

live and to make all its payments and the grudged exceptional grants which it asked for now and then under especial strain – the decline of the King's income would have led to parliaments being more and more constantly called to make up for the deficiency between the regular income of the Crown and its expenditure. But as a fact they were not so called, because there had also grown up another source of income for the Crown which was a sort of half-way house between the exceptional grants or gifts and the regular royal income. This separate and increasing revenue came from the Customs† levied at the ports both on exports and imports, where goods came into and left the country; they fell principally, of course, upon imports.

At the beginning, in the Middle Ages, the Customs had been a grant, exceptional like the rest, but they soon became a permanent set of payments collected by the officers of the King day by day and year by year as ships came into and out of the ports with merchandise, and formed part of the regular royal revenue. Whenever a new King came to the Throne one of these exceptional gatherings – a Parliament – would be summoned, usually for quite a short time, and among other things they would, before dispersing, grant the King the customs for life. It soon became a mere matter of form, and by the time of which we speak, the year 1600, the thing had gone on without interruption for so long that there was no further question of it. The dues were levied at a rate which depended upon the monarch's will, and what had originally been a grant was now, in practice – and had so been for long before any family tradition could reach back, for hundreds of years – a normal part of the King's regular income. It had come to be as regular a part of the King's income as the rents paid to him from his private lands, from the forests and wardships and all the rest of the personal sources of his revenue.

Just as the modern state was growing and adding to the expenditure of the Crown, so the trade of England began to grow; and it increased regularly from the very end of this period, the turn of the century marked by the year 1600 onwards. The colonisation and development of the Americas had brought the western ports of

---

† The word "Customs" is ambiguous. Sometimes it is used in a special sense distinguishing it from "Tonnage and Poundage." I am here using it in its most general sense; all dues on goods leaving or entering the country.

CHARLES I

Europe into prominence, so that they were gradually taking the place which the old Mediterranean ports had once held, when the main stream of trade had flowed from the east. At the same time the way to the east also was changed. The cheaper sea-road round the Cape of Good Hope had fully developed, and this increased the importance of merchant centres lying on the Atlantic, Channel and North Sea coasts. The Netherlands, Portugal, France – all felt the new advantage and England felt it with them. With the increase of trade came automatically an increase of customs revenue, and this increasing revenue from the customs partly filled the gap between the rapidly declining income of the Crown and the increasing expenses thereof; at any rate it put a brake on what would otherwise have been a catastrophic growth of deficit.

Side by side with all this there had come a great economic change in the structure of English society during that same half-century and more. By this change what were called on the Continent "the nobles," what we called in England "the squires," that is, the lords of land had *in England* become richer in proportion to the peasantry and richer also in proportion to the Crown. The least of them, who gathered dues from one village only, had in the last hundred years increased their incomes at the expense of the peasantry and that increase was continuing. The greatest of them, who had many such village estates, were becoming wealthier and wealthier as the government got poorer and poorer.

This economic revolution was of capital importance. It had begun with the seizure of the endowments of religion by Elizabeth's father, Henry VIII, more than sixty years before this date, in a process extending from the year 1536 onwards. To begin with all the monasteries had been seized, dissolved, and their lands confiscated to the King; the collegiate institutions as well, including many of the schools and hospitals. The loot was on a vast scale, and it had continued on uninterrupted after Henry's death. The nobles who governed in the place of the little diseased boy King roped in most of what was left though the colleges of Oxford and Cambridge, which had been marked down for destruction, were spared in time by Henry's timely passing. The endowments of the Bishoprics were cut down; the endowments for masses were confiscated, so were Guild funds. There

THE CIRCUMSTANCE

seemed to be no end to the transference of corporate property from its rightful owners to the Crown, or to those who stood for it.

It looked at one moment – from 1536 to about 1545 – as though the Crown of England were about to become the most economically powerful over its subjects of all European governments.

It turned out just the other way, and this wholesale loot of religious and of corporate property which was to have vastly enriched the Kings, put them under a curse and ruined them.

For the wealth thus looted did not remain in the hands of the monarchy; it was rapidly dissipated, the first examples being set by Henry himself immediately after his origination of these thefts. The spoils passed mainly into the hands of the squires great and small, including those very wealthy families, men such as the Cromwells, the Wriothesleys, the Russells – whose new millions had been accumulated rapidly from the seizing of Church and Collegiate lands. Within the villages this new economic power of the squire enabled him to buy up further dues, rights and land, to continue those enclosures which had already begun in the Middle Ages, and in general to count for more and more while the free peasantry, though still forming a very large part of the nation, were correspondingly depreciated.

As against the monarchy this economic change meant that a class of great new wealth, widely spread, was now set up over against the embarrassed Crown. But these rich men were the very men who appeared as "The Lords" and "The Commons" whenever the so rare and fitful national councils called "Parliaments" were summoned.

The Houses of Parliament were, in effect, twin committees of the great landowners, with that admixture of rich merchants and lawyers which I have mentioned.

But here must be noted a point of some moment. Though the squires now dominated the countrysides and the hundreds of big villages and small towns called "Boroughs," yet their financial interests were often identical with those of a large number of lesser men. When the King asked help from the landholders most of the money had to be provided by the squires, large and small; but the levy would also be spread over a host of smaller owners all over the country. England in those days was largely composed of a *Peasantry* – a force now long forgotten. From the substantial yeomen with his fifty,

37

hundred, two hundred acres, down to the cottager with a small croft of four, five or ten, all were assessed and had to contribute in some degree to a grant voted by great men in the Commons House. How many English families thus possessed the land on which they lived we have no exact record to inform us, but it may well have been half the nation. For the English freeholders were not only those who owned their land out-and-out; they included those who might have to pay dues – a fixed rent, etc. – to the squire, but who could not be turned out so long as they paid regularly. This was the system of which the commonest form was "Fee-Farm Tenure." A peasant holding his land in "fee-farm" held it hereditarily. It passed of right to his heirs and he was as much an owner as the man who paid no dues at all to the local magnate. The rent paid for a fee-farm holding was small – often negligible – and constant. It was always small, and often negligible, because the fall in the value of money had made it so. Where the original rent paid by a small man had meant, some centuries ago, the value of say, half a dozen pigs, it had come to be the value of only one pig. For the rent in terms of *money* could not be changed. Where he had been called on for the value of six bushels of corn, he now had to pay only the value of one; and even the original rent had never been a full competitive rent nor anything like it. It had been what we call today a "ground rent."

Now with this great mass of small owners of land in being the great landlords in Parliament had a weight of opinion behind them. No one likes to pay an exceptional sum of money, even a small one, over and above his regular expenses, and when the King asked for an exceptional grant, not only the big landlords of the House of Commons, but a very large part of the nation, perhaps a half, had to pay each in his degree. When John Hampden was asked to pay 2 ½ per cent. of his enormous income, it meant that the man with fifty acres had also to pay, in modern money, say twenty-five shillings; no crushing burden but noticeable. To say that the House of Commons in those days "represented" the nation, in the sense of our modern fiction of representation is nonsense. The opinion and action of the House of Commons on religion, foreign policy, everything but a grant, were the opinion and action of a small rich class, supported now by one section of opinion, now by another. But when it came

THE CIRCUMSTANCE

to refusing or reducing a grant of money, its action directly benefited not only its own wealthy membership but a great part of a nation, then mainly agricultural. Moreover the gentry who sat as members for the hundreds of little boroughs, though they virtually appointed themselves in most cases or were appointed by men wealthier than themselves, had to speak for lesser men who, in the little towns and big villages, often owned the houses in which they lived, and were therefore assessable. Of voting in our modern fashion there was little even in the towns and less, of course, in the counties; but in legal right, anyone in the counties with from fifteen to twenty acres of land was a voter and in the boroughs, for all the diversity of voting rights and the indifference or impossibility of their exercise, the great number of assessed owners of houses were concerned with resistance to, or reduction of, or delay in the granting of exceptional demands by the government, the "grants in aid." Pym for example, sat for little Tavistock, as a hanger-on of the Russell family which dominated that place. But he could not have sat for it in violent opposition to the assessed burgesses.

All this must be remembered as we follow the struggle for power between the wealthier classes and the King. In the main it was a struggle for *power* between the New Wealth of the gentry and the impoverished Crown.

With their struggle for *power*, the mass of the nation had little concern. The King seemed to it the national ruler. But in the first phases of this struggle for *power* the New Wealth, acting through Parliament, had considerable popular backing in the financial side of the conflict. The New Wealth was only using that financial side as an instrument to obtain new political power, just as it used the religious passion of a section of the nation as an instrument, but still, so far as finance alone was concerned the New Wealth was in a certain measure representative. It had, at least, a widespread popular backing.

The political effect of this new wealth among the squires and their consequent new power, began to be felt after 1560, half a lifetime after the first loot of religion. In the Parliaments summoned under the power of William Cecil, and largely formed of his nominees, the new strength of this class began to appear. The Commons already slightly intrude upon what has been the unquestioned rights of the

Crown; they comment upon policy, they complain of royal acts. The instinct for new political power which, inseparable from new wealth, arose and was ready to threaten the immemorial right to government still held by the embarrassed Crown.

But the process was very slow. The idea of supplanting kingship by the rule of the rich was not conscious for a lifetime. Its progress was the effect of that instinct, just mentioned, not of calculation.

As yet, by 1600, the effects of this instinct were sporadic and rare, but they had appeared. Evidently as the needs of the Crown would get more and more pressing with the development of the modern state still in progress and with the purchasing power of the royal revenue still going down, the monarch would need to summon Parliaments for special grants, and when those Parliaments should come together the wealthy landlords with their newly acquired economic power would begin to take advantage of the half-ruined Throne.

In 1600, all this was for the future. The seed was sown but no one noticed its growing. Those who were to benefit by the change and to substitute their power for that of the King – the landed class and the great merchants – were not themselves conscious as yet of any usurping motive; only they felt themselves to be stronger and stronger, and like all things which grow in strength were less and less inclined to be governed from above and more and more inclined to take over the ordering of their affairs into their own hands. But I say again, of all this there was no outward manifestation, all the forms of monarchy and its grandeur, the belief of all men in it and its own belief in itself remained intact, though it was being eaten up from within. Nor was it only the squires and great merchants who had in them such a beginning of a new ruling class there was allied with them and forming socially a part of their own body the increasing power of the Lawyers' Guild.

It was the lawyers who, in the generation succeeding to the year 1600 – the generation in which this royal boy, Charles, grew up to manhood – began, at first tentatively, later in greater numbers and with more determination, to ally themselves with the revolutionary movement which was to substitute aristocracy for monarchy and a governing class in the place of the King. Their decisions, their interest, but also (to do them justice) their whole habit of mind were the most salient, if not the strongest, factors in that great change.

THE CIRCUMSTANCE

It would be a great mistake, however, to regard this intermixture of the lawyers with the landed gentry as anything novel or peculiar to the beginning of the seventeenth century in England. The power of lawyers had, since the early Middle Ages, been a growing feature of life throughout western Christendom. What was novel about the lawyers' power in England after 1600 was that once the landed gentry had begun to take up a revolutionary – that is, by definition, an illegal – attitude, the lawyers gradually slipped into alliance with it and supported it with all the moral force of their extremely powerful traditional position and their strict organisation and "trade unionship." From the central Middle Ages onwards successful lawyers had in every country, as in England, risen into the territorial class. Theirs was a trade in which large sums of money could be made, larger even sometimes than the mercantile fortunes; and the higher posts accessible to lawyers were of such prestige that the transition thence to nobility was natural. The family of Howard, for instance, was founded by a lawyer more than two centuries before the life of Charles begins. One of the great distinctions between the Christian and Mohammedan culture was that the purchase of justice is abhorrent to the Mohammedan mind, whereas ever since the Roman Empire and especially in the last few centuries it has been acceptable to the western mind. A man in Christendom having suffered a wrong cannot obtain redress without paying tribute to the Lawyers' Guild and we all know to what a degree this tribute has grown.

The power of the lawyers differed slightly in kind with each province of Christendom. In England one characteristic mark of it was the comparatively small number of high judges who represented the authority of the King in his Courts of Justice. Another characteristic of very real advantage to the political revolution which destroyed was the old monarchy, was the fact that the Lawyers' Guild, in England was not divided into several bodies which the monarch could play off one against the other. Even judges in England were more and more drawn from the advocates; the whole body of lawyers, therefore, were already standing together in their trade interest and the solidity of their professional organization by the time they prepared to turn against the King.

Hitherto, not only up to the year 1600 but for some years after it, the judges still felt themselves to be the servants of the King and the community rather than of their own Lawyers' Guild and of the gentry with which it mixed. However wealthy the judges might be, however great lords they became, they were still, at the very opening of the seventeenth century, the supporters of the Crown rather than of the rich. But they discharged, besides their judicial duties in the Courts of Justice, a special political function which was to make all the difference to the struggle between the King and his wealthier subjects when the sympathies of the judges changed.

That special political function was the power of making law indirectly by their decisions.

In England, as in all other Christian countries, the judges were consulted as to what was sacred custom: it was their business and trust to declare what was and what was not of custom, and therefore (by all the ideas of the time) of *right*. On grave occasions the King would consult them as to whether a proposed act of his was too violently in contrast with custom to be acceptable in their eyes. Their decision was not final; the King's decision was final. The power of the judges advising the King was consultative only, not executive. But when it came to particular cases involving a trial of rights in the Courts, the King must accept their decision. He might, on rare occasions act against it, but so to do was always violent and out of place.

We shall see in what follows how the lawyers helped to undermine the Crown, which hitherto they had served. We shall see, first, hesitation on their part as to how far they should serve the King and how far the rising power of the gentry. They begin to hesitate more and more, and to limit, not only by their decisions but by their counsel and general pronouncements, the royal power. It becomes more and more difficult for kingship to deal with them, save by the grave and rare measure of dismissing a rebellious judge and appointing a loyal one in his place. At last, when nothing but the shadow of monarchy remained, the final triumph of the gentry was scaled by their making it impossible for the King to remove a judge at all. The position of the judges was made absolute. They became irremovable save by the action of the gentry themselves in Parliament. As yet, however, in the circumstances of the year 1600, they were still attached to the old constitutional power of the King, they were *his* servants, it was their business to support *his* place in the commonwealth and his function of government by their decisions.

THE CIRCUMSTANCE

But here let us note a curious and significant point. Not only were the lawyers tending to make common cause with the gentry in what was to be the rising of that class against the King, but the intermixture of the legal with the aristocratic body was made more thorough and the boundary between the two more vague, by a habit the landed families were taking up of putting their sons to a course of legal study. That formed a feature peculiar to the time. In the years when Charles was at issue with the landed class not only did it expect support from the judges, but many of its members were competent to argue legal points for themselves.

Such was the social, economic and dynastic Circumstance surrounding the birth and growth of Charles.

England was, in the years after 1600, gradually turning from its now diminishing Catholic tradition towards the opposite thereof. The years of the Gunpowder Plot – 1605–1606 – may be taken as the turning point. A very large though slowly lessening minority remained vaguely Catholic in sentiment, a considerable minority remained admittedly Catholic in affirmation, a respectable minority, perhaps a sixth,† remained ready and determined to practice Catholic worship if the persecuting laws should be relaxed, a nucleus was active for Catholicism and sacrificed all for their conviction, but by, say, 1625, the centre of gravity had so shifted that not only official England but the bulk of the people and especially the City of London had become definitely Protestant – anti-Catholic – in general tone, and within that field was developing a contrast between the Calvinist temper and the political rather than doctrinal relations of the newly established church. And all the while both the general Protestantism of England *and* the tendency of the Calvinist feeling against the Established Church, were accentuated by the presence in the commonwealth of a widespread Catholic tradition.

To recognise the extent and character of the remaining Catholicism throughout the seventeenth century, but especially in the lifetime of those who were born round about 1600 – the contemporaries of King Charles – is the very first necessity for those who would understand the England of that day. The historical truth is that so early as the year 1600 something like half the English people were still living

---

† As late as the Popish Plot, nearly a lifetime after, one eighth of London consented to leave the town rather than renounce Catholicism.

in the moral and spiritual traditions of their fathers. It was much more than half, if one were to test those moral and spiritual traditions by language and habit rather than by acts. The plays of Shakespeare are the standing monument to this truth. They are obviously written in what we should call a Catholic atmosphere: and after all, common sense, which is the essential guide to all historical interpretation and without which documents only mislead, could come to no other conclusion. It was barely fifty years since every Catholic practice had been universal throughout the country – that is, up to the death of Henry VIII in 1547.

There had been fifty years before, especially among the learned men, mainly among serious clerics and scholars, a small number of active intellects which were definitely hostile to the whole Catholic idea, to the sacramental spirit in all its forms, particularly to the sacramental powers of the hierarchy and the priesthood, to the Mass, therefore, and to the whole philosophy which moulds and colours life in that air. But these few intensely active minds were but a fraction of what was itself but a small minority of Reformers, the most of whom would have rejected with indignation the accusation that they were not Catholic or that they were rebels against the visible Church.

Calvin, the piercing French mind which gave and gives all its form to the anti-Catholic spirit, strongly influenced these zealous few; but he and his doctrine and his followers were repugnant to the English mind as a whole. For a few years after Henry VIII's death, when there was a sort of chaos under the brief nominal rule of the boy-King his son, Edward VI, a new Liturgy was forcibly imposed for a few months by a little detested group of rich men who in no way represented the nation, nor was it imposed without violent popular rebellions; and before it had been fully founded Mary had come to the throne with the strongest popular support behind her.

The persecution in her short reign of the anti-Catholic-minded minority, which was growing but was still small, may have produced something of a reaction, but there is nothing in the evidence of the time to show that such a reaction was widespread or deep; all that generation had been brought up in the ordinary practices of Catholicism and found them natural. The driving power behind the changes that followed on Mary's death was not hatred of Catholicism, but a

THE CIRCUMSTANCE

determination on the part of the wealthier class to keep the economic results of the Reformation – the new fortunes founded on the confiscation of monastic and other clerical land.

Until as late as thirty years before Charles Stuart's birth, there had been no active pressure put upon the mass of Englishmen to make them abandon that atmosphere of Catholicism in which they had been bred. William Cecil, in forming the new Establishment and causing the reluctant Elizabeth to set her hand to it, had not during all the first decade of the reign made a frontal attack upon what I have thus called "The Catholic atmosphere." He had renewed the breach with the Papacy – though Elizabeth had wanted to send bishops to the Council of Trent and to receive the Papal Nuncio. He had favoured such as were Calvinistically minded among the clergy, he had given them again the Liturgy in English which it had been attempted to impose with such difficulty a few years before, and, again in spite of Elizabeth who detested it, he had permitted and even encouraged the marriage of that clergy. But it is significant that the envoys of the King of Spain pleaded with the Pope for the new Liturgy, urging that it might be reconciled with Catholicism; and even the Oath of Supremacy, which was capital to the carrying out of Cecil's plans, was not universally imposed. In many parishes where men took Communion in the Anglican form they also continued to take it privately in the Roman.

When the real change did come, after 1569, the persecution of Catholicism was always represented not as a persecution of religion, but of treason. The English people were gradually forgetting Catholic practices because the Catholic system had been suppressed. Save here and there, and perilously, in a few private houses and at disjointed times and, when he could enter them, in the chapels of the foreign Embassies in London, Englishman could have the opportunity of hearing Mass – the very habit was for forgotten. But the older men had been brought up under that habit and in the Catholic tone.

The general tone of England then, round about 1600, was religious indifference under an official Church and with a strong savour or memory of Catholicism. Nonetheless, there was gradually growing up with the later years of the century before 1600 a generation moulded in a new way, and – most potent influence of all – the mass of the nation was, agreeably to Cecil's plans, substituting the worship of the nation itself for the old universal Catholic ideals: "Patriotism, the religion of the English." If you had taken the younger men only in the year 1600, the actually anti-Catholic minority among them would have already been found to be fairly large, and of course it would grow. But still, so early as this, Catholic ideas in the vague, the Catholic atmosphere, was, as I say, surviving in something like half the nation, and of the other half not all, nor perhaps most, were repelled by Catholicism, though the now large minority which did feel repulsion felt it intensely

When, therefore, the question is asked, "How many Catholics were there in England about 1600?" the answer will differ vastly according to what we mean by the word "Catholic." If we extend it to mean those who were still under the influence of the old traditions, we may include a very large body indeed which may have been, as I say, half or even more than half the nation. If we mean those who were conscious supporters of the Catholic system and would, had they had full freedom, expressed their desire for its return, it was a somewhat smaller body. If again we mean those who preferred the Catholic ideal to the national and who abhorred the Oath of Supremacy, it would be a much smaller body. And if we mean those who were prepared to suffer in goods and in prospects for the open declaration of Catholicism in the fullest sense of that word – the acceptation of the Papacy, the admission of its power to inmix in English affairs – why, those who were prepared by such a declaration to suffer even a partial martyrdom were few indeed. A man of any substance who did not frequent the Established Liturgy in the parish church could by law be more than half ruined, and even poorer men whom it was less worthwhile looting could be and often were molested. The numbers of those who had laid themselves open to such molestation among the poorer men, and to ruin among the richer men, was necessarily small; but to estimate, by the numbers of these "recusants," as they were called, the strength of Catholicism in England at that time is grossly unhistorical. You might as well estimate the numbers of those who were disappointed at the results of the Great War and wearied with its continuance, by the numbers of conscientious objectors actually in jail: and even that would be an insufficient parallel, because

THE CIRCUMSTANCE

all conscientious objectors who did not belong to the very wealthy families were listed and known, the machinery of conscription was at work, and he who resisted it was automatically marked. But it was not so even with the active, convinced, strongly Papal minority, in the year 1600. For the pressure put upon Catholics to conform was haphazard, not universal. Its exercise depended upon the caprice of those who wanted to make money out of them, upon whether they thought they had the power to do so. Often a great local Catholic landlord was somebody whom the persecutor would hesitate to tackle. With the masses of poorer people even less trouble would be taken, and even "recusants" who were favourable targets for the collectors of fines largely escaped. Bribes were often taken from them to secure immunity and they would conceal their position by an occasional conformity.

The presence of this very large body of people, who in varying degrees, from a mere vague sentiment or tradition to an active desire for restoring Catholic life, were out of sympathy with Protestantism, stood perpetually in the mind of the government itself; for the Authorities were, from the accession of Elizabeth onward, officially anti-Catholic. It stood far more vividly in the mind of that now growing body which was Calvinist in sentiment, actively anti-Catholic (as an Orangeman, for instance, is anti-Catholic in Ireland today). These were always in dread lest mere official opposition should prove too lukewarm, lest a compromise should be made between the official Established Church and the Roman Communion. It was this feeling which led men to what reads to us today like nonsense, when we find, forty years on, the Puritan leaders accusing Charles of commanding "Papist" armies.

If we take for a rough test the opinion of neighbours upon a man's religious sympathies (that such and such a one among them could be called "Catholic" though he never did or could practise), there are occasions when it can be discovered from contemporary evidence. It is, of course, an inferior limit, for the number of those who more or less sympathised with Catholicism must have been much larger, but still, noting what foreign exiles claimed, what numbers were called Catholic in the Civil War, later in the Popish Plot, we can see the numbers of those generally called Catholic gradually diminishing throughout the seventeenth century; from not one-third at the beginning of the period, they are perhaps a sixth in the middle of it and an eighth at its close. But it took time for such a diminution to proceed as it always takes time for deeply rooted social traditions to disappear.

Such was the state in 1600 and onward of that large but decaying Catholic tradition in England.

Over against it was the more powerful part of the nation, Protestant in temper as a whole but divided in its sympathies, passing from a strongly Calvinist and Puritan left wing, to a right wing which was strong in reaction against it. But it was not at first a quarrel between the Established Church and her opponents. It was rather a struggle for influencing that body. There was as yet, in the early seventeenth century, no large Non-conformist body: the great mass of Englishmen – including even those of strongly Catholic tradition – attended the parish churches and sat under clergymen who, various in opinion and including many clearly Calvinistic in doctrine, were not in favour of the Presbyterian Church organisation. The Church of England as a political organization – with its Bishops appointed by the Crown, and those bishops ruling their dioceses wherein all the clergymen were of the Established Church, whatever their variety of opinion – was not only in theory but in practice the Church of the English people. Save for London there were no great towns and only one or two of moderate size. Outside this restricted urban population all England was agricultural, and the great majority of England church-going. But within that organisation of the Established Church there was wide difference of attitude from a strong, long-established and growing body of what was essentially Calvinist opinion in such men as Archbishop Abbot, opposed to the sacramental idea and all its consequences, and a minority of such as Goodman, who recalled Catholicism with sympathy.

The state of affairs in Scotland was of double effect upon all this. An active and intensely convinced part of the Scottish people had early declared themselves effectively for Calvinism as an actual mode of life and worship and were now, by 1600, grown like the great mass of Scotchmen. Even in accepting the framework of the Established Church they worked it in a Presbyterian fashion. Remoter

THE CIRCUMSTANCE

districts in the mountains and the isles maintained the Catholic tradition and even here and there the Catholic practice, but the more densely inhabited cultivated lands of the south and of the east coast were angrily anti-Catholic.

It may be argued that such a state of affairs could not have been reached but for the personal interests served by the Reformation. It immediately enriched the great Scottish families who profited directly by it, and in Scotland the great families did all. Nevertheless, at the moment of which we speak, the determining thing was that the Scottish people as an active political force were intensely Calvinist in spirit, particularly in their capital of Edinburgh. Now in one way this would tend to make Englishmen suspicious of the Calvinist temper, for Scotland was still the hereditary enemy and a Scotchman still an alien in England, as was an Englishman in the eyes of Scotchmen. But on the other hand the presence of an active example abroad is always of great support to those who are of the same opinion at home. The number of Communists, for instance, in Western Europe is comparatively small today; but leanings towards Communism are certainly supported and increased by the presence of Communism in action among the Russians. Scotland, therefore, was a focus of Calvinism which, upon balance, tended to increase the forces of that spirit already growing in England and soon to be formidable. It was not yet formidable in the sense that there were many desiring to establish the Presbyterian form of Church government – that came later and was ephemeral. It was formidable only in the sense that there were already many and would soon be many more who were seriously convinced of those doctrines upon which Calvinism rests, who were inspired by that spirit which has well been called "the quintessence of Protestantism" – for Calvinism is exactly that – and who carried out in their lives the practical effects of such a religion. English Puritanism was planted and was extended during the early years of Charles Stuart, and although as yet it was still unpopular, it was determined and would grow.

In the background of all this was something too often forgotten; the example of the Seven Dutch Provinces. Here at the very doors of England, in close commercial converse with England, speaking a language nearer to English than any other Continental speech, was a

CHARLES I

body of wealthy merchants and territorial lords who had successfully resisted monarchy in the person of Philip the Second.

The proportions were somewhat different, mercantile interests counted more and territorial interests counted less than in England, but the Seven Provinces (which we later came to call Holland) were an example which no one in England engaged in the struggle against the Crown could fail to follow. The parallel runs close through the story, and it is always the Dutch who give the example and come first in date. It was they who began to give their revolt a religious and Calvinist character, a lifetime before the same thing happened in England. It was they who first began to adopt (paradoxically enough) the Jesuit doctrine of Popular Sovereignty and put it at the disposal of the great fortunes which were in rebellion against the Crown. It was they who set the example of coercing and persecuting their large Catholic minority – though they proved at the end more tolerant than did the government of England. They were even the inventors of such a detail as revolution by explosion, and it was possibly the Netherlands plot to blow up a powder-barge in order to destroy the authorities which later inspired Cecil (or the conspirators – whichever were the true originators of that anti-climax) with the idea of the Gunpowder Plot.

Throughout the century and on until William of Orange usurped the Throne of England the Dutch example colours everything.

*****

Here, in its broad lines, you have the Circumstance in which the child, just born at the end of 1600, was to be placed when, in his third year, his father came south of the Border to occupy the Throne of England in succession to Elizabeth.

In such a Circumstance the monarch, which this child was to be, would necessarily come into conflict with a revolutionary movement mainly financial, largely, religious, among his greater subjects. He would necessarily feel his power more and more challenged, more and more sapped. He would also necessarily come to be a target for opposition or attack from the one and another section of his subjects.

He would certainly, whatever he was, be closely and suspiciously watched by those who had benefited in fortune through the great

THE CIRCUMSTANCE

religions revolution of the last generation and who were determined to maintain the new economic position they had seized. *The least move towards an attempt to recover Church lands or dues in any part of his dominions would certainly lead at last to an explosion.* One might even argue that with so many elements of discord around him, and especially with the presence of that violent contrast between the claims and appearance of the Crown on one side and its declining power on the other, there was bound to be armed rebellion. And so it fell out. The threat to recover certain Church lands in Scotland began his troubles, the necessity for supplementing the falling revenue continued it, Puritan exasperation inflamed it. Any character surrounded by such a Circumstance would have been doomed to conflict. But the conflict would differ in form and in result with the character involved in it.

What fortunes the reign should have, what form the policy of the day should take, and its issue, must depend upon the reaction of this particular monarch's character to the Circumstance in which he grew up and, as a young man, assumed the Crown. We must turn, then, to consider what this character was; to what that life was which, meeting such Circumstance, surrounded by it, suffered the fate it did: defeat and a violent death.

STUART

A MONG THE OTHER GREAT HOUSES OF WESTERN CHRISTENDOM sprung from Normandy appears, already established full nine centuries ago, the house of one Foald. His son Alan came to England with William, the bastard of Falaise, the Conqueror, and was granted after Hastings the rents of Oswestry and its lands in the west. Now this Alan had two sons, the elder called William, the younger Walter. William, inheriting his father's land, became known as Fitzalan, that is (in his own French tongue) "Alan's son," and from him were the Fitzalans descended in right line. But Walter went north, to Scotland, taking service there with David the King. To him David gave the title of "Steward," that is, administrator and head of the royal household, and this office, passing to his own posterity, became the name by which they were known.

Son after son inherited name and office, growing in power until the sixth in the line, nearly 300 years after its founder, having married the daughter and heiress of the Bruce, their child Robert was made Scottish King. It was in the days when Wyclif was theologising and Chaucer writing verse in England.

But more than a hundred years before this the fourth Stuart, a man famous in battle, had married a certain younger son of his to a great heiress, and from him ran a line of wealthy Stuarts, *cousins-cadet* to the kingly Stuarts of whom Robert had been the first.

In the year 1546, just before the active Reformation in England had begun, while Henry VIII was still alive and the Mass everywhere still said and established, this younger line of the Stuarts saw born to it a son Henry, who was called Lord Darnley, after one of his family lands.

He was brought up in England and had been kept in Catholic practice as a boy in the years when Cecil was imposing his great change and his newly established Church. But he was at Elizabeth's

STUART

Court, and as he approached manhood his name was prominent, for while he counted as a full Catholic and might therefore attract the attention of the whole Catholic body he was also a claimant to the Throne of England, and might be its heir. His claim came through his grandmother, the daughter of Henry VII and sister of Henry VIII.† She had first been married to the King of Scotland, but after his death she married again, and of this second marriage Darnley was the grandson. There was another claimant, who was, by right, the true Queen of England at the time when Cecil and the King of Spain between them had put Elizabeth upon the Throne; this was Darnley's cousin, Mary Stuart, the granddaughter of that same Tudor Queen by her first marriage with the Scottish King.

Mary was three years older than Darnley, and from before Darnley's birth had been true and accepted Queen of Scotland, the only child and heiress of the last King, James V. She also, of course, had been brought up a Catholic. She had been sent to France, where she was to marry the heir to the throne, who died very young and left her a widow. After that Mary returned to Scotland, to rule there as best she might; for the whole country was in a state of violent religious revolution, with a strong Calvinist faction which was getting rapidly more powerful, which was supported by the English government under Cecil, and which had for its protectors and principal strength the nobles, who desired still further to loot the Church lands.

Into this turmoil the young widow Mary, Queen of Scots, plunged; and at such a moment she committed the prime error of demanding her cousin Darnley in marriage. Elizabeth had been reluc-

---

† The Stuart hereditary right to the Throne of England.

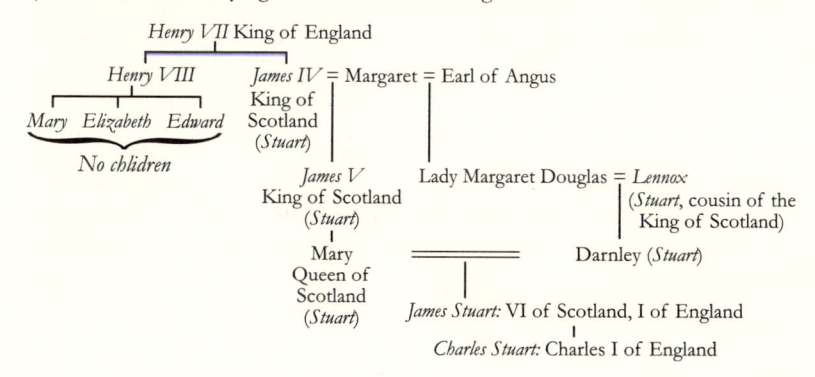

Henry VII King of England
├── Henry VIII
│   ├── Mary
│   ├── Elizabeth
│   └── Edward
│   No chlidren
└── *James IV* = Margaret = Earl of Angus
    King of Scotland
    (*Stuart*)
    │
    James V   Lady Margaret Douglas = *Lennox*
    King of Scotland   (*Stuart*, cousin of the
    (*Stuart*)   King of Scotland)
    │
    Mary   ════════════   Darnley (*Stuart*)
    Queen of
    Scotland
    (*Stuart*)   *James Stuart:* VI of Scotland, I of England
                 │
                 Charles Stuart: Charles I of England

CHARLES I

tant to let him go; she knew (though others were only beginning to suspect it) that she could never have a child. She was a warped, frustrated woman, sensitive to the accusation of bastardy under which she suffered in the eyes of Christendom (for when her mother Anne Boleyn, the mistress of Henry VIII, gave birth to her, the King's legitimate wife was alive); and, to check her masters under whose management she chafed, she would never acknowledge *any* heir – though heir there must be some time in the natural course of things. However, she let Darnley go, and now Darnley in Scotland married this young Queen of the country, Mary – or rather she married him. She was not yet twenty-three, he was not yet twenty. What concerns us is the blood inherited from this marriage by Charles of England, who was the grandson of it.

Darnley was hopeless. He was already a drunkard, debauched, probably also already diseased, though this had not yet affected his appearance. He was tall and handsome, and Mary's attraction to him – not without political reasons – was not mainly political, though with that marriage two claims to the English Crown merged.

Within a few weeks of the wedding the marriage began to go to pieces. Darnley was no support whatsoever, and Mary relied for her public work upon a secretary and factotum called Rizzio.

In the month of March, 1566, on the 9th thereof, the unhappy marriage being now some seven months past, and Mary already some six months gone with child, Rizzio was seized and murdered by men of the Court before Mary's very eyes, shrieking to her for protection, while she, trying to intervene, was gripped by Darnley and threatened with a pistol, the iron of which she could feel through her dress. Rizzio was dragged from the room and stabbed in the doorway.

This was the horrible night which put its stamp upon the mother and her child, and there was more to follow. For later, flying for her life with the child yet unborn, Darnley, in terror of his life also, compelled the horse on which she was riding pillion to gallop through the night though her agony was more than she could bear and she cried out; but he replied that he could spare the life of the unborn child – that they must save their – that he must save his!

Three months later, after a bitter interval in which Mary had had to feign affection again for Darnley in order to manage him and save herself and the country from such a character, the child was born, on the 19th of June, 1566. It was a boy; and they gave him, after his grandfather the last King, the name of James.

There followed for the young mother error after error, disaster upon disaster, with which we are not here concerned save in that they presage so much of what was to come to her grandson Charles. Darnley was murdered by rebel nobles. She was accused of complicity, without proof. She married the man who was in reality most guilty though publicly acquitted. In a further violent rebellion against her she was imprisoned, escaped, was defeated, fled over the border to England for sanctuary and there fell into the hands of Cecil, who kept her a closer and closer prisoner because she was the Catholic rival to Elizabeth. Further, when, nearly nineteen years later, Elizabeth had one of the worst of her fits of sickness and seemed likely to die, Cecil and his lot saw to it that Mary should be put to death – for with a Catholic heiress alive on Elizabeth's death there would have been a Catholic rising and, had it succeeded, Cecil and his were doomed.

Meanwhile during all those years the child James, King of Scotland now, was brought up as the pawn and later as the prey of factions, the great nobles contending overtly for or against the change in religion, but much more, in reality, for money. They had put the crown on his head while he was yet a baby; and he fell ultimately into the hands of that faction which was determined upon a change in religion as the best means of enriching its members; for during all that time, even before the baby's birth and when the young Mary, Queen of Scots, had first come to her kingdom, there had arisen and was now rising higher a storm of Calvinist enthusiasm, centred chiefly in Edinburgh, but present everywhere in the Lowlands and intense in its hatred of the old religion.

All that movement Cecil, the master of England, fostered and supported. This lad who was nominally head of the kingdom of Scotland, James, grew up with the taint of his origins manifest upon him. If there were upon the Stuarts, as an ancient and confused tradition would have it, a curse, in him physically it was exemplified. His body was big and strong enough but his legs weak; he seemed not to have full control of his mouth, from which the tongue would loll out, nor of his eyes, which rolled perpetually in his head. He could not stand properly for any length of time, but would lean for support against whoever was next him, and though perhaps he was not actively vicious he was at least abnormal.

But it is a very imperfect understanding of this King James, who, from his nineteenth year, was the acting King of a small and very poor northern people, to think of him only as the displeasing physical thing he was. He had good judgment and an alert sharp intellect; he had humour; he was not devoid of strong feeling. He had married, after a romantic journey of his own initiative, a sprightly woman of striking character, Anne, Princess of Denmark. He showed in his decisions a sound understanding of what Europe then was, but especially of how to attain the two ends which he had ever steadily before him – the recovery of the royal power, and the attainment, when Elizabeth should die, of the Crown of England. His youth, nurtured in the domination of the rebels, confirmed him in the first object; as for the second, he would not have attained it, though he was the rightful heir, but for the support of the Cecils, father and son, who were the direct government of England. He lived in part upon a subsidy which they paid him, and he looked to their support to bring him into England the moment Elizabeth should die.

He had never known his mother. He was fully acquainted with her religion, the old religion; he was not out of sympathy with it; but he had been trained by the Calvinists, and he knew well that, save with the support of the dominant Calvinist faction, of his own great nobles in Scotland and of the established Protestant rulers in England, with the Cecils at their head, King of England he would never be.

Now to be King of England meant everything to James. England was at least four times, perhaps five times, as populous as the land, mainly barren and mountainous, sparse in crops, lacking in towns, which he had inherited. And it was immensely wealthier. From that impoverished restricted little Court in the north he hoped to pass before the best of his life was spent (Elizabeth was more than thirty years his senior) to real power and to something like splendour. Meanwhile he perfected, thought out, proclaimed, argued, insisted upon, the supreme rights of kingship – of which his own position was so pitiful an example. It was in part the reaction against the miseries of his childhood; in part, and perhaps more, the work of a really active first-class brain dealing with the main political problem of

STUART

the time. For the days of James's reign were those in which the great struggle between Monarchy and Rule by the Rich was being fought out all over Europe.

The active dark-eyed vivacious Anne, his consort, bore him there in Scotland children, some of whom died early, but three of whom survived. The eldest, Henry, born in 1594, seemed to have escaped the taint in blood and grew up to be a find handsome boy full of vigour like herself; the next, Elizabeth, also vigorous and, by the testimony of contemporaries, charming; and lastly, six years younger than Henry, the baby Charles, puny, distressful – as it seemed hardly destined to live. The Queen bore him in Dunfermline, on the 19th of November, 1600; and down there in the south the unfortunate old Elizabeth still lingered.

For two full years and somewhat more, James waited impatiently for the end, knowing still what slips there might be between the death of the Old Queen in England and his own succession to her. And in Dunfermline the baby Charles, sickly, crawling or carried because he had not the strength to walk even at three years old, just survived, obscurely. Then one day, early in the year 1603, came the great news and the change.

To understand what next followed we must again go back to the origin of all these people, the first stirrings of Henry VIII's schism and the subsequent English religious revolution, which had begun a long lifetime ago – some sixty to seventy years – just within the memory of the oldest men alive in 1603. Henry VIII had taken for one of his mistresses a certain Mary Boleyn. She was the daughter of a very rich man of mercantile origin and (what was more important) of his wife – herself the daughter of the head of the Howard family.

Mary Boleyn consented to be Henry's mistress without terms. She was facile; and when Henry tired of her (which he soon did) he passed on these leavings of his to one William Carey, a gentleman about his Court. Henry then, feeling a general craving for the family type, turned to Mary's sister Anne in order to make a mistress of her in her turn. But Anne had such ambition as her sister had not had – she refused the King until he should somehow or other manage to have her crowned Queen.

We are not concerned with what followed – the Pope's hesitation both political and religious, his putting off and putting off

CHARLES I

the annulment of the King's marriage with his own legitimate wife Katherine. Henry's cutting things off short by getting Anne's creature Crammer to pronounce a divorce – after which he had her crowned in Westminster Abbey, to the disgust of his people and the indignation of Europe. The interest lies in this:— An illegitimate daughter was born to Anne soon afterwards – in 1533: we must always remember that she *was* illegitimate by all the standards of the times both for the English and for the mass of Europe. This bastard daughter lived to be that Queen Elizabeth who was now, in 1603, dying.

Meanwhile, Mary Boleyn had had by her complacent husband, Carey, an only son whom Elizabeth, his cousin, created Lord Hunsdon and made Chamberlain of her Household.

Now this man, the first Lord Hunsdon, had a seventh and youngest son who had been born about 1560 and was, therefore, at this moment – 1603 – rather over forty years of age; by name Robert – Robert Carey. As a young man this Robert Carey had already been seen in Scotland in the train of Walsingham, and had there come across young James, half a dozen years younger than himself. Later he had been employed all during the last years of Elizabeth variously, on the Scottish border, which gave him further opportunities for following what was happening in Scotland and keeping at rare intervals in touch with the Scottish Court. There had already reached James at his palace in the north news that Elizabeth could now last but a few days. She died at three o'clock in the early morning of Friday, the 24th of March, 1603.

The all-powerful man in England at that time was (and so remained till his death) the second Cecil, Robert, the son of the great Lord Burleigh and the continuator of his father's policy. It was he who had made certain of James's succession to the English Throne, although with his usual caution he had used a go-between, Henry Howard, the uncle of that Arundel who would have been Duke of Norfolk, had not the title been attainted at that moment, since William Cecil had managed to get his father to put to death more than thirty years before. It was Cecil who worked what followed, but he needed an agent who would be successful in carrying out a difficult piece of work and he found that agent in the person of this Robert Carey.

Horses had been got ready all along the Great North Road for many days past, and Robert Carey, on the morning of that same

STUART

March day, Friday, the 24th, at about nine o'clock, set forth in secret and with great speed.

The distance he had to cover was 397 miles. He brought the last of his weary galloping relay horses into the courtyard of Holyrood late on the following Sunday evening, having ridden the 397 miles in sixty hours. It was one of the great rides of history. One may ridicule Carey, and there was a good deal that was ridiculous about him, but at any rate no one can ridicule his riding. And for this exploit Carey was to have his reward.

James set forth at once for England. There was astonishment and not a little disgust at the first shock of his appearance, his almost incomprehensible Scottish accent, and his pompous assertive manner which went ill with his lumbering ill-supported frame and his big uncouth face and uneasy glance. The children were left behind; the rigorous young Henry, now nine years old, Elizabeth, who was six and a half, and baby Charles. Later Henry and Elizabeth went south to join their parents, but Charles was left behind. It is just possible that this baby carried on through life some slight memory of those days; events very striking do sometimes remain in the mind even from so tender an age. At any rate Charles was left secluded in Dunfermline. He was not neglected. Everything was done to foster his constantly failing health and his apparently doomed little weak body – but he lacked companionship. That first isolation of his during all those very early years must be remarked, and counted among the things which formed him. It was not till the next year, 1604, that the doctors thought he could, at some risk, be moved, and the little child was brought down south with every precaution, slowly, stage by stage, to meet his parents.

James loved his children; he was anxious to see baby Charles again; he came out a long way to meet him, even as far as Northampton, and there took the poor little thing up in his arms and kissed it and set it down again, certainly noting – for though his gaze was so uncertain and clumsy he was as sharp as a ferret to note what was going on about him – the ill-effect produced by that small unhappy morsel of humanity upon the women and even the men of the Court about him. But now Carey's wife was to be given the custody of that child, and a year later he himself was to be put at the head of the little Prince's household. It was a good stroke of fortune for the Careys

CHARLES I

— the administration of what we should call today about £6,000 a year with the perquisites thereof and separate salaries of their own as well. As for Lady Carey, she was one of those women who know how to manage and delight in doing it. She was a success, and her success forms part of English history, for it was she who saved little Charles.

She had been a Trevannion before her first marriage; her present husband was her second one, she was of good birth, of Cornish stock, and, as I say, energetic, resourceful and of good judgment. James, alarmed at the way in which the months went by and the child not able to walk properly though in his fifth year, wanted to have set on either side of his legs those irons which are sometimes used for strengthening children so afflicted; the little boy's ankles were so weak that some thought they were disjointed, and his father seriously feared that he would grow up a cripple. But Lady Carey would have nothing of irons; she believed that Nature would set things right, and Nature, approving of her determination and judgment, obeyed her commands — as did James. But there was yet another affliction in this afflicted childhood — an affliction which Charles never wholly grew out of, though he grew out of all the others, and this was his difficulty in speech.

He was naturally very nervous, and his hesitation had been increased by the way he had been kept apart; but the impediment in his speech was also a definite mechanical thing. James was for having a slight operation performed and the ligament at the base of the tongue cut, as is sometimes done in these circumstances. Again Lady Carey would have none of it. And she carried her point — as indeed she carried all her points, for she was of that kind. And it is to her, and her ability of thus having her own way, that we owe the life of Charles and the many years with which his own character quite as much as his tragedy ennobled the history of England. It was Lady Carey who saw that he should be as much as possible in the country, saving him from the fret and excitement of the Court, strong as would have been the temptation of any other woman to make the most of her charge in public and herself to enjoy the great world. He was but five years old and a few weeks more when there fell an occasion upon which her rule had to be relaxed, for the ceremony of his Duchy. He was carried by the Peers summoned for that office into the old vast hall of the Palace of Whitehall,† and there had enough and too much of

---

† Not the Banqueting Hall as we know it; that was not completed till much later.

60

STUART

excitement. *That* was certainly a day he remembered, when he sat thus solemnly silent at the head of the table on his big chair, all blazing with jewels. They made him understand when he went to bed that night that he was Duke of York. It was his first touch of grandeur.

Lady Carey looked after him not only during these years of babyhood but on till he was a boy half grown and she could rejoice in the achievement of her task.

Such was the prelude; there you have the pre-natal strains which had made of the father James the mixed thing he was, half efficient, half diseased; there you have the bent of inward-turning, the timid but tenacious mind thus formed in those first years, the moulding in the strong hands of a capable woman, the putting forth of the weak little figure upon feet, so to speak, and the introduction of it into life.

He was now in the middle of his boyhood, still something apart and secluded but his character had appeared and the formative years had opened.

Thomas Wentworth, First Earl of Strafford
AN OIL PAINTING OF THE STUDIO OF VAN DYCK CA. 1636

THE FORMATIVE YEARS

CHARLES ENTERED LIFE – THAT IS, THOSE YEARS IN WHICH A CHILD becomes fully conscious of the things about him, noting others and concerning himself with environment – still very reserved in one set of qualities, in another younger than his years. He was older in his gravity and detachment, both the product of his ill-health, his bad start in life, his continuing though decreasing weakness of body; but he was younger in the retardation of his development, his continuing moral, rather than physical, timidity.

He was not used to contact and still shrank from it. He heard and received patiently without reaction; though he was very sensitive in the matter of his defects, notably of his still weak legs and his halting speech. That speech was rare, though this sensitiveness would sometimes lead him to a burst of anger. Yet as a rule he was docile, if that was docility which was also mournfulness, for he was mournful from the first. His features in boyhood were his mother's – her long straight nose, high forehead and the exact oval of the face. Above that high forehead, which already had a stamp of nobility upon it, lay parted to fall on either side, very fine and silky brown hair which also he had inherited. His eyes again were Anne's; they were not illumined with the gaiety of hers, but they were dark and lustrous. One defect they had which they kept till the end – and that he had from his father – the too great prominence of the eye-balls; it was not very marked but it characterised his expression. His manners, apart from those rare fits of temper which soon left him, were very perfect: dignified, quiet and growing in form; and his hesitating voice was discovered to have great charm about it: it was a point which all noticed who remembered him.

In one thing the effects of that early debility from which Lady Carey had saved him were noticeable: he did not grow. He arrived too early at the fullest stature he would ever reach and remained all his

CHARLES I

life so short a man that the lack of inches was remarkable.† Perhaps a guess at 5 ft. 4 in. or 5 ft. 5 in. or something of the kind would be approximate.

The roughness and buffoonery, the coarseness, but also the hearty vitality of that strange Court little affected the boy. He did not protest against it; he did not notice it. He stood apart from it as a spectator, thinking his own thoughts. He had already a passionate affection, though hidden, and this solace was the companionship (not too frequent, for by the time he was ten she was already taken up in the life of high policy and alliances) of his sister Elizabeth. The love he had for her, her vivacity, her sudden smiles, lasted with him unchanged throughout her own troubled life – next only in its misfortunes to his own.

He was eleven before he was thought sufficiently developed for Lady Carey to terminate her charge, but already he was upstanding and his small body was saved. He might still have continued slowly maturing and reluctant to impress himself upon his surroundings, still retiring within himself wholly, had not there fallen upon the family in the next year – just at the end of his twelfth – a blow which changed all things. Henry, the beloved handsome elder brother, the idol now in his eighteenth year, suddenly, in a few days, died. It was perhaps pneumonia, for he was delirious and the first trouble had come upon him after a violent game of tennis which he had left too heated and after which he had caught a chill; but for some weeks before that those about him had feared he might be ailing. None of his own were near the boy when he died, the doctors would not have it – even Elizabeth, who adored him, was turned back when she tried to reach his bedside in disguise. And upon the 6th of November, 1612, he was gone. Suddenly Charles stood under new stars; he was become heir to England.

His whole position had changed; his whole meaning to those about him had changed; but the boy, still quite young, too young for his age, and always shrinking too much from contact, made nothing of it. There it was, and so it must be. He was heir to England; but he did not understand at all how that situation would develop.

---

† I have not been able to find any indication of his exact height in manhood, though we ought to have some record of it somewhere, seeing that his grave was opened and his body recognized many generations after his death. Was it not measured?

THE FORMATIVE YEARS

He was occupied with his own self and therein he showed not a little iron. He knew bitterly enough in what he was deficient, and very young as he was he had begun to determine the strengthening of himself. It was but a year since he had left what might almost be called the tutelage of a nurse, yet he struck out upon his own. And this early rooting in him of a determination to pursue his own affairs grew to be a permanent part of his character, making him strong not as a block of stone is strong but strong as a plastic material may be strong. There were fibres of inflexible determination within him, now rooted, and they exercised their influence upon the most important things: upon his determination to do his duty and therefore to fulfil the tasks of his royal office later on: upon his determination to be loyal to every affection: upon his determination to keep a goal in view. Also there grew in him, from these roots thus planted in the turn between childhood and early adolescence, a determination to fix certain boundaries to action beyond which, in any negotiation, he would not retreat.

These things at such an age, when a lad is entering his teens, are nebulous enough – they are nonetheless determinant of character. Such determinants nourished his formative years, and that is why, towards the end of that life which was just beginning, you find what the foolish call obstinacy, and for which the wise have found no name; for no wise man has given Charles Stuart as yet his due praise.

I may compare the effects of his inward strength to the effects produced by one kind of resistance against an impact.

When men plan to make impact against resistance in the will of another they expect, and commonly find, at first a resistance. They proceed to wear it down. If it gets less, they are introduced to a last struggle in which, when they have taken all the outworks, they may naturally expect to succeed. So it was with the pressure brought against the boy's father, James I, in the first beginnings of the revolt of the gentry against him. James's Parliaments – that is, the country gentlemen – pushed him further and further. Such an action is like a siege, it can have but one end, and as we know, James, fighting from trench to trench, always, in the end, gave way.

Then again, there is the kind of resistance offered by men who are adamant from the beginning. They bluntly refuse, and if you lost your first battle against them you can go no further.

CHARLES I

But Charles was to be neither of these. His nature, trained in isolation, was fluid against the first onset of attack; then there came a moment when the attack reached something quite different from the first fluid resistance – a stone wall. It was thus that he came to his death. Men were led on to think him pliable; when they came unexpectedly on rigidity, they were infuriated.

Now this distinction, I take it, between his fixity upon certain things, well defined in his own mind, and his indecision or rather lack of convinced *cause* for resistance on the rest – this quality in him which kept in reserve and hidden an ultimate power of complete refusal reserve (even to martyrdom) took root, I say, in these very early years when he was compelled, almost against himself, to consider in private what remedy he could find for his defects.

He was heir to England now; good; but apart from that, he would not, as puberty came upon him, consent to be insignificant.

What he first showed was an industrious resolve to redeem his body. Being already very short in stature and slight, he would probably remain so; since he stammered, and was ashamed of it, his face fell before the gaze of others; he could still remember how in childhood his limbs would hardly support him. Now he methodically took to exercise; he played his tennis, having before him the athletic example of that elder brother, now dead, whom he had so much admired; but especially was he determined to be a good rider.

Now here you have something remarkable. For most men seem either to be born riders, or never to ride well at all; and if a boy be short in stature, weak in the legs, and know himself to be timid at that, riding the great horse (distinguished in those days from the hackney and involving much more strength, skill and courage) would be the last thing one would expect him to undertake. It was here precisely that Charles set himself to excel, and there he certainly showed what will he had in him. Before three years had passed, when he was fifteen, his ungainly father was surprised and delighted to see the little figure, graceful, well set, and controlling from its high saddle the big mettlesome mount on which it rode. James had a queer confusion in the mind, at seeing what had been the neglected baby but was now necessarily the heir, developing this new power. This horsemanship, acquired so early by strength of will, Charles retained to the end. He rode, sitting loose but well, all his life, and we must remember him as a horseman.

THE FORMATIVE YEARS

But the business of the Court, though one cannot say that it repelled him, left him spiritually aside. He was not affected by it in those early boyish years. It was well enough for him that it should be so, for that Court was lowering the already imperilled position of monarchy in England.

The Court's virtues quite as much as its vices diminished that prestige without which nothing can govern. The frankness and the gaiety of Anne the Queen did not make for ceremony. The intimate nationalism of the King, with many Scottish companions, a Scottish tongue and, one may say, a Scottish mind, in that day when Scotland was enemy and alien to England, was to his honour, but not to the strengthening of kingship. And while it was good that the Court should be splendid (which it was beyond its means) and gay, which it also was, and of no great harm to England or to itself that it should be coarse, yet it was of great harm to itself and to England – or at any rate to the kingly dignity – that it should be morally extravagant, full of things unseemly.

Of this the worst was James's irrational and inconsequent attachment to favourites. And this attachment was not only irrational and inconsequent, it was blatant. All England knew and despised one Carr, a Scottish lad – of tolerable birth – whom he had brought with him, putting him into the peerage and giving him the highest honours. Then he grew tired of the favourite's airs and domination, and the base fellow exceeded on his side. He fell under conditions that are notorious.

All that happened in those first years when Charles had just become heir, when he was absorbed in his exercises and unwilling to be too much put forward publicly. We may guess (we cannot affirm) what effect such an atmosphere in the Court had upon the lad. He may have been disgusted; he may have been too young to be other than indifferent; but probably at the end of the business he had already begun, as he approached his sixteenth birthday and a certain knowledge of things and of men, to be offended with this atmosphere of favouritism. For in what followed we shall see him thus moved.

What followed was the supplanting of the ridiculous and offensive Carr by a young brave, gallant, and very distinctive English gentleman, George Villiers. The story of the way in which this new favourite of his father's, from being an offence to Charles became his companion, his friend, and at last the chief influence over his early life, is the heart of the Prince's story in the next five years.

While yet Carr (under the title of Somerset – grotesque enough in such a connection!) was still unquestioned, though the observant could perceive the beginnings of his decline, this young man George Villiers, a younger son of ancient lineage in Leicestershire, came to London, and was seen at Court. Fortune he had none, and his object in coming up to town was to obtain as a wife, the daughter and heiress of Sir Roger Ashton, one of King James's gentlemen of the bedchamber. The marriage had been recommended and apparently approached – or suggested sufficiently for these first steps to be taken. The young man was just twenty-two, he had come back from a long tour on the Continent, upon which his widowed mother had sent him by way of completing his education. We must particularly remember that on this journey he had for companion a young man of much the same rank as his own, and with plenty of cash, which Villiers had not; this rich young man was the son of a certain Cornish squire, by name John Elliot who formed a friendship for Villiers – and later betrayed him.

For some three years, George Villiers had travelled thus, had become well acquainted with French, and had rubbed shoulders with the great world abroad; he had learnt the manners and habits of a Court far more refined and cultivated than ever was the Court of James I. Though he was a younger son, and thus poor, he was certain to reach some position, for he made friends easily, was gracious, well mannered, exceedingly good-looking, courageous, tall, active and excellent in the use of the body. He had also, not in excess and not to the degree of cunning but in a degree sufficient to be of great service, the faculty of waiting. It was not in his nature to plot and intrigue much, though he certainly wanted to advance – as all such younger sons of the landed gentry did. To aid him in this advance he had not only the quality, rare in the young, of being able to wait, but also a remarkable absence of touchiness. One might almost have said, in this first youth of his, he was unable to quarrel. He seems to have had a natural inclination for making friends with those who had at first resented his presence. His beauty of feature was striking; that and the tall shapeliness of his person, the natural grace of his gesture, were what was first noted by any who saw him – they are the first things appearing in the memory of contemporaries. James being what he

THE FORMATIVE YEARS

was, such a newcomer to the Court could not but be a candidate at least for his favour.

But at that moment, August, 1614, when Charles was still no more than a boy and socially a rather backward boy, only just realising what it meant to be heir to the Throne, intent upon the task of strengthening his health and perfecting himself in exercise and horsemanship, the favourite still in the ascendant was the ignoble Carr with his thick alien accent and forward offensive manner. James had not yet got rid of him, though perhaps he was becoming a little tired. Young Villiers had so far advanced in the King's favour that by the autumn he was given the minor post of cup-bearer, but it was a post that brought him continually before the King, and meanwhile Graham, a courtier of some influence, approached the young man and dissuaded him from his intended marriage.

At this point it must be appreciated that there was a powerful body making against the influence of Carr, and the stars were fighting in their favour. The reason was that Carr had become too much of a scandal altogether – he and his wife between them, and her relatives the Howards, who hoped by Carr's influence with the King to get the greater offices and thus to add to their incomes. Indeed, nothing is more remarkable in this reign than the way in which, while the prestige of the Crown sank lower and lower, the great families served it more and more subserviently. The story of Carr's downfall is this:—

The boy who was the son of the unfortunate Essex (he who had been sacrificed to the old age and depravity of Elizabeth) was married at the age of thirteen to a Howard girl of his own age, the daughter of Lord Suffolk, Frances by name. He was then sent off to sea, and when he came back three years later she, though nominally his wife, would have nothing to do with him. With repulsive wickedness this young slut of sixteen plotted to obtain a nullity suit, with the object of marrying Carr, the King's favourite, and her father, her brother and her uncle (yet another Howard peer) supported her in the outrageous plan. For if she were to marry Carr she would not only have the great income which the King had arranged for him but, through her husband, the favourite, her relations would be able to get out of the King all that they might desire.

Carr had in those days a sort of necessary man, a person who did everything for him, had a considerable influence over him and

69

CHARLES I

planned to rise with his master's fortunes; a certain Overbury. Overbury tried to interfere with this idea of Carr's marrying Lady Frances after she should have obtained her divorce. For some reason not very easy to discover the proposed marriage did not suit his book. Frances Howard, Lady Essex, first got Overbury into the Tower, and then paid people to poison him. The man was thus poisoned and died on the 15th September, 1613. Ten days later a commission (on which the deciding people were the Bishops, after the fashion of the old Church Courts in such affairs) granted Frances Howard her verdict and her marriage with Essex was pronounced null, so that she was free to marry Carr. But it was noticed that among the Bishops who dissented the Archbishop Abbot was prominent. Henceforward it was Abbot who was to do all he could to fight the Howard faction and to procure the fall of the favourite. It was he, therefore, who pushed the coming fortune of Villiers, and he who persuaded the Queen to help him in that task. Later the task was amply fulfilled: the mystery of Overbury's death was inquired into, the immediate poisoners and their abettors were put to death. Carr (Somerset) and his detestable wife, Frances Howard, ought to have suffered as the principal culprits. They were pardoned; but their title was over and the field was free for the advance of the new favourite.

Two powerful influences had therefore been brought to bear in favour of young George Villiers's advancement; the influence of the Queen and the influence of the patriarchal Archbishop Abbot. The former was always listened to by the King, although he had but very little of the affection of a husband for her, and the latter made so much of the young cup-bearer that he called him, on the growth of their intimacy, "his son," and in little more than a year he was writing letters to him which began, "my George." All this bore rapid fruit. On St. George's Day the young man was knighted by James, who had already told off Graham help him on. He was, at the direct instance of the Queen, made a Gentleman of the Bedchamber, and soon there was set apart for him out of the funds of the Court of Wards the equivalent of what we should call in modern terms six to eight thousand a year. On the New Year's Day of the third year in this very rapid ascent he was made Master of the Horse, rather more than half a year after he was raised to the peerage, and a full year later he was an Earl and a Privy Councillor under the title of Buckingham.

THE FORMATIVE YEARS

George Villiers was now enjoying a total income of what we should call a hundred thousand a year. It was the most astonishing progress that had ever been made for a man by royal favour – and that man still so young and only two or three years before unknown. Meanwhile Carr had crashed. He lingered on under his title of Somerset, but in obscurity; he no longer counted in the councils of the state nor was anything to the King; and to the Englishmen who, all secretly and some of them openly, resented the presence of Scotchmen and the favours given to them at Court, and the presence of so many adventurers among their number, it was a blessed relief. In their eyes young George Villiers formed a most welcome contrast.

But how did Charles, who was now in his later boyhood and growing to be almost a young man, take this new close friendship his father had formed? Villiers (Buckingham, as we must now call him) was to become not only the chief friend of Charles, but the dominating influence in his early life, yet in those first years no one would have thought such a thing possible. The young heir to England was angry beyond the common limits of his reserved temper. He could not help contrasting himself and his lack of initiative and opportunity with this brilliant fellow, easy, tall, gay and of brilliant conversation, pleasing all, while he – Charles – short, and in the background, only once making a public figure in the Court (when he was proclaimed Prince of Wales) was something of a second order and lived upon another plane. Moreover, there was eight years difference between them, and that, though it is not a rational cause of jealousy was still a cause of jealousy between a boy approaching manhood and a young man whose manhood was achieved – and so brilliantly achieved! Though jealousy was not part of Charles's nature, yet there was jealousy in his attitude, as well as a constant irritation, and as he grew towards the end of his teens and Buckingham towards the end of his twenties, there were scenes which angered King James to petulance and, once at least, to violence.

Now it is characteristic of Buckingham, and perhaps the thing that best enables us to understand him, that he not only overcame this hostility in the lad who later would be King, but turned it gradually into a close acquaintance. This became at last an attachment so strong that it led the Prince to accept guidance from, and to fall wholly under the influence of, that older and more conspicuous friend. Nor is it in keeping with Buckingham's character – as that was revealed in all the actions of a very open and vigorous life – to follow in this anything of a plan. He loved to get on with all those around him, he hated to offend, and insofar as it is possible for a man of strong body and mind and active will not to offend, he did succeed in being friends with the world in spite of the envies which so astonishing a career aroused. Charles, I say, had changed altogether in regard to him; and that change was to be of the greatest consequence to both men. Through it the senior by eight years became not only the leader but the mentor. This early and most vivid affection was never forgotten by the young Prince. It was sealed in a tragedy, and after that tragedy you can feel the memory of Buckingham standing fixed, unchanging, in Charles's mind until he died. But if you would know what image it was that thus affected Charles Stuart, you cannot get it better than in one sentence left as a brief record by one who had known intimately all his contemporaries: "He was as inwardly beautiful as he was outwardly, and the world had not a gentleman of more genius."†

You will get the truest knowledge of Buckingham if you consider him as a young soldier. For this had Nature formed him. Had he been thrown by Fate into chances such as Marceau had, or Hoche, or young Edward Plantagenet (Edward IV of England) we should have had in Buckingham one of those gallant and arresting figures – youth in arms. It will be seen later how well he understood the problems of conflict and indeed, in spite of the heavy handicap against him – the failure of the revenue – came very near to adding a decisive page to the annals of England's amphibian wars.

It is characteristic of Buckingham that he grasped, as no one did in that day, the essential character of England's power reposing upon the sea. The country was small compared with the great Continental monarchies; it had no trained forces nor experience in Continental warfare, but its geographical position at the moment when the Atlantic had become the scene of traffic, the excellence of its seamen and their numbers, its command of the narrow seas and the Straits – all these made it possible for England to count more through sea-power

---

† The phrase in the original is not "of genius" but "ingenious." I have put it in the modern form because the word "ingenious" has since that time changed its meaning: thus another, nearly contemporary, speaking in admiration of William Shakespeare, calls him also "ingenious."

THE FORMATIVE YEARS

than in any other way, and with an organised marine to converse almost as an equal with Spain and France. The rapacity and corruption of the Court during the reign of the unfortunate Elizabeth had delayed and warped this maritime advantage; it had been frittered away in piracies and no one under the Cecil governments grasped the meaning of an effective, continuous, official organised armed force at sea.

Such a force – which for nearly three centuries was to remain the very essence of English strength – was the creation of the Stuarts, and especially of James, Duke of York, later James II. But at the origin of it all stands George Villiers. His great concern was for the creation of such a fleet and for the use of it, and as good a day's work as ever was done by the personal power of a King was the appointment of these very young, but fervid talents to the post of High Admiral of England. So determined was Buckingham to make the machine work that when he took it out of the incompetent and corrupt hands of old Nottingham (who is better known as Lord Howard of Effingham, the bitter anti-Catholic, who had held the post ever since Elizabeth's time) he paid a very large sum to his predecessor and, what is more, to ensure unity of command, he paid a further large sum for the purchase, from its existing possessor, of the Wardenship of the Cinque Ports.

He showed in every task he undertook energy and a determination to rule, and he had the particular quality of *lucidity*, of seeing what the problem was and how it should be tackled, which is the very mark of efficient command. But he was handicapped by three things; by weaknesses in himself; by the fact that he was contemporary with a greater rival, Richelieu; and above all by the impossibility of obtaining the financial means for the strengthening of England under his guidance.

Moreover, Buckingham was handicapped from within by diversity of aim, the perpetually recurrent weakness of ambitious men. He ardently desired glory, he also desired to achieve – and the two desires are never quite compatible and often at active issue one with the other. He desired wealth, he desired splendour, and with all this though he could wait and though he could understand a problem clearly, he was too passionate. Passion will not destroy a leader in arms if he be granted victories, but it destroys diplomacy; and Buckingham never had a diplomat to do his work for him. He was not a man of passionate angers; on the contrary, most of his charm lay in the perpetual gaiety of his nature and in his avoidance of bad blood, but he was passionate against a declared enemy, especially an insulting one, and thus allowed a minor personal thing to interfere with large impersonal plans. Connected with and part of this passion in him was his lack of self-control in the matter of women. It was natural enough; he was immensely admired, he was treated like a young god, and all the rest of it. But to be without restraint in this matter is a peril; continued, it rots men of fine texture.

We must not call it a weakness in him that he abased himself in the service of ambition which a single-minded man would not do; the attitude is a morally evil one, but it does not diminish the strength of public men, and all those who have advanced at Courts and in Parliaments have taken it. It had led him to a marriage which might surely have contented him, for the woman adored him and seemed to think herself sufficiently fortunate in being allowed but a part of his favours. Moreover, that marriage was part of the making of him, for she was a Manners – that is, a daughter of one of the greatest names as well as one of the greatest fortunes of the time. Her father, the Earl of Rutland, was not only immensely wealthy and of the greatest lineage among the old nobility, but one of that important minority among the Catholics who chose doggedly to accept all the evils which publicly proclaiming and practising the old religion involved. On that account he had at first opposed the marriage strongly; but he yielded, and the connection put Villiers still more strongly into contrast with the opposing Howard faction which had been the supporters of the late favourite, Carr. For the Howards as a group were anti-Catholic: the head of the family, who would have been Duke of Norfolk but for the attainder, was conspicuously so, disinheriting a nephew for returning to the religion of his ancestors.

Had there not been, contemporary with Villiers and set up in a sort of rivalry with him, the far greater figure of Richelieu, he might have been more. It was Richelieu who defeated Buckingham in his main effort under arms, it was the tenacity, the pre-vision, the energy of Richelieu which just at the critical moment decided the fate of the expedition in aid of La Rochelle.

THE FORMATIVE YEARS

The two men rose in something of the same fashion – through the favour of royalty (and the partiality of Marie de' Medici for Richelieu was not much more dignified than that of James for George Villiers). They differed in age, and Richelieu, the senior by seven years, came into active power later in life. There was no intention of rivalry; indeed, Richelieu would have been surprised to hear that Buckingham could have been considered a rival in any sense, but circumstances set up the one man against the other and when it came to scheming or even to tenacity there could be no comparison between them. For Richelieu, apart from his far superior talents, was a man of wholly single purpose – the establishment of French unity within the natural frontiers of France; "no enemies but those of the State." Lacking ambition, Richelieu completely achieved.

But the third handicap was the most serious. George Villiers would have made England such a power at sea as could have transported troops at will, occupied key positions upon the coasts of Europe, and thus have been an almost necessary ally to one of two rival Continental powers such as were at the moment France and Spain; but for such a plan great sums of money were vital and he came just at the moment when the regular revenue of England's Crown was sinking and sinking. He came at a moment when it was impossible to carry on save by the goodwill of the wealthier classes, shown in voluntary grants, and that goodwill was very conspicuously lacking. Government, and especially the Admiralty, had to scrape along as best it could on occasional grudging grants from the gentry in their organised form – the House of Commons – on gifts, or loans, begged for and with difficulty obtained; it never had one-third of what it ought to have had to create such a naval power as England needed and should have possessed. It was therefore impossible to recruit good crews or to keep them up to the mark, even to feed them properly, let alone to pay them. That obstacle George Villiers could never overcome. Yet even in spite of that obstacle he all but won the game in front of La Rochelle.

There stands the brilliant leader who was to fascinate with his warmth (and, it must be added, with his real affection) the still shrinking character of Charles. And Charles became at last, as he entered early manhood, wholly devoted in his turn to such a captain.

CHARLES I

Charles Stuart, the lonelier from the nature of his spiritual seclusion, found a friend, and to that friend he bound himself with all the passionate attachment of lonely souls. That well-remembered elder brother Henry, who had seemed like the sunlight to him, had died while he was yet a boy; his other great love, his sister, had married very shortly afterwards, and he never could forget the last vivid days when he was with her in Kent before her sailing to her German principality, having been recalled to London by his father, never to see her again. A third attachment of a lesser sort was for his mother, but it was much weaker, and though after her eldest son's death all her affection had gone out to the one remaining boy, she influenced him little. Her Catholicism, which was sincere but thwarted (she died under the ministrations of the Church of England) never affected him at all, and during the last years of her life, when boys begin to understand how a mother should be treated, she was failing in health so rapidly and so grievously that he had little chance of understanding what she might have been to him, like as he was to her in feature and in taste, though with no particle of her vivacity.

James had long been indifferent to his wife before that sad end of hers; Charles had then stayed with his mother – the only member of her family who did so – but the memory of his mother was never strong upon him. After her death, however, he was left without anything his silent need of affection could feed upon, until he came under the fascination of this true, warm and shining friend, Buckingham.

Such was Charles Stuart at the end of his formative years, in that age when Kings were thought to be competent to govern, and when his own father had been first permitted full power, for he was approaching his nineteenth year. Henceforward we must understand and see him wholly in the light of Buckingham; it was under the reflection of this light that he entered manhood, a still reserved, still ill-approachable and sensitive short slight figure of eighteen, looking to, hearing and following the energies of this young leader of twenty-seven, towering and vigorous in his astonishing success.

BUCKINGHAM

I. The Spanish Match

THE FIRST INTRODUCTION OF CHARLES STUART TO PUBLIC LIFE and the affairs of Europe, the first part he was called upon to play in person, was in connection with his proposed marriage to a Princess of Spain, the Infanta Maria.

It is important at the outset to understand how and why such a project had arisen and what effect it had upon the politics of England.

This young man Charles Stuart was not only the heir to England, but the sole surviving son of the King. His marriage would presumably mean an alliance with that power in whose family the bride was chosen, and with such an alliance not only the support of that power but a tendency (at least) for the English Government to support that power in their Continental policy.

James was at the head of a nation officially Protestant, and one where Protestant opinion was in the saddle. How large the Catholic-minded part of the English people was we know; we know also that the intensely anti-Catholic feeling was the feeling of a faction – a very large faction, but a faction nonetheless. It was a faction which felt so strongly in the matter as to blind it to all other considerations in foreign policy. Very many men of the greatest weight, who were quite as much opposed to Catholicism politically and in religion as their fellows, supported the Spanish marriage as a piece of policy: for instance, Wentworth. But, surrounding that faction, and radiating from it, the various degrees of anti-Catholic feeling, down to mere indifference, affected the majority at least of the nation. Though anti-Catholicism might not yet – by 1621–22 – command a large majority, a numerical majority it had, and especially was anti-Catholic feeling strong in London, where everything official was centred, where all

CHARLES I

public action passed: the capital whose moral atmosphere surrounded and impressed the Court.

Further, the most powerful section of all the English people, the wealthy landlords, both Lords and Commons, were for the most part by tradition attached to the anti-Catholic policy even when they had no strong religious feelings. A certain proportion of them, even a large proportion, and a growing one, were in personal religion opposed to Catholicism, but far more powerful were the family traditions of the squires great and small. From millionaires like the Hampdens, the Wentworths or the Cromwells down to the men with one country house only and one set of village rents for income, Protestantism meant, for them and their class, secure wealth, and the return of the old religion a menace of impoverishment. The origins of that tradition lay back eighty years in the past, when the first loot of the Church had begun to trickle into the coffers of the landed families, old and new. It was sixty years since the thing had been clinched and made permanent by the advent of the Cecils and their government. So long a use had only slightly dulled the sense of peril, for all the time renewed confiscations of Catholic land had fed the victors, land which, under a reaction, might be taken from them. On the other hand so long a use had given the feeling deep roots. Upon the change of national religion were the new landed fortunes established, by the same had the old landed fortunes been increased; to maintain the success of that economic revolution had been the main anxiety of its beneficiaries throughout the whole of the past reign, when, under Cecil, with Elizabeth as head of the State, the general policy of the country had been permanently established of the new Protestant religious settlement.

But Charles having this position of sole remaining son and heir to England, his marriage lay between one of two Catholic Courts – it must be either a Spanish marriage or a French one. Unthinking men (outside the large minority which was still in sympathy, slightly or strongly, with the old and now dying religious traditions of the nation) would have suggested a Protestant marriage for Charles on the ground of no more than religious sentiment: but there was now no Protestant marriage worthy of the occasion or that could sufficiently enhance the position of England in Europe. There must be connection with one of the great powers and all these were Catholic. France and Spain in their strong and increasing rivalry were yet both officially Catholic, and their Princesses sincerely Catholic.

There were two problems, therefore, before anyone with a sense of statesmanship in England at that day:—

(i) Which of these two rivals, France or Spain, should be chosen as the side to which England should lean through the marriage of the heir; and

(ii) When a decision had been come to, how such a marriage could be reconciled with the now permanently and definitely established Protestant policy and the now rooted Protestant opinion not only of those who were organised for the conduct of the State – the mass of the landed gentry – but also the bulk of the commercial middle classes – the great majority of it certainly in the towns – and above all the wealthy city of London?

A Catholic wife would certainly not abandon her religion; such a proposal would have been abhorrent to the traditions of the French Court, just recovering from the long horror of the religious wars; to the Spanish Court it would have been inconceivable. Yet a Catholic Queen, to be the mother presumably of children over whom she would have influence, a Catholic Queen, moreover, having her own train and Court, and inevitably her own clergy, would be, in London, a source of friction between the City and the Court. The more thoroughly the future was safeguarded against the influence of such a Queen, the more would that friction be alleviated. On the other hand, the more thoroughly it was safeguarded the more danger there was of a quarrel and war with the Queen's foreign relations.

As to the first point, there had been some hesitation as to which of the two alliances, Spanish or French, should be chosen. The tendency, the strength of which increased as time went on, to decide for Spain lay in these points:—

France was near at hand and, potentially, a very dangerous enemy.

Spain, possessed of what looked, at the time, like half the earth, was (in the eyes of the time) inexhaustibly rich. That judgment was wrong; the power of Spain was already declining. But so things appeared to contemporaries who are always misled by their immediate past and the remaining externals of it. How much greater France was to become during the lifetime upon which the younger men were embarked no one had guessed; but there may have been some element of instinct in this affair, a hardly conscious feeling that safeguarding against France was important.

The tendencies for the Spanish marriage were therefore in the ascendant; it was the issue which was expected, and negotiations for it were well advanced, when there fell abroad an accident which made all the difference and greatly increased the desire or necessity for the Spanish match.

This accident was the breakdown of the Elector Palatine, who had married James's only daughter Elizabeth, Princess of England, seven years before.

There lies in the midst of Europe a strong little square country called Bohemia, cut off by mountains upon three sides and looking southward through the open side towards the Danube and the power of Austria, with its capital at Vienna. Bohemia was and is Slav; but the fringe of it is German: the Germans being most numerous in the mountain ranges and in the plains to the south and east of them. Bohemia had at that moment for its rightful sovereign the Emperor at Vienna, that is, the Austrian Crown: not because Bohemia formed part of Austria, which it did not, but because the Ferdinand of Hapsburg, who was later elected Emperor, had been duly elected monarch of Bohemia, holding it as a separate Crown.

Now the Slavs of Bohemia had, since long before the Reformation, resented the domination of the German-speaking great lords on their soil and of a German-speaking Emperor. This feeling had such strength that it had even led some to religious revolt against that orthodoxy for which the Emperor stood, and there had been, in the later Middle Ages, outbreaks of heresy particularly intense among the Bohemian Slavs. Slav hatred of Germans made the Hussite movement – the chief revolt against the united religion of Christendom in the century before the Reformation. Afterwards there was arranged a large measure of toleration; and now, in these early years of the seventeenth century, the two religions in Bohemia lived on side by side. The mass of the population Catholic of course, but with a certain minority, especially of the well-to-do, Protestant. Now in this arrangement was a certain clause relative to episcopal lands. The Protestants might put up Churches where they would, but not (so the Catholics claimed) upon episcopal lands. The Protestants, supported by Slav national feeling even in the case of men who were not Protestant, were moved to a quarrel on that point. On the 23rd of May, 1618, rather more than five years after the young Elector Palatine (who stood for Calvinism among the Germans) had married the English Princess Elizabeth, the delegates of Ferdinand in Prague, the capital of Bohemia, had been seized and thrown out of the window by the leaders of the rebels. It was the famous incident, the beginning of the great religious German war, described with unconscious humour as the "Defenestration of Prague." When one sees the place where the "Defenestration" happened one wonders how the "Defenestrated" survived – it is a horribly high wall down from that window! Happily there was a large dung-heap on to which the Imperial victims fell immune.

But their immunity did not make the incident less sensational; the rebel faction having seized power illegally offered the Crown of Bohemia – as though the Throne were vacant – to James's son-in-law, the young Calvinist Elector Palatine, who very foolishly accepted it. He went to Prague, and proposed to act there as though he were King, against the legitimate monarch of the House of Austria. It was a mad proposal, because the Hapsburg monarch of Austria was not only in the right, but would certainly be supported by his cousin the Hapsburg of Spain. The forces of the usurping Elector Palatine were quickly destroyed, he fled, was put to the Ban of the Empire, and lost not only Bohemia but his own principality of the Palatinate, which was confiscated by the Emperor and overrun by the best troops in Europe, the Spaniards under Spinola.

All this produced an urgent political need, and a personal need also, for James to rescue his unfortunate daughter and her husband in order that her descendants might rule where their father had ruled and that the dishonour done to his family might be wiped out. Now it was hoped by the Spanish marriage to effect this. With a Spanish Princess married to Charles, the heir of England, Spain would, it was hoped, lend her weight to the English theme and help to succour the Palatine and his English wife and restore them, not, of course, to Bohemia but to the rightfully inherited lands of the Palatinate. Here, then, was James, the Stuart King of England with every motive for proceeding with the Spanish marriage for his son: his health was failing, he might not live long, and he intensely desired to see the thing done before he died.

It almost seemed as though the thing had been settled. The clauses of the settlement were being arranged one by one, and a large dowry, which James hoped would be paid immediately in cash, was no small part of it. The religious difficulty had been tackled; there seemed to be hopes that the Pope, who was very reluctant, would be induced to grant a dispensation.

It is possible that if things had gone normally, conducted through James's accredited Envoy at Madrid, a conclusion would have been reached and the proposed marriage brought off, in spite of its unpopularity with what was most powerful among James's subjects: most powerful in numbers as in wealth and in organisation, and in particular the merchants of London and their mob.

But a strange incident interfered. Charles being now close on his twenty-second birthday, in the latter part of the year 1622, Buckingham a man of thirty and now in everything Charles's support and guide and inspirer, the young men came to the King with a project for going off to Spain themselves incognito – a romantic adventure which had something of the schoolboy about it.

But the plan was not a mere escapade of theirs; it was not a mere folly; it had not even originated with them – not even with Buckingham, let alone with Charles – it had originated with a very able man, perhaps the ablest diplomat in an age of able diplomats, Gondomar, the Spanish Ambassador at James's Court. It was he who had suggested to the young men the plan which fired their imagination, and possibly it was he who got Buckingham to work upon Charles until he was as enthusiastic as his leader for the idea.

Gondomar's motive should be plain; he wanted to produce a shock. He thought that with the Prince actually present in the Spanish Court, by surprise as it were, the long-drawn-out negotiations would be clinched and the hesitations of the young King of Spain (and, what was more important of his great minister Olivares), would be broken down.

James, Gondomar perceived, would certainly have the wisdom to doubt the thing having any such effects, and that was why Gon-

BUCKINGHAM

domar had not worked through James, but through Buckingham. But Buckingham was no dupe, he knew the Continent fairly well, his excellent intelligence worked clearly in the matter, and he is not to be blamed if his own judgment agreed with that of so deservedly admired a statesman as Gondomar. Buckingham and Charles pleaded with the King for leave to go. James, surprised and worried gave way, resisted, and gave way again; but he shook his head over it as he finally consented. He did not know more of the duplicity and complexity of public life than did Gondomar – for no one could know more – but he judged the problem as a whole better than Gondomar had judged it. He believed that the shock would produce a reaction, that the two young men would act rashly and unwisely – especially Buckingham – and arouse opposition. He was right.

However, he let the young men go, and off they started in mid-February, 1623, in the highest of spirits; hardly attended, and later (what is rather absurd) disguised. As they passed through Paris they attended (in false wigs) the Court of the young King, where Charles saw the little Henrietta Maria, a girl of thirteen, dancing gracefully enough.

It was on Friday, March the 7th, 1623, that Buckingham and Charles entered Madrid as Mr. Thomas Smith and servant. The two had left their few attendants behind on the road by half a day's posting. It was about eight o'clock at night, dark, when Buckingham went up, alone and holding a suitcase, to the door of what we should call today the English Embassy, the house in which James's permanent Ambassador, Digby, Lord Bristol, a Catholic, lived and from which he had been carrying on his negotiations with the Spanish Court. After some little difficulty Buckingham was admitted and Charles, who had been waiting on the other side of the street, crossed and passed through the door into the lighted rooms within. Whether the surprise were complete or no, Bristol and the young Spanish King acted as though it were, and certainly the first interviews were cordial. The thing seemed to be going exactly as Gondomar had hoped it would – and then, as James had foreseen, everything began to go wrong.

Poor little Princess Maria, charming, innocent and good, with her fair Flemish face, neither liked what she saw of Charles nor could stomach the thought of his religion. When, upon a certain occasion, the Prince was urged (perhaps a little reluctant) to play a minor surprise and to scramble over a wall into the private garden where she was walking, she ran from him screaming. She implored to be allowed to take the veil.

But such human obstacles would not have counted had it not been that the real power in Spain, the great minister Olivares, elderly, experienced, dark, ugly, determined and strong, was more and more set against the whole affair. It was he, if we read the muddle as a whole and balance one thing against the other, who appears as the true author of the breakdown. He so acted that even Buckingham, the least quarrelsome of men, savoured insult, and was stung to a violent annoyance. Olivares made every delay. He counted on the growing weariness of Charles himself and on the certain revulsion of feeling in Buckingham, and he was not disappointed. All the careful work which Bristol had undertaken crumbled, and then Olivares played his trump card. He said (what he certainly did not think!) that he took Charles's conversion to Catholicism for granted. Bristol's game was lost, and the match with it. The thing was made the more certain by formal efforts at Charles's conversion. The dispensation from Rome arrived indeed, but under conditions which showed clearly what the end would be; the children of the marriage were to brought up Catholic, they were not to be disqualified from succeeding should they remain Catholic when they grew up; and the Spanish secular policy was on the same lines, demanding the fullest toleration for James's Catholic subjects.

Against all this Charles reacted more and more. It offended his dignity, of which very young men are so full; it offended also in him what, through all his life, was a fixed principle, most sincerely held, that the Church of England, of which he would be the supreme Governor on earth (and especially the Church of England as opposed to Rome) was the guardian and enunciator of the purest doctrine.

The summer dragged on. Buckingham and Charles still talked in their letters home as though things were going well, and even promised that at the end of August, when they were to begin their return journey, they would bring the Infanta with them.

There fell in the midst of all this a further significant incident. Among the few companions of Charles was a certain Henry Washington, who fell ill in that hot Spanish summer, and, at the approach of death, did what so many Englishmen did in those days; he sent for a Catholic priest. Thereupon another of his companions, Verney (who was of the other side) barricaded the door of Washington's room, and, when the priest came, hit that cleric in the face. The incident had an exaggerated effect, because it was symbolic; when at last the two young men, now knowing well enough that they had gone on a fool's errand, rode northwards, they were determined; and the most determined of them was Charles himself. Yet outwardly things were still going well, officially Charles was returning to put everything before his father and the marriage was to be held by proxy when a new dispensation from Rome should come, which would be necessary because the Pope who had given the first one had died. But before leaving Santander, whence he sailed, the Prince himself sent a note back to Bristol, forbidding the proxy for the marriage to be used until he could be satisfied about the Infanta's not entering a convent. It was obviously a ruse for delay, and Bristol was not deceived. He also, being in close touch with the English Catholic body, understood what had been the real cause of the rupture.

Buckingham and Charles landed at Portsmouth on the 15th of October, 1623, and immediately all men knew that the Spanish match was done for. Whereupon the powerful English imagination, which breeds such sudden enthusiasms, got to work in London, and the mass of the populace who had disliked the match, the lesser number who had hated it, went wild with joy. Since there was no corresponding enthusiasm among the restricted few who had seen the wisdom of James's policy, the celebrants had it all their own way. The streets were filled with shouting and cheering, and Buckingham (or rather an imaginary, deified Buckingham) became the God of the hour. And to him it was very sweet. He had tasted power and had used it. He had always desired glory, and now by the very fact of his failure and his rebuff, glory, popular fame and acclamation were upon him; though it broke old James's heart to see the patient labour of so many years undone.

And here it must be remembered that in these wild demonstrations which put Buckingham briefly into so fierce a blaze of popularity there entered, not as yet perhaps very consciously but nonetheless deeply, the opposition to kingship which had been steadily growing

CHARLES I

as the leaders of English society recognised their power. Such of the gentry as were in Town, also the rich merchants, the financiers of the City, in general the great taxpayers, more and more in the mood for resistance, were doubly glad. It was not only that the most of them had disliked the Spanish match and that some of them actually hated it; it was also that the Spanish match had been the King's creation, and to see it break down was to see one more step in the decline of the monarchy which in due time they were to supplant.

I say again, this instinct of theirs for depressing the Crown was not as yet conscious, or only partly conscious, or conscious only in a very few. But it is always so in the great revolutions of history; before they appear upon the surface they are running in the hearts of men, ill-recognised, sometimes not recognised at all, but on the move. It is like that tide which you may see in some dredged harbours, where the flood runs along the bottom of the fairway while on the top of the water the ebb still flows till long after its due hour for turning. But a time comes when the flood reaches the surface, and all can see with their own eyes that the tide has turned. The tide which put the gentry into power – and with them their allies the lawyers and the great merchants who now made part of the same social body – the tide which substituted aristocracy for monarchy in England, was not to be apparent to the eye for some years, but in the depths it was moving.

Buckingham, in this new fury of popular acclaim (for those who disapproved were silent) did what men of a conquering temper will always do – but in his case at this this moment it was a blunder. It was not a blunder to determine to feed the flame of popularity, for upon popular support (or at any rate upon the support of the more intense and the more powerful) ambition thrives and careers are advanced; but it was a blunder for him to let it take the particular form it did. *Buckingham urged the King to call a Parliament.*

I have used the word "blunder." Perhaps an apology is owed to the shade of Buckingham for using such a word. We know it to have been a blunder by its consequences, but we cannot say confidently that it could have been avoided, though its effect was the beginning of all the troubles, for what had happened was going to lead to war. Now this war Buckingham ardently desired; but war added suddenly and enormously to the already desperate financial straits of

BUCKINGHAM

the Government, and there was no source from which extraordinary payments — abnormal occasional supplies — could be obtained save from Parliament. Indeed Parliaments were rarely summoned save with the object of furnishing such exceptional sums of money. They were summoned as a matter of course at the beginning of a reign; they had been summoned more than once to support policy (to get a sort of ratification to the policy of the King from the richer and more important classes of the community) but the normal function of Parliaments, to fulfil which alone they were occasionally and reluctantly summoned by the Government, was to discuss what the rich could voluntarily arrange to supply for sudden and exceptional needs, arising out of the ordinary course, which the ordinary revenue could not be expected to meet.

At the risk of repetition this truth must be made to stand out, for if we read into the seventeenth century our modern idea of permanent Parliament we miss all the character of the time.

Well, the chance was taken, a Parliament was summoned and the risk of disturbance deliberately faced.

When we look back on that critical moment we see the desperate pity of it. England had been at peace for twenty years. There had never been known by any then living so long a stretch of prosperity and content. Only the Crown was embarrassed. The nation was rolling in wealth. Trade was increasing and the Customs revenue with it. The Government might have pulled through financially in the long run and the Old Constitution partly saved. But with *war* must come gravely increased financial strain. There would follow the dependence of the Crown upon the wealthy in their organised committees, the House of Commons and the House of Lords. The rightful government of the country, the Monarch who stood for all men, great and small, would have to go, hat in hand, to the rich. These would press their advantage, gradually advance claims which would at last destroy kingship and set themselves in the seat of power.

Buckingham had another intention in thus urging upon James the summoning of a Parliament. He desired to use that Parliament for ending whatever remained of support for the Spanish match.

The symbol of its destruction must be the undoing of Lionel Cranfield, Earl of Middlesex, and — this was the essential point

– Lord Treasurer: that is, financial adviser to and agent of the Government. Cranfield was not naturally opposed to Buckingham, the two men were complementary one to the other, and had not Cranfield now appeared, not only as a sort of symbol of support for the Spanish match but also as the most obvious man of which to make an example, he might not have fallen. But he had openly spoken in Buckingham's and Charles's presence and before the King in favour of proceeding with the Spanish match, using the word "honour." He had said that "honour" demanded of Charles that he should proceed with it. And that word "honour" – the insinuation that he was lacking in *honour* – was something Charles, Prince of Wales, would not tolerate, as Buckingham well knew.

Cranfield had risen from the middle class; he had begun as an apprentice to a City man of business into whose family he had married and whose affairs he had inherited, and Charles told him now, in words such as he very rarely used, for he was by nature courteous, that as for honour, Cranfield might keep his advice to himself and concern himself with money matters, in which he was competent enough no doubt. Let him deal with the mercantile concerns from which he sprang, but let him not talk of honour to gentlemen.

Cranfield would have enemies on all sides, for he had been a strict financial reformer and it was as such that he had hitherto worked hand in hand with Buckingham himself; Buckingham by reducing and putting into order the national expenses, especially those of the King's household, and Cranfield by a wise administration of the Treasury and a proper use of the Customs in a period of increasing trade (for under the excellent administration of the Stuarts the trade of England rose regularly and fast). Cranfield had made a fortune in the process of saving the fortunes of the State; such commissions and perquisites were the admitted habit of the time, but could always be used as accusations against anyone whom powerful men wished to impugn. It had been a favourite trick with every Government for generations past, when they wanted to break a public man, to accuse him of what all public men did – the taking of such perquisites and commissions. But to break Cranfield, and with Cranfield as an example, all the remaining strong and intelligent support of James's Spanish policy, Buckingham could work more solemnly and thoroughly through a Parliament than through a trial for peculation before one of the ordinary Courts or by mere dismissal.

For these reasons, then, Buckingham desired and urged the now failing old King to summon a Parliament; one might almost say he commanded; he certainly insisted. And James – for whom money was now an urgent necessity, since Spain had refused to help the Elector Palatine actively, and England would be compelled to intervene – James agreed. A Parliament should be summoned and it could be used to impeach Cranfield. But he told his son, and he told his son's leader and guide and masterful friend, something which those young men could not understand. To Buckingham he said that in resorting to the use of a Parliament he was making a rod for his own back; and to his son he said (in a prophecy more awful than he knew) "that he would have his bellyful of impeachments."

In early 1624 that fatal Parliament was summoned. James had but one more year to live. Buckingham, in almost royal fashion, addressed the assembled Lords and Commons (that is, the gentry of England) not in their own place but in the King's Palace, in the Great Hall where it had been James's custom, when such assemblies were occasionally summoned, to appear. The tall, vigorous young man with the short silent Prince at his side made an admirable speech to the two Houses. He was not only a good commander nor only a clear thinker, but one of the best orators of his time – if we may call him an orator who uses no rhetoric, but only persuades by a right marshalling of arguments and a firm reliance upon the truth.

Buckingham now told the Houses nothing but the truth. He told them what his adventures had been, how the Spanish Government had certainly not intended to carry out the policy of which they had made a pretence; and, with deliberation, in clear-cut phrases, he told them how much had turned upon Charles's devotion to the Protestant cause – how steadfast he had been in his support of the claims of the Church of England. He told them that Bristol had been the dupe of the Spanish Court, or their servant (in this alone there was exaggeration), and he ended by asking them whether, things being so, they would continue the Spanish Treaties?

He had an overwhelming success. Buckingham's abnormal career had offended many among the great families, none more than the Herberts, of whom Pembroke was the head. But even Pembroke voted with the rest. There was no going against the current. The Parliament met, and though it was all in favour of open war against Spain it did what might have been foreseen – it began at once to quarrel with the Government's demand for money. It extravagantly landed Buckingham, and that peculiarly offensive old man, the Lawyer Coke, who had married his daughter to Buckingham's brother and had called Buckingham himself a "saviour," demanded the impeachment of Cranfield the Treasurer, Lord Middlesex.

Thus was the instrument, or weapon, of impeachment launched. It was to be used later, as James had foreseen, against those who had so imprudently revived it.

Such impeachment was an innovation; and by a dreadful irony Buckingham himself was the author of that innovation! The process against Bacon had in its time, three years before, been called an impeachment; it was not a true impeachment; but the use now of Parliament for a political condemnation, unknown since the Middle Ages, was in effect allowing Parliament to taste blood. For in an impeachment the Commons of old used to arraign a victim of theirs or of the Government, accusing him to the House of Lords, who were to judge the case and could condemn the man at the bar to any penalty – to death. The time was to come when Parliament was to use this new revived, forgotten weapon of impeachment as a weapon not of those in power but of its own, a weapon indeed with which to destroy those in power because those in power were in truth less powerful than the Gentry assembled in Parliament who were about to replace the authority of the King by their own. Cranfield was impeached, condemned, not put to death but ruined; and with him all chance of the Spanish alliance disappeared.

What was left of James's reign was but a waiting for the end. There belong to those months the first negotiations of what was to be the alternative French marriage, and the disastrous Mansfield expedition. The first of these more properly belongs to what followed upon the old King's death; as to the second, the story is a simple one and should have been a warning to Buckingham of how impossible it is to carry out a military plan if he who has the power of command has not also the necessary supply. After so many years of peace that policy which the Protestant merchants of London and the great landowners had so much desired, the support of the Protestant cause in Europe, that which James had (before these last few months of decay had come upon him) so vigorously aimed at was realised. To aid in recovering the Palatinate in spite of Spain, twelve thousand men were to be sent as a beginning. It was with enthusiasm that the wealthy in their Parliament supported the expedition; with an equal enthusiasm they ultimately refused to provide the funds necessary for war. The troops were ill-paid, ill-fed, and at last not paid at all. They landed at last on Dutch soil at Flushing, but in the heart of the winter. Through February and March the wretched men, partly pressed and partly hired from the poorest of the people, fell in sickness and in death. As March, 1625, drew to its end there remained perhaps four thousand of the original twelve valid for a service which they were never to perform. On Friday the 27th of the same month of March the old King, on his last bed, had for one moment lifted his head from his pillow and said gently, "*Vene Domine Jesu*," and died in peace.

II. THE ATTACK BEGINS

Here was Charles Stuart, King: and a very young man. It was only three months since his twenty-fourth birthday, and he was still younger than his years in all things save a certain melancholy. He did not laugh.

He was younger than his years in lack of experience, lack of opportunity to watch men, in lack of knowledge for judging them; and younger also in his continued inability to deal with the complexity of life. His few principles were absolute, and that was a strength in him; but the knowledge of how many principles – they are an infinity – must be called upon in meeting the actual world had never been given him by experience or by teaching, still less by intuition. For his nature was simple and direct, dealing with few categories, infused by this strong, this profound affection for the glorious older friend who was now so firmly fixed in his heart. But, more than all else, Charles was resolute on the duty of kingship: the restraint of the powerful in the interests of all.

CHARLES I

In all this Charles was right, but though right, insufficient. But even had he had by nature subtlety, or the experience of years, could he have succeeded in the coming struggle? It would become of necessity a struggle between a Government without financial resources and an increasingly rich class which could not but grow determined to usurp the kingly power.

To vanquish that potential rebellion, which was soon to become active rebellion, two things would have been necessary: an army, and the support of the common people. An army could not be found, nor was it sought or thought of yet; had it been thought of it could not have been called into existence for two reasons: first, the Government had not the revenue to pay for it, nor could have such revenue without the voluntary consent and grant of the rich expressed through their two committees, the House of Lords and the House of Commons: secondly, the *cadres* of such an army could only be, must be, drawn from the gentry: and it was precisely against the gentry that the army would have had to be used.

But if an army was lacking, still more lacking was that other essential, the support of a populace naturally antagonistic to a rebellion of the wealthy against their King whose function it was to protect the many against the few. In spite of the gradual enrichment of the squires and their increasing grasp upon the land of the villages, their increasing power in local administration, there remained a mass of lesser men who were themselves freeholders, and were therefore reluctant to be assessed for grants. The mass of English agricultural families in 1625 were living on farms which even when they paid dues to the squires, were hereditable. They lived on their own land. Such freeholders could always be relied upon to support the gentry, while the landless men had no tradition of resistance to the rich leaders of the English countrysides. In the towns the greater commercial men were virtually part of the gentry, and the poorer men were mainly at their orders – notably in London.

It was with the odds thus heavily against him, though he did not appreciate them and though his enemies did not yet appreciate them, save in some measure by instinct, that this young man Charles, the King, faced his opponents.

What it meant for him to be King, in such circumstances and so young, must be judged not only from his own character with its determination upon maintaining its rights, nor only by the strong effect in those days of the monarchic principle throughout Europe, a general atmosphere of authority upon which he himself too much relied, but also by the aspect in which the gentry, the men of the country houses large and small, the average peer, the average local landlord, would see their sovereign who governed them.

In their eyes he was most vulnerable; there was no such tradition behind Charles as there had been behind James his father. All during the reign of that father, twenty-two years of it, the strength of the gentry had been growing and the strength of the Crown declining, once and again and yet again in those twenty-two years the gentry had shown their power of resistance through the organisation of their two Houses, Lords and Commons. They had increasingly shown their determination to have their way in the religious struggle (in the struggle against Catholicism) and in the curbing of authority by stinting supply. But so long as James lived there was the momentum of his earlier years and the unbroken tradition of monarchy which he had inherited from the sixteenth century. James had been a man already mature when he had come among them at their King; he had had weight and, in a fashion, increasing weight, in spite of his declining power, throughout those twenty-two years; and it had been a time of prosperity and peace, rising commerce and good livelihood. Now they had only this young man before them, without practice in government or a known personality.

Further, they might well believe him to be pliable. They had seen him following without question a character dominating his own; they conceived of Charles as being without initiative, and one who might be the better resisted. But there was this especial point which made all the difference to their position in 1625. Their one necessary instrument, the thing through which they could work – their two Houses – must of right and custom be called into being at once. They could not be put off.

By all constitutional custom a new King must summon a new Parliament, if only to give formal expression to the "States of the Realm" and to symbolise the unity and support of the nation. In these first Parliaments every new King took contact with his greater subjects in ritual fashion and received from them the ratification of his rights, whereof by far the most practically important was the

CHARLES I

Customs, including under that general term Tonnage and Poundage. These were the dues levied on merchandise at the ports. They formed not only the largest part of the government's regular income, but a part which was getting larger every year.

That revenue had been unquestioned for many generations, but it had, as a matter of ceremony, to be confirmed by Parliament near the beginning of each reign. That the King should be granted the Customs for life by such first Parliaments was a matter of course; but the ritual must be performed.

The first Parliament of a reign had a different character than from those which might or might not be summoned at shorter or longer intervals for brief or for considerable seasons later on. The first Parliament was, as it were, of necessity, and had about it a solemn confirmatory character, setting a seal upon kingship second only to the rite of Coronation.

The first Parliament of Charles was summoned. It met, and with its meeting the revolution began.

But before we begin the story of the struggle between the new young King and the great men who might or might not grant him exceptional supply we must deal with two points. The first is of the highest importance though at the moment almost unnoticed; the second introduced directly the religious question, and indirectly the question of supply. These two points are the Scottish Revocation and the French marriage.

The Scottish Revocation does not come strictly first in order of time, but it must be first dealt with because it is first in order of importance. It is rare that the first seed, the springs, of great events are emphasised in history. The Scottish Revocation is commonly left isolated or casually noted as an early incident of Charles's reign. It is worthy of far more attention, indeed of principal consideration in any survey of the time, for it was the seed of all. It was the origin of all that followed, down to the axe and the block.

In the Kingdom of Scotland there was vested in the Crown a right of revoking to itself properties which had been alienated during the minority of a sovereign. It was appreciated that while the sovereign was not his own master those in power might, and probably would, abuse their position by taking over rents which were of right the King's; such acts were, by a compromise, not regarded as criminal but as terminable, and when the King was old enough to exercise his power he could demand the return to the Crown of what had been alienated from it. Charles, therefore, very early in his reign, in its first weeks, announced his intention of revoking the concessions made in the name of his father during his father's minority. That alone would take one back a long lifetime ago, nearly sixty years; but to this another twenty was added by including the loot which had been seized before his grandmother, Mary, Queen of Scots, was in a position to affirm the rights of the Crown. In all, titles to land over a space of eighty years were affected.

In making this demand Charles was not only just but most moderate. These had been a very riot of robbing the Crown north of the border. The great Scottish nobles, from the fatal day of Solway onwards, or rather from the death of their King which had followed immediately upon that battle, had looted public property at will; and particularly the lands of the Church — on which form of spoil the Reformation was everywhere based, but nowhere more than in Scotland. The Revocation, therefore, threatened to diminish the incomes of the rich. But it was not only the great nobles who were thus affected; one might say that almost all landed families in Scotland, and even not a few of the smaller freeholders, felt themselves to be in peril of seeing their incomes lessened.

Charles's declared intention of revocation was, I say, most moderate. A much wider recovery of Government and public property would have been justified, but his restricted design was only to recover Church land sufficient for the endowment of the Scottish Church — moneys which were lacking, and necessary, to the maintenance of the new national religion. To England the act meant little or nothing and was not deeply marked; but through all the Scottish Lowlands it was a menace and a warning. It was from this origin that the Scottish troubles were to arise in the future, and from those troubles again arose the active conflict in which Charles was to lose his crown and his life. Action was delayed; but the principle had been enunciated and we must bear it constantly in mind through all that followed.

The French marriage had been arranged after the breakdown of the Spanish match, and for what reasons has already been described.

CHARLES I

But though it was necessary, it provided another opportunity for resistance to kingship, because it involved, as the Spanish marriage would have done, the presence of a Catholic Queen.

To begin with, the whole business was badly handled. France at the moment would have proved to England a most valuable ally. She was about to become, under the growing influence of Richelieu, the strongest power in Western Europe. Her policy was fixedly opposed to Spain – a matter which did not directly concern England though it agreed with the general resentment against the Spanish connection – but it was also directed against the other branch of the Hapsburgs, the house of Austria, that is, the Emperor. Therefore the support of Richelieu's France, properly managed, not too much forced, might have been used by the English Government for the recovery of the Palatinate. The French Court, and Richelieu directing it, had no intention of open hostility as yet against the house of Austria, but they intended to weaken that house by supporting the smaller Protestant states in the Germanies of the north. Richelieu had prevented the Mansfield expedition from passing through French territory and had therefore, in a measure, led to the disasters following its landing at Flushing and the ruin of the English Expeditionary Force; yet with patience and skill England and France might have worked together and in the long run the young King of England's brother-in-law, the Elector Palatine, might have recovered his estates; though of course he could never have recovered that Crown of Bohemia which he had so foolishly usurped. The Ban of the Empire might have been lifted from him, his lands (which had been given to the loyal Elector of Bavaria) might have been restored – and the French match meant all that.

How was it mishandled? In two ways. First of all through lack of patience on the part of Charles, a purely personal thing which made the first years of his marriage go wrong. Secondly, through Charles's desire to placate the anti-Catholic feeling of the two Houses, Lords and Commons, with the city of London at their back. Thirdly (and though it was but a personal incident it was perhaps the most important thing), through an impetuous love affair of Buckingham's, which proved fatal to the whole scheme.

The little French Princess, Henrietta Maria, was but a child, just fifteen. She was still growing, and even when she reached her full stature she was tiny, appearing short even beside the diminutive figure of the King, her husband. She had inherited from her mother, Marie de' Medici, from her father, Henry of Navarre, great energy; from her mother a hot temper and from her father decision. The marriage was to be made by proxy on the 1st of May, 1625, that is, barely two months after Charles's accession; and it was duly solemnised upon that May Day in front of Notre-Dame on a platform there erected, with the Duc de Chévreuse representing the King of England. A week later Buckingham appeared at the French Court in a royal splendour of his own; his carriage, his vivacity, his courage, wit and manners, the splendour of his retinue and his person, produced a vivid effect in that Court which he had already known in early manhood, which he had revisited two years before incognito, and with which he now mixed so splendidly in his thirty-third year, the very climax of his manhood. The new little Queen set out for the Straits, Buckingham and his retinue and certain English ladies with her as well as her own mother, and her sister-in-law, Anne of Austria, the French Queen, wife of her brother the reigning King, Louis XIII.

Now this Anne of Austria who thus went northwards with all her train was in a false position. She had been with child by her husband, and had promised him an heir; she had suffered, through her own imprudence, a miscarriage. The King had not forgiven her and she was neglected.

She was *completely* neglected. The indifference of Louis XIII to his wife was the talk of the kingdom and of much of Europe besides, and it was taken for granted that there would be now no children. To this woman Buckingham now made violent love. The origins, the motives, the sincerity of that passionate passage we shall never know. Perhaps the lovers hardly knew themselves. Perhaps it was the fault of both. At any rate, if such an affair, which under the circumstances was a huge political blunder, was to be undertaken at all, it should have been managed by Buckingham with the utmost secrecy. He showed no discretion at all – he allowed his passion to become a matter of public comment. But this much seems to be certain, Anne had not yet yielded to it, when, in one critical evening at Amiens, in the park, she was heard suddenly crying aloud for her ladies, who came up to find her frightened and indignant, and Buckingham at once rode northward as though in disgrace. Yet the next morning he was kneeling at her bedside, having turned rein and ridden back through the night. For a Queen to receive in her bedroom before rising, in the presence of her ladies, was the custom of the time, and there was present when Buckingham thus appeared one of the gravest of the Queen's women. She rebuked him for the violence of his protestations and he was dismissed. On that incident as much as on anything turned the breakdown of what might have been a fruitful alliance between the French and English governments. Buckingham never saw Anne of Austria again. For the matter of that he was never again allowed to set foot as a friend upon French soil. He had given mortal offence, for Louis the King had been told all; and Richelieu, though reserved and far-seeing in plan, though desirous of avoiding any breach with England, remained permanently moved by the memory of the insult.

When the little Queen landed in England and was at Charles's side the second part of the blunder was committed. She was too young, and yet at the same time too vivacious. That he felt no affection for her as yet might seem natural; she was a child in his eyes, nearly nine years younger than he. But he also allowed himself to be impatient with what was inevitable – her foreignness, and especially her Catholicism. Charles disliked the French – indeed he disliked all foreigners – and Catholicism he hated. He hated it more thus in youth perhaps than he did later, for he was filled with memories of his rebuff in Spain and these embittered him. He quarrelled with his little wife's great train of French attendants. He was in particular exasperated with the many priests about her. On the day when she first heard Mass he forbade any of his Court to attend, and after months of increasing annoyance he suddenly turned out nearly all the members of her household, driving them back home (to use his own phrase) "like wild beasts"; and thereby he openly broke an essential clause of the marriage treaty, and insulted the French Royal family.

She also, in those early quarrels, was at issue with him. Charles was chaste. I might have written "too chaste" save that the phrase is bad in morals. Had it been the chastity of a powerful nature controlled by affection or religious rule it would have been a source of strength: *Timeo Hominem Unius Mulieris*. "A man who keeps to one woman is formidable." But his chastity as yet was not of this sort; it was timid, or, at any rate, indifferent.

BUCKINGHAM

But of really more importance and perhaps equally as strong in motive as his personal feelings was his consideration in all this of the Parliament, the Parliament which was, the majority of it, so determined to wear down the large body of Catholic tradition in England.

All Charles could do to placate his Parliament must be done, for it was a crying necessity that the grossly insufficient income of the Government should be supplemented by voluntary grants from the squires. One of their spokesmen in the matter, a typical great landowner, and what is more (as his name shows) a man typical of the Reformation tradition and of the fortunes founded upon that religious revolution, Philips, the baronet from that beautiful palace called Montacute House in Somersetshire, gave full emphasis to the feeling. In a speech he estimated the Catholic subjects of the King as still amounting to half the total number. He exaggerated. Even counting in all sympathisers they were not now, by 1625, a half, and those openly Catholic were much less. But they were very numerous. To put pressure upon that large body, gradually to change the spirit of its less courageous or less attached members, to prevent their practising their religion by destroying the hunted remains of the priesthood, to drain the wealthier ones by recurrent great fines – all this was a principal purpose of a majority in the House of Commons, and it found sympathy with a majority of the Lords. It was a temptation, or perhaps a necessity, for Charles to support this anti-Catholic policy, a necessity if he were to obtain supply, and a temptation because it agreed with his own strong feelings against the old religion.

But in so supporting the anti-Catholic policy he was compelled to break the Treaty with France in more ways than by his treatment of his wife, for he was compelled to break definite promises agreed to in writing, signed by himself and his father, and giving as much toleration to the Catholics in England as was given to the actively rebellious Huguenots in France.

The virtues of Charles largely helped to disarm him. It was a lack in his character throughout his life that he did not know how to lie. For here let it be remarked (though the truth, like most truths, is unpleasant) that human negotiation is based upon falsehood. The three greatest diplomats in modern history, Talleyrand, Richelieu and Bismarck, are all examples of highly skilled liars.

CHARLES I

All through Charles's life, and markedly here at the beginning, his inability to conceal motive or even to promise two opposing policies in such words that he might be free to choose either, his perpetual falling into bald true statement when he should have been ambiguous, and into mere contradictory promises where a skilful deceiver would have left nothing but anxiety in the minds of his rivals, made Charles's plans go wrong over and over again. So it was here. He had affirmed one thing to the French Court; he affirmed its contrary to the more powerful of his own subjects. What a contrast with Richelieu, perpetually giving the English Government to understand that he was with them in the matter of the Germanies, but always finding language which left him free to dupe them when it came to action!

This first Parliament of the reign had met on the 18th of June of this first year of the reign, 1625, and after its attack upon Catholicism it had to deal with the necessities of the Crown. No one had demanded a war with Spain more eagerly than these same great landowners, or at least those who counted most among them and who led the bulk of the rest; but to carry on such a war, even only by sea, would mean a voluntary aid to be granted by the rich in addition to the insufficient regular revenues of the Government. Their desire to show their power over the Crown was too strong to be denied; they knew that the fleet which was being prepared for the attack upon Spain would cost close upon a third of a million pounds. They supplied less than half that sum, and even then bargained upon its application!

While they so resisted the new reign, while they so manœuvred to raise and still further to raise their status against the regular government of the country, there appeared among them a spokesman of singular effect, a man who in all the first stages of the struggle between the King and the squires must be regarded as their protagonist.

This man was that same John Elliot whom we saw travelling as a lad with Buckingham on the Continent years before.

He was now in Parliament, a wealthy Cornish knight, made wealthier by a great marriage, typical of his class in every way, save that he was an artist. For he was a great orator, as yet undiscovered; and the way in which that power of his over the Word was used, the effect it had, the sword it became in the hands of the new revolutionary movement, can only be understood through Elliot's relations with Buckingham.

BUCKINGHAM

To attack the King directly was not the morals of the time; the King was still sacrosanct. But one could attack him through a Minister; and Buckingham, all-powerful, was necessarily the target of the attack on Monarchy. To destroy Buckingham was to show that they could, if they willed it, ultimately master the King. Moreover, in the vigorous offensive now launched against Buckingham there was a special motive apart from the fact that he was the screen by breaking down which the King in the background could be reached. Buckingham's power was excessive and abnormal; it had already been so in the last years of the old King; it had perhaps been hoped that there would be a change with the new reign, but the exact opposite was discovered, and Buckingham, so deeply, passionately loved by Charles, was more Royal than ever.

It so happened that John Elliot was exactly suited to the affair in hand, for he had been led to hate his former companion, by a long series of personal incidents; a personal grudge, a personal hatred, fed and inflamed his rhetorical power. This intense personal hatred of Buckingham quite overlay all other things in John Elliot's mind. It made his rhetoric triumphant, and gave it an edge and a drive which no abstract principles would have done.

But how was this? We last heard of this same John Elliot as a companion in very early youth, perhaps the somewhat patronising companion, of the then unknown and much poorer George Villiers, when they made, as young men, their Grand Tour together on the Continent. That was not a dozen years ago. How then in the interval had John Elliot become the inflamed enemy and, in effect, the murderer of Buckingham?

The process was this:—

Buckingham, full of good nature and always ready to advance those of his connection, remembered with warm affection this old travelling companion of his youth. During his own prodigious rise it did not occur to him to drop the man who at one moment had been his superior in wealth and connections. When he himself, Buckingham, was made Lord High Admiral, he gave to this old comrade and friend the lucrative post of Vice-Admiral of Devon. The holder of such a post got all manner of receipts, of which he could keep half himself and give the other half to the Lord High Admiral; he had wreckage, and salvage and fines in his courts, captures, etc., which

101

CHARLES I

made up a large income – but Elliot was one of those men to whom it is very dangerous to be kind! There went with his feverish oratorical talent the touchiness of the artist, and, almost inevitably, the vanity thereof. Further, there was to be found in that temperament, as is so often the case, a certain looseness about money. Under an opportunity for illicit gain he does not seem to have been quite dependable.

While Buckingham had been away in Spain two years before with the Prince, in 1623, there took place an incident in John Elliot's Vice-Admiralty which particularly compromised him. He had got hold of one Nutt, who had committed piracies, but who had also, like so many of the maritime free-lances of those days done useful work for the country in the New World. He had there helped Calvert, now one of the Secretaries of State, to develop a grant of land and seems to have served faithfully enough. According to Nutt's story Elliot had sent him messengers secretly proposing that Nutt should capture certain ships recently come in to Dartmouth from Spain, and with the money he would find upon them pay Elliot £500 for his pardon. Nutt also accused Elliot of stealing part of the cargo of one of the ships he had captured; and Elliot was sent for by the authorities and put in preventative prison in London while the thing was gone into.

Meanwhile a certain number of suits were brought against Elliot for other malpractices, notably by the owners of ships which he ought to have released but from which, it was affirmed, he had made private profit.

Elliot under examination denied Nutt's charges and those of the others who complained. The man whom he had sent as messenger to Nutt also (of course) denied that his master had tempted Nutt to piracy against the ships in Dartmouth; but he was forced under cross-examination to admit that he had pointed out to Nutt the ships in Dartmouth and the large sums of money they had on board them, and this admission, wrung from a reluctant witness, made Elliot's case look very bad. However, Buckingham was still his friend, and upon Buckingham's return from Spain Elliot was released, presumably by Buckingham's orders, and went back to his duties in Devon.

But he went back wounded in pride and in something more. He thought that Buckingham ought to have vindicated his character in some public and striking way. There is a letter from him to Buckingham in the November of that same year, 1623, fulsome enough, but protesting his innocence; telling Buckingham that he was so noble that scandals of this sort could not affect him – but evidently begging for support. Also he wanted the suits which were out against him stopped, and Buckingham would not do this. There was no reason why he should prevent private citizens from obtaining justice – if indeed Elliot had committed the thefts which were complained of.

Three months later, at the end of February, 1624, Buckingham received a second begging letter from Elliot. The profits from the northern shore of the Devon coast had belonged to the old Lord Bath who was dead; Elliot tells Buckingham how he has heard a rumour that these profits are not to be given to him – the Vice-Admiral – as he had hoped, but to the new Lord Bath; he begs Buckingham to let him have the money almost as though it was his right. He ends by calling himself Buckingham's "creature," saying that his word in all things may dispose of Elliot as he wills, and calling himself Buckingham's "thrice humble servant."

Buckingham did not answer except to thank him in general for his work. It seems that he thought of having Elliot in his train when he went to France at that moment, to begin negotiations for the French marriage. But if that were so, Elliot was disappointed again. He had got only as far as Exeter when he was turned back.

He wrote again, just after James's death, hoping that it was only Buckingham's grief for his old master that had prevented his remembering a friend; yet, once more, on his way up to London to see Buckingham he was turned back at Exeter by an order from the Council.

The truth was that Buckingham was beginning to suspect Elliot's honesty. The Admiralty was not getting its full dues from Devon. So a certain Baggs was sent down to the West to make particular accounts of the receipts, on which he and Sir John Drake (of the great local family) were to take their commission. Elliot's pride was thus still further wounded; and he was a violent man, be it remembered: one who in early youth had stabbed a neighbour with his sword, and in general suffering all the weaknesses which often accompany talents of his kind.

A report was sent up to the authorities that Elliot was sulking and refusing to do his work, but the good-natured Buckingham still kept him on as Vice-Admiral of Devon, remembering his old friendship and not wishing to penalise him too much; and Elliot (who had been returned again to Parliament, for he had already sat in the last Parliament of James, where he had clamoured for war with Spain) was still regarded by his colleagues as Buckingham's friend.

It was on this account that, in the early days of July, 1625, just when the big trouble was on between Charles and the House of Commons, Elliot was approached by May, who asked him, as a friend of Buckingham's, to prevent Buckingham from pressing for more supplies. The House would not give them, and to ask for them would only lead to further conflict between the Government and the Commons, which it was ardently hoped might be prevented.

It was on Thursday, the 7th of July, 1625, that this message reached Elliot in his acerbity and smouldering anger against his old patron, and now feeling his power as a member whose eloquence had already moved the House of Commons. That message sent him off for a last interview with the Duke. He called at York House early the next morning, Friday, the 8th of July, and was shown into the bedroom where Buckingham was in bed with his wife and there received. He said he had important public matters to lay before the Duke, and the Duchess went off in her dressing-gown to the next room. Elliot then – who, even in such circumstances, could not avoid quoting Tacitus – took up his new attitude of defiance. Buckingham, unwilling to quarrel, said with great justice that in this matter of a war which the Commons themselves had demanded (and no one more eloquently than Elliot himself) the State must not be prejudiced through parsimony. If they wanted ships, ships must be paid for. But Elliot's bitterness had overflowed and his hatred of Buckingham, supported by his own new-found position prompted him to defiance. "Very well," he said in effect, "ask for the money if you like – but you will fail to get it!" Thenceforward he had burnt his boats. There was nothing more to be got out of Buckingham, and Elliot henceforward concentrated on one thing – to avenge himself. Yet Buckingham, month after month maintained his old friend as Vice-Admiral, even after that murderous attack of which we shall read.

It was high summer, Parliament had been dissolved on the 12th of August, after being taken to Oxford because a pestilence

BUCKINGHAM

in London endangered the lives of the members and had reduced their attendance by three-quarters. The Commons had taken the first revolutionary steps: they had refused Tonnage and Poundage for life, granting it only for one year, and even so the Bill had not yet been passed. They had refused any proper supplies for the fleet – yet the war must somehow be carried on.

The ships sailed from Plymouth for Spain on the 8th of October. They were commanded by one of the Cecils, who had been made Lord Wimbledon for the occasion, and who had for second the neuter, ineffective and very doubtfully loyal Essex. It was a doomed fleet, because Parliament had refused the necessary funds. There was not sufficient provisions nor proper pay for the men; the ships were ill-found – and the expedition completely failed, mainly from the breakdown of discipline, which breakdown in its turn arose from the miseries and misfortunes of the under-fed, under-paid private soldiers. From that harbour of Cadiz where the father of Essex had captured such vast sums (and put them into his own pocket in spite of poor Elizabeth's outcries) – Essex, having done nothing nor Wimbledon either, returned. When the commander's ship touched at Kinsale they had taken no treasure, they had missed the galleons from America, and on reaching the Irish coast the flagship, like her consorts, had the plague aboard: more than a hundred men had been buried at sea and not far short of two hundred were incapacitated by illness.

It was the second disaster, coming so soon after the Mansfield expedition, and though the fault lay wholly at the door of the squires in Parliament, their faction was of course the loudest to complain. That Buckingham should not have led the fleet in person (he had been occupied at Charles's command in negotiations with the Hague for the war that should relieve the Palatinate) was made a reproach to him – as it would certainly have been made a reproach to him if he had led it in person.

In such a crisis the expedition to Cadiz having come to nothing and with no further supplies at the expense of Spain, there was nothing for it but, in desperation, to summon the Commons again, and see whether it might not be possible to get a grant – if not sufficient for the foreign policy of the country, at any rate enough to carry on from hand to mouth. The country was at war, and the need for supply was acute. Supply of some sort was an absolute necessity. An attempt to raise something at least by loan, though the requests were made in the most conciliatory terms, appealing to the loyalty of the wealthier men, produced nothing sufficient, and the second Parliament of Charles met, after so brief an interval, on the 6th of February, 1626.

That Parliament made itself famous, or infamous, by the impeachment of Buckingham. It turned against himself that weapon, Impeachment, which old James had warned him was a most dangerous one for him to have resurrected after all those centuries.

The articles of the impeachment were false, the worst of them absurdly so: that he had bought public offices, notably that of Lord High Admiral, by bribes; that he (who was the renovator of the English Navy!) had neglected his duties as Admiral; that he (who had brought order into the financial affairs of the country) had corruptly muddled the national accounts to conceal his own peculations – and the conclusion was the monstrous accusation that James had been poisoned by a medicine given him by Buckingham, the implication being that he was guilty of the old King's death. The "managers" of the impeachment (as they were called) dealt each of them with one section of these false charges. Among them, of course, was Elliot; and because he would be the most violent and would also have the most effect, he was put up to speak last, upon the third day.

It was a fine piece of rhetoric, now hackneyed by too much repetition – perhaps to our modern taste a little marred by that perpetual citation of Latin tags which was the custom of the time. Though the thing is so well-worn, its sentences in every text-book, its ringing appeal among the most familiar things in history, I will quote the conclusion. After speaking of "foul extortion," "bribery," "corruption," and of the Duke's having "preyed" upon justice, Elliot called him a "cancer," compared him to fabulous beasts, and ended, addressing the Peers who were to be the judges of the accused man, "My Lords, I have done! You see the man.... By him came all these evils, in him we find the cause, and on him we expect the remedies, and to this we meet Your Lordships in conference.... We cannot doubt but that in Your Lordships' wisdom, greatness and power, he shall in due time find judgment as he deserves."

Though none had spoken with more murderous venom and power than Elliot, yet another of the managers, Digges, had, in a way,

BUCKINGHAM

gone further, and what he did is evidence of how strong the Commons felt themselves to be against a declining monarchy. For Digges had implied that Charles himself "was privy to the poisoning of King James his father."

It was on the 8th of June, 1626, exactly one calendar month after the opening of the impeachment, that Buckingham stood up in the House of Lords to reply. It was a finer speech than any which the Lords had heard, not for its eloquence, which was not attempted, but for its sobriety, humour and truth. He showed no anger, he allowed himself to fall into no haste, he answered the charges (worthless as they were) quietly one after the other, and he proclaimed what all knew to be the truth, his intense affection for the King, his readiness to lay down his life and fortune in the service of the Crown. As for bribery, he had compensated Howard, the former Admiral, Earl of Nottingham,† who was thus in old age losing his post; and as for unfitness, he had always worked with a professional committee appointed by James. He had recouped, as was right, the Warden of the Cinque Ports when he desired to unify the Admiralty. So he went on with one charge after another and dealt at last in the same quiet clear manner with the impossible falsehood of his having poisoned his old master. It was a complete reply, and one which made a profound impression. The King urged the Commons to abandon their position; they replied by a "Remonstrance," which insisted upon Buckingham's dismissal. Buckingham himself was willing to stand his trial in regular form before a court of justice, and that way out might have been possible had not Elliot refused to give evidence – for indeed he had none.

There was no more to be done, and the second Parliament, a week later, on the 15th of June, 1626, was dissolved. A first lunge had been made and parried; the next one would be deadly.

III. The Blow

The Government of Charles was approaching war with France. It was a policy favoured by Buckingham, though he was not the one who spoke of it first, and though he came to it reluctantly.

---

† He was that Howard of Effingham, who, nearly 40 years before, had been Admiral against the Armada. He was Elizabeth's cousin but fiercely anti-Catholic not (*cont'd*)

CHARLES I

Many things were combining towards hostilities between Charles and his brother-in-law, Louis XIII. There was the purely personal set of grievances, Buckingham's annoyance at not being allowed to return to Paris (he had brought it on himself), the young King's quarrel with his still younger wife, the strong feeling of Louis that he had received a private insult through the action of Charles when the Treaty was broken and the Queen's household sent away. There was the quarrel about prizes at sea, the right of search and of capture exercised by the English ships which were predominant at sea, for France had *as yet* no navy to speak of. These captures were made on the plea that foreign ships, though not belonging to a nation with which England was at war, might be carrying goods to and from Spain, with which country she *was* at war: and there was the fact that France – that is, Richelieu – had led the English Government on to believing that some sort of active alliance would be made for the recovery of the Palatinate, and yet had continuously disappointed the English King and his minister, always postponing such an alliance and doing nothing active. It was this which had led to the expenditure of a million of money to no purpose and the loss of ten thousand men on the Mansfield expedition. It was argued that if England were to show herself strong by taking action against France, that strength would make her valuable as a partner against Spain, and so a true alliance for the recovery of the Palatinate might be reached, which apparently could not be got by diplomatic means.

All these causes were at work, and the last was almost sufficient to explain why, though the Government was at the last gasp for money and was already saddled with the Spanish conflict, it should have undertaken one more throw, and added the French Court to its enemies.

But truth lies in proportion, and to understand the situation we must appreciate that all these causes together did not weigh as much as the supreme necessity under which Charles and Buckingham lay to placate as best might be the wealthy classes organised in Parliament. It was the strong Protestantism of the majority there, their determination to destroy Catholicism in England, their delight in seeing

---

only by interest but by conviction. He had died two years before in 1624 – a very old man of 86, but still intensely fanatical. One of his last acts was handing over a friend and guest to be persecuted for Catholicism.

it attacked abroad, which weighed more with Buckingham and his young master than anything else. This is the key to the problem, this is the understanding of what would otherwise be inexplicable. A false legend has made out the personal motives to have been the most important: on the contrary, they were the least. The motive of foreign policy was strong, but the motive of playing up to the anti-Catholic feeling of the majority of the Lords and Commons was far stronger and decided the issue.

The King in his desire to soothe the Parliament now posed not only as the *mediator* between the French King and the great Protestant families with their middle-class following who were rebels against him, but also, more recently, as the *Protector* of the French Protestants at large. It was an exasperating claim and a claim intended to be exasperating. The French Court repudiated it with vigour. Charles now had an opportunity to act up to this claim, and the chances were that if he took that opportunity England would emerge from a short conflict victorious by sea. Now an England commanding the sea, basing her new power upon the sea, was Buckingham's main aim. He stands at the beginning of that idea which later was so greatly to develop. France, having in those years no ships, would not, if she were attacked quickly enough by sea, be able to meet the shock: there would be an English triumph and, thenceforward, an England courted and respected for her sea power.

The maritime weakness of France and the religious opportunity combined had already been very well illustrated in the Pennington business.

The French Government had proposed to hire certain English ships. They were sent under the command of Pennington to be taken over at Dieppe. But both Buckingham and Charles were secretly intending to make trouble. A rumour was spread that the ships were going to be used against the French Protestants, whose maritime power on the western seaboard centred in the strongly Protestant privileged town of La Rochelle. A mutiny was worked up among the crews, who were led to protest against being used by a Catholic power against its Protestant rebels. This mutiny provided an excuse against the crews being used. The incident therefore served two purposes at once – it emphasised the Protestant character of the English policy and it exposed the weakness of the French at sea.

CHARLES I

The first definite step towards active warfare was the reception by the English Government of two Huguenot envoys, Soubise (one of the greatest of Huguenot names, the brother of the Rohan) and Brancard. After this comforting and supporting of the enemies of the French King there was no going back, and a technical ground of offence was chosen in that Louis had not dismantled (as the Huguenots claimed he had promised to do) the new fort raised just outside La Rochelle to overawe that town and to command the entrance to its harbour.

These things being so, in the summer of 1627 an expedition was launched, and the first point we must note, the first example of Buckingham's military talent, was the first-rate strategical surprise which he effected.

The destination of the expedition was kept secret. The French Government were in doubt as to whither it would proceed; probably to Spain, perhaps to the Mediterranean. It sailed in strength under the command of Buckingham from Stokes Bay at the mouth of Portsmouth harbour with more than 100 sail all told, of which 42 were armed ships and 34 the main transports. It carried altogether nearly 8,000 men, of whom some 6,000 were infantry, a few cavalry, some gunners and the rest sailors, the soldiers drawing rations and pay being 6,884 in number.

The expedition set forth on the 27th of June (O.S.) and ran before a strong northerly breeze down within sight of the Breton shores and across the Bay, making straight for La Rochelle. It came before that port in a few days. The strategical surprise was, I say, excellently carried out, and was the first proof of Buckingham's practical talent in command. But other proofs were to follow in the selection made of the field of action. He did not land for the garrisoning or defence of La Rochelle itself; it is true that even if he had desired to do so the Senate of that quasi-independent maritime city-state hesitated, by receiving the English troops, to declare open war against their King. But Buckingham's intention was not so to act. The district was malarious, indeed the danger of the marshes surrounding the city had been always one of its principal sources of strength; to have shut himself up behind fortifications condemned ultimately to a siege from the much greater forces which the French Government could ultimately

BUCKINGHAM

raise would have been a great error. What Buckingham determined on was the capture and occupation of the island of Rhé.† The choice of Rhé as an objective was admirable. It was the first example of that strategic policy which England thenceforward pursued, the policy which all states aiming at maritime supremacy have always pursued, to wit, the seizing of isolated points which cannot be attacked from the land but which threaten the approaches to the land and can be used as bases for a fleet.

There are two islands outside the narrow bay at the head of which the port of La Rochelle stands; the southern one called Oléron is the larger, therefore the more difficult to occupy and also the further from the port; but Rhé, the northern one, stands right on the flank of any fleet, mercantile or armed, making for La Rochelle. The sound between Rhé and the mainland acts as a sort of great cistern, through the southern end of which, narrowing down to a sort of funnel, the tide races; it is hardly navigable save to the local pilots, and these were all in sympathy with the Huguenots of the neighbouring town, to which most of them belonged. If Rhé could be conquered and held – and the odds were in favour of its being so held and conquered – it would form not only a permanent base for English operations nor only a permanent menace to the French power, but a guarantee that no one without leave of the maritime power possessing Rhé could approach La Rochelle.

It was about a fortnight after the sailing from Stokes Bay, on the 12th of July (O.S.) that the attack was delivered. There was on Rhé at this moment a garrison of no more than a thousand men with a few horses; there was a small fort and a single small fortified town on that arm of the sea which lies between Rhé and the mainland – a town called St. Martin. The command of its defence was in the hands of Toiras, a man of determination and ability, but here hopelessly outnumbered. The landing, though difficult through the softness of the sand and also through the ill-training of the rapidly raised and pressed English recruits, was successfully made under the guns of the fleet – not without slight loss, but loss that could be easily afforded compared with the corresponding loss on the side of the defenders.

---

† I give the old spelling, though already the common French form was "Ré" without the "h" and it is now universally known under that form.

CHARLES I

The defence fell back on the fortifications of St. Martin, and three days later the effort at reducing that stronghold began, upon the 15th of July (O.S.).

The siege followed all the stages proper to the time; it began with the regulation effort to storm, which was always a chance worth trying, though the odds of success were usually against it. If one succeeded in an initial effort of that sort the thing was done at a blow – if not, one could fall back on sap and blockade. This first attempt at storming did not succeed, and the siege proper began.

Toiras had upon paper, and was thought by his Government really to have, about two months supply; but what with the flocking of the inhabitants of the countrysides into the town for refuge, and what with the margin always present between nominal and real supply, he had, of full rations, not much more than thirty days. But he acted with vigour and imposed strict discipline, eking out all he could by half rations early in the affair. He was still holding out at the very end of August, but he had sent word to his Government on the mainland that he then had only six days rations left. Meanwhile the forces of the besiegers had been reinforced. They had suffered, as a besieging force nearly always does (and particularly under the circumstances of that time) from disease; it had suffered also from the fire of the defenders, which killed among others one of the best English soldiers, Burrough, a man more timid than Buckingham and one who exaggerated the difficulties of the task, but loyal and sincere and of considerable experience, for he had served long in the Flemish wars. His death gives us an opportunity for measuring the devotion of Buckingham's officers to their leader, for his own son says in writing home and describing Buckingham's loyal respect for the fallen man, "that such a tribute from such a commander was a sufficient encouragement for dying."

It is almost invariably the case when a military operation is undertaken by someone understanding the art of war, that civilians at home and Allies abroad will be at a loss to comprehend him. When his effort is prolonged without immediate glory or apparent tangible result, it is also a perpetually recurrent phenomenon in history that the grumbling grows louder and the complaints of the critics more vocal. The Protestant forces in Germany and the Netherlands could make nothing of this diversion of the English action on to the

BUCKINGHAM

French coast, and to their sympathisers in England it seemed equally inexplicable – waste of effort and a risk taken for no valid object. But Buckingham, to whom some echoes of these ignorant objections came, was not moved by them. He went on with his task, and came within an ace of a success which would have changed history.

The garrison of St. Martin had eaten all that was fit to be eaten and a good deal more. They had not only eaten the horses, but boiled the leather of the harness to make what soup they could of that. They were down to just so much of the last few biscuits as would keep body and soul together, when an accident of weather intervened in their favour. Certain light craft manned by Basques, which Richelieu had gathered on the mainland coast in a small harbour to the north, ran down through the night of Tuesday to Wednesday, the 4th and 5th of September (O.S.) in an attempt to relieve St. Martin. The large English armed fleet was of course blockading the place, riding in the open roads outside, and across the mouth of the harbour Buckingham had thrown a boom of spars, securely lashed. The task set to the light Basque craft seemed impossible, especially on that date. The spring tides were over; there had only recently ceased a storm which still left a heavy sea running, and they would come under the guns of the very numerous British vessels maintaining the blockade. But in the course of that night as the wind dropped a thick fog gathered, and it was under cover of this that, on the Wednesday morning, the Basque boats suddenly appeared at the mouth of the harbour. The blockaders only saw them when it was too late, just as the flat open boats were lifting over the boom on the successive crests of the rollers, urged by the young flood tide.

The garrison of St. Martin was reprovisioned, not indeed for very long, but enough to give it time to await the large relief forces which were at last preparing. This day of the first re-provisioning by the Basque boats was the decisive one; and this operation, which had been planned and brought to success by the genius of Richelieu, who had chosen the right craft and the right crews (difficult to obtain on that coast), but who had also been thus favoured by the weather. Richelieu lay behind the whole thing, pitted against, and now successful against, the talent of Buckingham.

St. Martin having thus been relieved, the English chance of victory grew less and less. When the French had gathered a sufficient

CHARLES I

body of large craft to engage the blockade they were indeed beaten off at first in a fine action fought in half a gale, one in which Buckingham himself showed the greatest courage and initiative on the English decks, but it was impossible to prevent a second reprovisioning.

Buckingham made an error in not retiring by mid-October; a fresh French force had sailed before, at the very end of the month (O.S.) and he was compelled at last, with the bitterness of defeat in his heart, to allow the re-embarkation of his force and to abandon the island.

But what could have been done easily a fortnight before was now, with fresh French forces at hand (though they were inferior in number), very difficult; for a force cannot fight and embark at the same time. He had, however, a sufficiency of troops to cover the operation, though not without severe loss. The way to the ships led over a causeway where the English, stretched out in a narrow column, were vulnerable to the French fire. There was confusion; men were pushed off the causeway and drowned; some 1,200 men (the French claimed 2,000) were lost, and the French claimed twenty guns as well, before the last man of those who remained to the expedition was on board.

Buckingham himself was that last man. He would not leave the beach until all others had gone before him, maintaining to the end that intrepid courage which he had displayed throughout all the operations and which always shone in him under a strain, in contrast with the ordinary impetuosity of his nature. What a heavy toll this prolonged effort had taken can be seen by the pay-roll and the distribution of rations on the fleet's reaching England.

The disaster turned the course of English history, or at least deflected it. By this I do not mean that, Buckingham returning victorious, Rhé permanently held by an English garrison, La Rochelle saved and the Protestant cause there triumphant – and all the rest of it – would have averted that general revolution whereby the monarchy in England declined and aristocracy took its place. But the change would perhaps have come in another form, with the Crown less degraded, with its enemies more ready to treat. Something might have been saved of the old popular monarchy of England, and some brake put upon the increasing economic power of the great landlords. It is even possible that if the expedition to La Rochelle had succeeded we should still have something of a peasantry in England.

But all these are conjectures. It failed; and its failure was the loss of one more prop from the tottering structure of kingly power in England. Now indeed would the two Houses when they should be summoned be encouraged to charge home against Buckingham and his King! Now indeed was there an argument, loudly appealing to every assessed man, not to supply voluntary aid for further misfortunes! They had seen the ruin of the Mansfield expedition; they had seen the fiasco of the attack on Cadiz; here was a *third* breakdown; and starving men, broken with disease, their numbers more than halved, landed, once more defeated, in their native country.

The straits of the Government for money grew worse and worse; it was impossible to withdraw from the war without ruining the position of England, another expedition must be provided – but how should it be paid for? If there were to be another attempt at a forced loan there was risk of rebellion. Not without dread and hesitation the Council decided to risk yet another Parliament.

Charles's third Parliament, therefore, was summoned at the opening of the New Year, towards the end of January, 1628, but some weeks would pass before it could meet, and meanwhile money must be had or the troops could not be gathered or equipped. The very smallest sum possible for the beginnings of such equipment and the payments incidental to the formation of a new force was fixed: considerably less than two hundred thousand pounds. It was hoped that this sum would be advanced in expectation of the Parliamentary payments, to be regularised when Parliament should meet, and a Commission was appointed to go the rounds collecting the assessed sums. But even this form of advance, not claimed as a right nor forced as a loan but only as a payment made a few weeks earlier, one which would in any case have to be made under Parliamentary sanction later, roused resistance everywhere. The Commission was revoked by proclamation, and the Crown, halfway between the issuing of the writs and the meeting of Parliament, promised that it would rely upon the only regular precedent for exceptional grants supplementary to the regular revenue – the agreement to such an especial grant by the House of Commons.

CHARLES I

To carry on in the interval, certain new duties were put on merchandise; but there was a very ominous sequel to that – for the first time in all this prolonged and increasing struggle between the King and his wealthy subjects the lawyers began to oppose the Crown. For the first time the judges were ranging themselves in a body (as they had often threatened hitherto to range themselves as individuals) against the Monarch. They gave advice that the new increased duties were illegal.

It was on the 17th of March, 1628, that the third Parliament of Charles met, and when he addressed them in what was in those days a reality – a Speech from the Throne – he put the issue clearly enough. He told them that he had called a Parliament because in a moment of crisis when more than the regular revenue must immediately be found "to secure ourselves and to save our friends from imminent ruin," a Parliament was "the ancient, the most speedy and the best way to obtain such succour." But he told them that it would be his duty – as indeed it was; the first duty of kingship – to see to the safety of the State whether they did their duty or no; and he added the famous words, "Take not this as threatening (I scorn to threaten any but my equals), but as an admonition from him that both by nature and duty has most cares of your preservations and prosperities."

It was the old Royal Majesty, the incarnation of the people of England in one man, speaking against that new and still swelling flood of territorial revolt which would not reach its height until it had supplanted the monarchy and put wealth into power.

Now is to be observed, immediately following this incident, the quality in what was soon to be the English governing class which has given that class its homogeneity and its political success at home and abroad. The great landlords and their fellows, the merchants and lawyers – all one body, as they still are, though the proportions have changed – acted with discipline and corporate unity. They planned and planned successfully as though they had not been hundreds of men but one. They passed a resolution granting supply, put it as high as five subsidies (which meant as much again as the whole natural revenue of the Crown – almost filling the gap between what was present in cash and what was imperatively needed to carry on). They made this Resolution the more tempting by saying that this sum of money, so much larger than any they had *willingly* voted before, should be paid rapidly within the next twelve months; *and having passed that Resolution refused to make it effective by putting it into a Bill.*

They were determined to manifest their new power and have it ratified before these moneys, upon which the life of the kingdom depended, should leave their pockets and those of the body of lesser freeholders who would also have to pay and who supported them in their discontent – with no idea, poor yeomen, that the Revolution would lead to their own destruction.

What the Commons demanded to be made permanent law before a penny of theirs should be forthcoming was drawn up in four clearly distinguished points, making between them what they called their "Petition of Right." "Right" it was not, it was Revolution; but the word matters not; what matters is, that the King was thus to be given the choice of seeing his strength threatened through immediate starvation, or more permanently imperilled through his own surrender of what had been, by all the traditions of the past, his due executive power over the State.

The first three of these points were designed to hamper the executive in its control by giving it no power of delay or of exercising authority without the concurrence of the lawyers. The King (it was proposed) might no longer restrain or imprison a subject without stating a "cause" – so that his action must be debated between the lawyers and decided by them. Any rebel so restrained or imprisoned could appeal of right to the lawyers to be released; and until a specific accusation, which could be debated before the lawyers in their courts, had been formulated against a subject he remained free to act at will against the Government.

There was no real distinction between these three first clauses of the Petition; they formed together one instrument designed to hobble the executive in its dealings with obstruction. No Government in practice has ever observed, or could observe, the spirit of such restrictions. It would be impossible to govern if they were seriously carried out. It is impossible to carry on against rebellion or even disaffection without the power of arrest and detention until a policy in each case shall be determined on. And when the governing class had succeeded at last in supplanting kingship it maintained these powers of arrest and detention in fact, though long carrying on as a pretence the theory of the revolutionary phrases then framed. A rebel against the governing class could appeal to the lawyers: but the lawyers were members of the governing class.

It is an excellent example of those equivocations the use of which makes aristocracy the best secured form of human society.

So much for the first three clauses.

But the fourth clause was another matter, and it was even more vital. The King was asked to agree to, and to make law, a statement that he would not supplement the now ruined revenue of the Crown. The goods of the subject (which meant, in practice, the wealthier subject) were to be the absolute possession of the individual owner and over them the State should have no claim; only the rich owners themselves, assembled in Parliament, could voluntarily give or withhold such "aids."

To admit that principle – and it was extended in intention even over the age-long right of the King to levy Customs upon import and export – was to destroy the power of the Crown, for there can be no power without revenue. The trick could only be played by pretending that the existing official revenue was still sufficient as it had been in the past for the purposes of the nation; by pretending that the income of the Government was the same as it had been when money could buy six times more and when the things and services to be bought by the Government were not half as numerous as they had already become in the development of the modern State.

All this was a manifest pretence, but by the use of it a further pretence of legality and of relying upon precedent could be upheld. It was as though you were to ask a man whose expenses had doubled and whose income, through the inflation of the currency, had fallen to a sixth, to carry on his life as of old, or alternatively to accept for his masters those who owed him goods and service.

The dilemma in which the monarchy found itself had no issue. It was ruin either way. But when a man is at the very last gasp for money he will, and must, of two ruinous alternatives take that which does at least provide ready cash. Charles made an effort at delay, and at half saving himself by assenting in general terms only to the revolutionary demands presented to him.

The King avoided the ritual phrase "*Que droit soit fait comme est désiré*" ("That the law might achieve what is required" —Ed.) which turned a Bill into statute law – "He had not the art of lying." He imagined that the use of words which were so vague that they might later have been given what interpretation he chose would be accepted by these men who were infinitely his superiors in the business of intrigue. That general evasion of his was promptly met. The Lords resented it and supported the Commons. The Commons were united – for the last time. The leader on that day was old Coke, the former Chief Justice, a man still vigorous after seventy-six years of a singularly evil life, filled with an immensity of legal learning. The weight he carried was not only due to his enormous fortune but to the reputation he had for precedent, and his motive was as personal as Elliot's. It was rancour. He had been refused the Treasurership, and he never forgave. He who had so recently called Buckingham the "Saviour," he who had sacrificed his little daughter of fourteen to Buckingham's wretched brother, now recalled all the disappointments of his life and charged with full weight against the Crown. To him more than to any other spokesman do we owe the valuable Magna Charta myth which still rules uninstructed minds. Elliot also spoke with all *his* wrongs boiling within him as might be expected, and raised the temperature of the Assembly to white heat. They locked the doors of their meeting-place, resolved that they were now a Committee to consult upon the public good. They demanded that the Petition of Right should be made *law* by the addition of the ritual phrase. Let the Speaker go and put before the King his impression of their temper; it was their intention to proceed to another open accusation of Buckingham as the cause of all the troubles, and thereby to strike at the King.

When the Speaker came back he brought with him the Royal order for an adjournment, and the Commons obeyed it. Forcible resistance was not yet necessary.

It was Thursday, the 5th of June, of that year, 1628, and the next day they carried on their protest and campaign, and on the day after that, Saturday, the 7th of June, in Whit-Week, Charles gave way. He was moved to submission by his desire to save Buckingham, for he understood that if he yielded Buckingham would be spared. Later, when he should have had time to organise and to consider new methods it might be possible to regain his constitutional status and to be what the Kings of England had always been.

He took his place upon the throne, prepared to answer the demand of the Lords and Commons combined for an explicit reply

CHARLES I

— understanding that the saving of Buckingham was part of the bargain — he ordered his first answer to be cut off the Bill, and added the traditional formula which made it law as it stood, *"Que droit soit fait comme désiré."*†

They cheered him, and no wonder, for they had won. And they passed the five subsidies at last.

But they followed up their victory, and continued to strike at the joint in the armour, breaking the implied agreement and bringing forth yet another Remonstrance denouncing Buckingham.

On the same day that the House of Commons was thus making ready to denounce Buckingham as the cause of all the evils, a hanger-on of his, a physician, one Lamb, had been murdered by bravos who set upon him in the street. It was the prelude of what was to follow.

The summer was advancing, a new expedition was prepared, Buckingham was at Portsmouth, his wife with him and all his train about him; the French Protestant Envoys were there and the fleet at anchor without.

It had indeed been privately determined, not that Buckingham should engage in yet another military expedition — that was only a feint — but that he should, under the use of its threat, after sailing down the French coast open a correspondence with Richelieu and attempt a public Treaty of Alliance. Full instructions were drawn up in London to be sent down to Buckingham at Portsmouth, and Charles himself was in the neighbourhood of that town to see his friend off and to bid him good-bye.

Upon the morning of the 23rd of August, a Saturday, Buckingham, with many of his train about him, was dressing for going forth in his carriage after he should have breakfasted. Soubise was there, and others of the Huguenot French. There came rumours that La Rochelle had been relieved. There was a buzz of conversation in the room where the Duke was and he told those about him that he would go off and tell the King the good news — which was in fact false. The house in which Buckingham was stopping stood in the High Street, and after the custom of the time (when public men were public indeed) people from the street went in and out as they willed and the press increased. Buckingham all that night had been wakeful and fe-

---

† The formula varies and today is in more than one form. See Stephen's *Commentaries*, Vol. II, p.383.

120

verish. A servant came in to tell the Duke, who had not finished his preparations for travel, that his breakfast was ready, and he moved towards the door which gave on to the main hall of the house, where the meal was served. They held the hangings up to let him pass. He had with him, on his left, Sir Thomas Fryer, a colonel in his army, and Sir Thomas Fryer was a short man, Buckingham a tall one. As he went through that door with the press of people about him he turned his head to the left and lowered it to speak to his shorter companion – just as he did so a man standing a little behind him and to his right leant forward round his body and stabbed him suddenly with a knife over the heart.

He gave one loud cry, "The villain hath killed me!" snatched out the knife and, with blood gushing from the wound and from his mouth, the tall figure stumbled forward, blundered against the table where the meal stood ready, and fell dead to the ground.

*****

There runs east and west, north of Portsmouth, a long sharp ridge of chalk, very even, some 300 feet high, defending the harbour from the north or landward side. It is called Portsdown. Where the road northward out of Portsmouth crosses this ridge, not far from the middle of it, a man standing upon that height can see upon either side a great prospect. To the south is the long grey line of the Isle of Wight and the broad belt of the Channel; at his feet the wide expanse at full tide of Portsmouth Harbour. If he turn to the north he sees a country still largely wooded and at that time counting in part as a Royal forest, the forest of Bere. Immediately at his feet, thus looking northward but a little to the west, is Southwick House, from which manorial place to Portsmouth harbour and the ships is some five miles. It was then the property of Sir Daniel Norton, and he it was who acted now as the King's host, for Charles lay there during these last days when he was awaiting the sailing of the fleet from the great harbour. He was to have gone into Portsmouth to meet Buckingham that very day.

Thither immediately spurred Sir Thomas Hippesley, through the morning northward, galloping up the road with the dreadful news of Buckingham's murder.

CHARLES I

He came booted into the house, as he was, without delay. He was told that the household was at divine service, as was the custom of a morning, and King Charles himself was kneeling at the head of that small domestic congregation. Sir Thomas Hippesley walked up to him and whispered the awful message in his ear. But the King would allow no interruption. His face remained impassive and his glance still fixed before him as he continued his prayers.

The service over, the frightened household gathered to glance furtively at the silent figure of the King as he moved out – still silent, still giving no sign – towards his own room.

Never had his determination to maintain the due order and sanctity of the Crown showed itself more strongly. But once behind the doors of his own room, and alone, Charles burst into a passionate fit of weeping which seemed to break him altogether. He had lost suddenly, at a stroke, all that to which his youth had been devoted; the deep friendship in which he had lived; and one who should have seen him thus might have thought that his strength would never rise again. But his nobility was far superior even to such agonies of grief. For some days, though he worked many hours, busying himself in all public things, there was apparent on him the weight of that terrible moment. At last this outward proof of the shattering thing could be concealed. It seemed to have passed. But the man had changed.

MATURITY

The King was alone. Men are upheld by their affections much more than they know, even when these are varied and dissipated, even when they are spread widely and even when they work only upon a nature naturally joyous and avid of many companions. To such a man as Charles Stuart, who had had this one intense affection, hitherto increasingly dominating his whole life – this profound affection for that elder, strong, vivacious genius whom he had followed since his boyhood – the sudden loss was a kicking away of all supports and such an ordeal as not one man in a hundred has to pass.

There was that in him such that by this business he was matured. The shock precipitated what was diffuse in him; he crystallised. His character henceforward is united and inwardly determined, though it must still suffer from that inheritance of blood, that puny childhood, that friendless and hesitating youth. His speech grew less rare, though it was as abrupt as ever and still suffering from the cause of that abruptness, a hardly conquered stammer: a physical hesitation which was the more marked through a Scottish accent of his which he never lost. The melancholy of his face grew settled and henceforward did not leave those dark, prominent grey eyes: but still, he was master of his grief always and of the memory of it, and if anything it strengthened the dignity of his carriage.

After the loss of a great affection there is nothing left but duty. Charles's duty was plain – to be King, to rule England. This he had always known, but the active work of it he had left to that Minister who had fallen in his service. He had felt the man to be so much abler and readier than himself that he could not do other; but now it was his business to act without such aid, to act single-handed, to make his own decisions, to look into all details himself, to master the whole affair and to be continually the Moderator of his Kingdom. He had duty to nourish him and clear principle; but the course in front of him was less clear, surely, than to any man before. It was his by the traditions of all time to be King; that is, to protect the humble against the mighty, the poor against the rich; to be himself the nation in the flesh; to see to the strength and prestige of England among her rivals, to her prosperity at home; it was his to give himself always to the public thing, and to be as it were in himself the people.

That was what he had to do; *that* was his task – the thing that now must wholly occupy his mind.

But where was the money? In all the long line of his ancestors, his predecessors in all the tradition of the Kings of England of whom he was now here the last, there had been sufficient endowment for the work to be done. That endowment had now failed. None can rule without resource in material things, none can fulfil a human plan at all without such resources – only one thing can be done without money, and that is the salvation of the individual soul.

The mere routine function of government required, in these years, the twenties of the seventeenth century, about double the revenue with which the Government was endowed. The breakdown of its endowment through the vast and continuing change in the value of money and through the looting to which the Royal property had been subjected since the Reformation, left between available income and necessary expenditure a gulf menacing immediate ruin. Charles, even with the strict economy Buckingham had provided, needed for administration and defence ten shillings yearly in money of the time, from each English family. His rents and dues and the rest only furnished five shillings. He needed, in modern values, £3 per family. He was getting but half. How was the gap to be filled, if he were now to act as King indeed? All those early years since his accession had been filled with expedients, and many of them would continue – "shifts of a poor throne in the midst of a rich nation."

There had been the abnormal devices which our official history has so absurdly over emphasised: loans begged for, half-enforced; magnates (such as Wentworth) imprisoned for refusing help – and then released.

There had been abortive efforts to compromise between the necessity of calling a Parliament to give grants and the necessity of curbing or eliminating the leaders of such Parliaments, as in the

MATURITY

famous experiment at nominating them to be sheriffs, so that they could not act in the Commons.

But all that effort failed – and even in its temporary successes produced no permanent supply.

There had been selling of the Royal plate, pawning of Royal estates to the usurers of London (aldermen of the Corporation) and all the rest of it. We have seen what his necessities had done during those first three years of his reign; how they had compelled him to go cap in hand to the rich and beg for grants – whether privately by loans or publicly through the machinery of their Parliament, and how they took advantage of the situation to attempt to draw away power from him and acquire it themselves, as the price of their aid. But then, there had been war upon war. Might it not be possible, if he insisted on peace, to be, with efficient and loyal service from those about him, King indeed and by using every right to raise a revenue sufficient? The wars could be ended; economy could be still more strict; and the Royal rights in land and dues could be used to the utmost by a strict examination of title and precedent.

He rose finely to his duty, for his character was now annealed – the character of that young man still in his twenty-eighth year, but having suffered after a fashion which made him ten years older.

Happily for him Charles had, to help him in this business and duty of his, men who would serve him well after the blow of Buckingham's death had fallen. He already had Weston the Treasurer, Laud the churchman, Noy the lawyer, and that great administrator, Thomas Wentworth, who, after so long a resistance, was now reconciled with the King.

These four must be considered. Weston was a man wholly devoted to his task. He had taken no part in the debates and struggles of the immediate past; he had good intelligence, good education, good birth; he desired no more than to serve his master and with this object he had been made Treasurer in that same summer of 1628, when those of the Parliament who opposed were wrestling with the King. He had been made Treasurer at the expense of Manchester – Manchester had hungered for the post and never forgot his disappointment – that must be remembered when we come to the Civil Wars and to the armed rebellion and the action therein of Manchester's son.

CHARLES I

It was, then, Weston's duty by economy of expenditure and strict administration, to balance the outgoings and incomings of the Crown. To him personally was due the success attained therein. But his integrity, his industry, his intelligence, his devotion were accompanied by certain defects. He was nervous, and though he had the courage to do what was right he troubled over the consequences. He was outspoken – perhaps too much so – yet also too anxious about the consequences of his free speech. Moreover his health was breaking, and though he was not old he had not very long to live.

It was a handle against Weston as against scores of others, that he was connected with the large Catholic section of the State. It was on this account that Clarendon, who detested Catholicism, has maligned him, though he has done so with that appearance of judicial impartiality which is one of the charms of his style. Not only were Weston's family avowedly and openly Catholic, but his domestics and familiars as well, those at least with whom he generally conversed; and of his own sympathies – though he conformed – there could be little doubt. Yet he did his duty, even in this matter. Indeed the only alternative to so doing would have been resignation. He got the utmost he could in money from that small minority among the large body of Catholics who stood out and were liable to heavy fines for not attending the services of what was now the national Church. He was concerned solely with the revenue, even in the matter of the persecuting laws, and that revenue he increased by collecting the fines as directly as possible, getting rid of as many go-betweens as he could, and effecting practical compromises whereby, for a promise of lesser but regular payments, he would be saved the expense of prosecutions and delays. It is a great testimony to his character that Charles, to whom Catholicism was so distasteful, respected and admired this honest servant.

Noy, the lawyer, was quite another case. He was not a merely gloomy man, for he had sardonic humour. Nor would it be just to call him repulsive; but he was aloof and almost sinister. He had a passion for independence. He was devoted entirely to his trade. He had been of course in the opposition to Charles like the bulk of his trade union, withstanding the Crown with legal arguments – but was ready now, like a true lawyer, to serve his present client and to give to the service of the King those same legal talents which he would have given to the

MATURITY

service of anyone else who should have paid him. He presumably had his personal reasons – as had most of those who now supported the Monarchy – for abandoning opposition; but his prime reason was the desire to ply his trade and he very honestly carried out the contract. Whatever legal ingenuity could do for the King, Noy was prepared to use in the discovery of precedent, and the spinning of arguments. Heaven knows the side which he had abandoned was keen enough on such tricks – and after all it was within the code of his profession to sell his ingenuity to the highest bidder.

Laud, on the other hand, had never been within a thousand miles of opposition to the Crown. He was much older than the others; he was nearer fifty-five, twenty-eight years older than the King, and he had all his active life been wholly occupied with two things which were the twin passions of his sincere and eager soul: love of the Church of England, and the unifying and adorning thereof. He had been born just late enough to belong to the generation which had never seen the Church of England other than a settled institution standing of itself. He had not known the Mass; he had no memories of his Church as a novelty; he had not passed through those early years of the Establishment when it was doubtful whether Cecil's experiment would succeed; he had never been one of those who were tempted to react towards Calvinism because they had known in youth what Catholicism really was.

To say that Laud had Catholic sympathies is to misuse words. Laud never felt for the Catholic Church that yearning which so many of his contemporaries and equals had felt. He ever regarded it as something separate and alien; the *national* quality of the *national* Established Church was his glory. Catholicism is not a body of doctrine, still less of opinions. It is a definite *thing* with a savour and quality all its own, which cannot be denied and in contrast to which, in the Western world, stands Protestantism. The main line of cleavage lay not between the Establishment and sundry dissident bodies, then small, but between the Catholic Church, with its Mass, its Papacy, above all, its claim to a unique divine authority, and the Protestant opponents of such a claim. Laud was one of the latter.

Because he was determined upon order in the Church, upon discipline within it and upon such ritual as he found necessary to its dignity and glory, the opposing wing accused him of what was furthest from him — an attachment to that attitude of universality and infallibility which is the essential of the Roman Communion. He had it not. "With Rome as she now is" (to quote his own best-known phrase), he would have nothing to do. The hearty dislike of Catholicism which Charles felt all his life found no obstacle in the character of Laud. To all this I shall later return.

Thomas Wentworth, much the greatest of the four, presents a certain problem upon which men have long debated and will continue to debate. Why did he now join the King's side in the battle? He who had hitherto been so prominent on the side of his class and its claims! The answer is not very difficult to give, though it is complex to state; but that the question can be put at all and that it can be put with such force is due to certain apparent contradictions.

Thomas Wentworth was exactly of that wood from which the opposition to kingship was now being carved. He was a great landowner, one of the very greatest in his own county of Yorkshire, a sort of little local king; he was Protestant after the manner of the Established Church with no approach to Catholicism whatsoever, and so little understanding of it that he quite missed the nature of Ireland, with which he was to be principally concerned. He had, like the rest of his sort, depended upon legal arguments against the Crown; he had been a leader of the struggle against the King in the earlier Parliaments. When he joined Charles in this summer of 1628 his fellows among the wealthy whom he represented talked of him as a traitor to their cause, yet the motives for his determination to serve his King should be clear enough, though they were not single.

There was in the first place a disgust with the futility (as it seemed to him) of the continuous Parliamentary wrangle. He had an appetite for order and for final solutions and there seemed no end to this see-saw of Remonstrance and Dissolution. Next, he was at once perplexed, disturbed and repelled by the greater and greater use made of Puritan enthusiasm by the revolutionaries. He disliked Revolution anyhow, and as for Puritanism, both the thing itself and the use of it for such a purpose were odious to him. Next, he reacted against the position into which Elliot had been raised. In this reaction of his against Elliot's fame there was something of vanity, perhaps, but certainly much more of disdain. Elliot was a man blown upon in mat-

MATURITY

ters of money, one who had risen by the friendship of Buckingham and then had turned upon him, one whose reputation lay wholly in his artistic powers as an orator and was based on a shouting extravagance. All this combined was disgusting to Wentworth. To see all this combined taking from him his old place of leadership was intolerable to him. It seemed to him that Elliot and those who followed him were heading for chaos. Now Thomas Wentworth knew himself to be a man made for administration; exaggeration of all kinds, but above all exaggeration which seemed to lead nowhere, exasperated him; he was for settlement and for strong government always, and by mid-1628 things had come to a pass where there was no settlement or strong government possible, in his eyes, save in the service of the King.

He was a man strongly emotional as well as highly intelligent, but emotional with the reserve of Yorkshire and the gentry, somewhat troubled in face, dark, intense of will, and one who – when he had undertaken to act – was determined to succeed.

But if you would have the key to what he and Laud, and Charles himself, whom they served, were inspired by, the answer is "Unity" – National Unity.

Laud saw the core of the thing (that is, of the business of Unity) in unity through the national religion or rather the national establishment. Wherein he had little objection to disorder of ideas so long as there was not disorder of language and of rite. Thomas Wentworth worked for unity of administration – or rather would have so worked had he been first Minister, which, to Charles's loss, he never was; for Charles was his own first Minister after he had lost Buckingham. Wentworth was first, after his adhesion to Charles, made President of the Council of the North, that is, Viceroy of the north of England; and then given the same task in Ireland. It would have been far better for the King had he been present always in the Council Chamber in London. As for the King, a desire for Unity, effected by and expressed in kingship, was the very centre of his being.

These three between them began the moulding of such a Unity – but they did not achieve it. They perished every one of them on the scaffold through their failure to achieve it. To none of them was it revealed that the apparent chaos then threatened by the revolt of wealth would in its turn breed unity when the monarchy should have been destroyed and aristocratic government established in its place. Today Great Britain presents the strongest example of political unity in the world, and of moral unity as well. And yet that unity is the fruit of aristocracy as it was established upon the ruins of the old monarchy. But it was late in coming; for a hundred years after Charles's death, disunion, not union, was the mark of political England, and these men supporting the King in 1628 foresaw it would be so unless they succeeded.

In the task to which Charles now set himself, he found his first check in a detail concerning Buckingham's murderer. The man who had stabbed Buckingham turned out to be one Felton, a man driven wild by personal wrongs (as he believed them to be), a minor officer in the army who had been refused promotion; he was further, and much more, inflamed by the storming of the politicians, those who were led by the eloquence of Elliot. Now it was apparent to Charles, as it must have been to everybody else, that Felton could not have acted alone. He therefore proposed that he should be put to "the question" – which is in plain English, torture – the regular procedure of the Courts in the past when it was necessary to obtain information of that kind which was refused. But whether Felton had accomplices or no, whether he had been prompted by greater men to act as he did we shall never know, for it was characteristic of the turning-point which we are reaching in English history that the lawyers again baulked the King. It was partly from the spirit of the time, it was more from a desire to strengthen the Lawyers' Guild against the executive, but it was also as a demonstration of opposition that they pronounced for an innovation in practice and decided, in the case of Felton, that torture should not be applied. They even called it illegal – though they were ready to allow it years later when their own skins were imperilled by a popular riot.

Felton was hanged on the 29th of November, three months after the murder he had committed. He died penitent and admitting his guilt.

Meanwhile La Rochelle had surrendered; and that was a further blow to the King's prestige; but it had to be endured: nothing more could be done. The fleet that Buckingham had gathered at Portsmouth started out for La Rochelle after his death, but found that it

MATURITY

could do nothing against the mole Richelieu had thrown up across the harbour mouth, and the King of England's proposal to be the protector of the French Huguenots was frustrated. But he had in any case made up his mind to have done with foreign wars, since everything now must be sacrificed to building up the revenue and cutting down expense for the sake of right government within the country. It is to be remarked in passing that the Envoy he sent to the French to negotiate peace, Montagu, Manchester's son, became a Catholic, a priest, and lived on as Confessor to the French Queen-Dowager.

It remained for Charles to ravel up the loose ends of the conflicts with France and Spain. He was putting an end to the foreign wars, he must now clean up what was left of the mess at home, and that meant, in the main, the getting rid of the obstructionist Parliament.

The King had promised to meet Parliament again; he kept his promise; it was summoned and met at Westminster on Tuesday, the 20th of January, 1629, and of course the trouble would begin all over again, but this time it should be met with decision. It had done its worst. Buckingham had been murdered. It was time to resist.

The Revolutionaries felt the new spirit they would have to face. They dreaded the swing of popular opinion towards the Crown. Their able leaders determined to ally themselves more closely than ever with that other Revolutionary force, Puritanism.

It was growing, it was fervid, it was sincere. Those leaders in Parliament were for the most part indifferent to Theology, but they had an unfailing sense of tactics, and they saw how an alliance with the Puritan minority of the nation, the confusion of its enthusiasm with an enthusiasm for political change would add driving power to their plans.

It was Elliot more than anyone else who shifted the new attack round to religion. Charles, anxious above all things to regularise the position of the revenue, begged them to settle once and for all the question of the Customs, Tonnage and Poundage. He was still outwardly for conciliation; he had to be, so long as the landed classes and the lawyers were in session. He was quite willing to admit that according to all precedent Tonnage and Poundage must be formally voted to him for life by the Parliament as they had been to his predecessors, and that technically he could not levy Customs at the ports

CHARLES I

until the Parliamentary vote had been taken. But in practice of course, the work at the ports of levying for duties had to go on as usual. All Charles asked for was the same source of revenue as his predecessors had received as a matter of course for hundreds of years, one without which it was quite impossible for the Government to carry on, with the Customs supplying every year a larger part of revenue. Yet the opposition in Parliament determined to press their advantage; they deliberately put off confirming the Customs, and began a loud religious debate, on a Resolution listened to by Oliver Cromwell, a new member hitherto unremarked, that "the affairs of the King of earth must give way to the affairs of the King of Heaven." Hume says of a phrase then used by Cromwell, "they were the amusing words of a fanatical hypocrite." The judgment is hardly just; the fanaticism was sincere, though there was hypocrisy in this special display of it at such a moment by Elliot because the religious quarrel between Puritan and High Church was only thrust forward in order to delay the settlement of Tonnage and Poundage.

We must remember throughout that the danger to history in all this affair is the exaggeration of the religious quarrel. Not to give it its full weight would be to write bad history indeed, for it played a very large part; but it was not the main driving force behind the whole movement. The main driving force behind the whole movement was the desire, already in part deliberate but still largely instinctive, of the gentry to supplant the King. What we are watching is the embryonic growth of aristocracy; which of all forms of government is the most anti-monarchical. This main quarrel driving towards the destruction of monarchy took the religious quarrel for an ally; the religious feeling was so vivid that, when it came to fighting, we can only see it in terms of the Puritans and their opponents, and before the fighting was over this religious enthusiasm had almost monopolised the attention of men; yet it remained throughout secondary, and while it profoundly affected the history of England it did not affect it as profoundly as did the complete political change which was at work. England today is largely though vaguely Puritan in religious tradition, but politically, although the aristocratic system is breaking down, modern England has been so wholly made by aristocracy that other forms of government are still almost incomprehensible to the average Englishman.

MATURITY

England is still the one aristocratic state in a Europe everywhere else egalitarian.

An excellent example and test of the way in which religious feeling was now being used by those who were preparing a political revolution – the leaders of the opposition in the Commons – was the business of the Ten Priests.

Of the many hundreds of Catholic priests in England, ten lay at that moment under sentence of death actually pronounced – such death being by hanging and quartering, the horrible details of which can never be too much insisted upon. The victim was cut down before he was wholly strangled, he was castrated, his stomach and chest were then ripped open, his heart was pulled out while he was still alive by the hand of the executioner, after which the dead body was cut into quarters which were burnt or boiled and the head cut off.—All that!

Such was the business of the King of Heaven. But the King of earth had but recently renewed the solemn promise made at his marriage to suspend these horrors. One of the victims was executed by inadvertence, the other nine he pardoned, and that pardon was treated as a horrid piece of tyranny on his part, to be denounced with all the zeal at the command of the opposition.

That, I say, is an example of the new spirit which had been called up to add vigour to the proposed revolutionary movement. But there was a general point as well, involving a sentiment which covered a much larger proportion of the Commons, for it brought in the lawyers, few of whom were fanatical, and it also brought in many half-way men who were all for the Established Church but feared innovations. This point was the publishing by the Government, that is, by the King, of the Thirty-Nine Articles of Religion, including a clause that the Church of England had a right to decree its own rites and ceremonies and had authority in matters of faith.

It might seem self-evident that any organised religious body should have authority in matters which concerned the creed of its members – but the denial of that self-evident point was a very good opportunity for the oratory of John Elliot. And those who were managing the affair, those for whom Elliot's eloquence was an aid but not a guide, arranged the debate carefully, as they always did. Elliot called upon the House to enter upon its journals "a vow" as he called it. The

CHARLES I

Commons – the assembled squires and lawyers – "avowed for truth the articles of religion which were established in Parliament in the thirteenth year of Queen Elizabeth." This had all the advantage of referring to precedent, for in that thirteenth year of Queen Elizabeth, a lifetime before, the obnoxious clause did not appear. It had been taken for granted.

And still nothing upon Tonnage and Poundage! Though the King did not claim this essential and growing part of his revenue as his right – which he could have done, for it was a thing established since the Middle Ages – though all he asked was that there should be the formal granting by a vote of Parliament as of old, the managers of the revolt still deliberately proposed postponement in order to maintain their power. And before they would turn to the discussion of the revenue necessary to the kingdom they brought up another quarrel on the Petition of Right.

The Government had done in connection with that contentious document something which could be so misrepresented that a false legend of it has come down to our own day and flourishes in every textbook where official history warps historical truth.

It will be remembered that Charles, when he had agreed to the Petition of Right in the summer before Buckingham's death, eight months before, had done so in a general form of words, saying that he intended to preserve the laws as they existed. He had not used the consecrated formula "*Soit droit fait, etc.*" which turned the proposition into a positive law. In other words, he had refused to make the Petition of Right a full Act of Parliament, which the judges, being lawyers and already inclined to support the class they belonged to, could use in their verdicts as an immutable piece of legislation. It will also be remembered that Charles had given away because there was a threat of a renewed attack upon Buckingham: to save Buckingham he had at last allowed the consecrated formula and thus turned the Petition into true and permanent law.

But the gist of the matter – which is too often omitted when the incident is described – is this:—

The final assent of the King had only been given as part of an implied bargain. He gave it in order to get rid of a renewed "Remonstrance" which was being got up against Buckingham on that Friday, 7th of June, Whit-Week, 1628. But when the opposition had

MATURITY

got the King to play his part, they refused to play theirs. They broke the implied contract and went on with the Remonstrance. The Commons, be it also remembered, had made no mention of Tonnage and Poundage in the Petition of Right. Their language spoke only of extraordinary and exceptional levies.† Yet when they had got the King to sign, they unexpectedly brought out Tonnage and Poundage again, like a Jack-in-the-Box, and used it as a bargaining point for purchasing the downfall and presumably the death of Buckingham. They even prepared a second Remonstrance, denying the King's right to Tonnage and Poundage, and it was only then that Charles had come down to the House, told them that there could be no question of Tonnage and Poundage, and dissolved the Parliament. Bearing all this in mind we can understand what follows, which would otherwise be incomprehensible.

The Government had the Petition of Right printed, 1,500 copies of it, and put at the end of it the *first* form of Royal assent, the general promise to maintain the laws. But the Parliament having broken their side of the contract the Government quite properly and wisely refused to be bound on its side; they did not print the formula which had been later added to the Petition as the price for saving Buckingham. That they should thus have acted (as they had every right to act after the breach of the implied contract) offered an excellent ground for further attacks upon the King in this session of early 1629.

Charles came down to the House and made a most conciliatory speech, once more affirming that he required no more than that they should pass the Bill for Tonnage and Poundage, so that he should have it, "as my ancestors have had it." He told them that he had taken for granted that they had not been lacking in goodwill, and had only delayed from want of time. He concluded by saying, "So make good your professions and put an end to all questions arising from the subject." *The feeling of the House* (as the phrase goes) *was with him*. That is, the large minority which was wholly on his side, and the big floating mass of perplexed moderate men in the middle thought that peace had been made, and there was general applause.

But the organised body which had made a determined plan and was carrying it out with such skill weighed more – as organisation

---

† Taxes, Tallage, Aids, or other like charges.

always does – than the confused general body. They did not refuse to vote the duties, but in order to cause further irritation and delay, they proposed as a condition, before they should vote the Customs, that reparation should be made for the goods which had been attached for payment by the Government's officers of the Customs until the vote was passed.

It was, I say, merely a trick; it could have no practical effect; it was exactly as though today somebody quarrelling with the fact that income-tax is often collected before the passing of the Budget when it is legally due should demand the refunding of the sums paid, and then, after they were refunded, have them paid a second time when the Budget had been passed.

This skilful move was worked on Monday, the 23rd of February, 1629. A week later, on Monday, the 2nd of March, John Elliot was in the midst of another violent speech against the Government and all its ways when the Speaker rose and told the House that he had received the Royal order for adjournment. The leaders of the opposition called upon him to put to the vote a Remonstrance against the levying of the Customs. He refused to be coerced, and rose to adjourn the House, as was his duty. Then did there take place that famous scene when Holles, the young aristocrat, and Valentine, held the Speaker down in his chair, and when a free fight broke out between those who were for and those who were against the proposed revolutionary changes. Swords were drawn, and at the door the plaintive voice of a boy was heard calling with a strong Welsh accent, "Let hur in! let hur in! To give my master his sword!" – for it seemed to this good servant from the mountains that if the gentlemen who were "Saints" proposed to stick the gentlemen who were not, these last ought at least to have something to fence with!

We have it from an eye-witness, Sir Simon Ewes, that the mass of members were still confused but growing more inflamed by the rhetoric about them – for Elliot went on with his passionate and eloquent shouting – when Holles proposed that anyone who should seek to bring in Popery or any other opinions differing from what he termed the orthodox Church should be judged worthy of death and that anyone who should advise the continued taking of the Customs at the ports should be held worthy of death, and that any merchant who paid the Customs should be held a traitor to his country.

MATURITY

After all this tumult the adjournment did take place, but not until the King had gone down to the House of Lords in person and threatened to break open the doors – which the leaders of the incipient rebellion had bolted. The adjournment was until Tuesday, the 10th of March, and on that day the King came down to the Lords and dissolved the Parliament. It was high time!

Ten of the ringleaders were summoned before the Council. Their technical offence was having rebelled against the King's authority by refusing to accept his adjournment of the debate; a thing which by all precedent he had a right to order. Among these ten of course were Holles and Valentine and Elliot. To Holles, who had been in the Court set and would be again, Charles quietly said, "*Et tu, Brute?*... We were fellow-revellers in a masque together!" But the man whom he noted most strictly was John Elliot. There stood that considerable artist who had used his art to foment sedition, and who was the true murderer of Buckingham – for though Felton had struck the blow it was the eloquence of Elliot which had inflamed his followers to the point of blood. Nor did Charles forget at that moment – nor ever – that Elliot had implied abominably that he had poisoned his own father.

When the accused had been sent to their prisons Charles, in obedience to a judicial decision, offered them their liberty on giving security for good behaviour. In course of time most of them yielded and were willing to promise, but among the few who stood out was Elliot.

Then was it seen with what courage an artist can die – and incidentally then was it also seen with what cunning an artist can plan. This great orator had "castled" as they say in chess, he had put his big fortune into the hands of trustees for his sons so that there was nothing out of which to pay his fines; and as for promising good behaviour, in his letters begging for release he carefully avoided the phrase. He remained in the Tower, writing a book to pass the hours; he fell into a consumption, and yet he would not yield; he claimed his liberty for the sake of his health but his determination stood and not even for life itself would he give up his point. It is so with the great rhetoricians. They persuade themselves, and are in their own eyes sacred prophets. His plea on the ground of health was not insincere, he was failing, and at the end of the third year, on November the 27th, 1632, he died. But his abominable accusations remained fixed in Charles's mind and that King, who had never in his life done anything cruel, was here stern to the last. To those who implored that Elliot's body should be taken from the Tower to be buried in his own land he answered, "Let Sir John Elliot be buried in the parish where he died."

When Charles dissolved Parliament on the Tuesday, the 10th of March, 1629, he had made a resolution to which he steadfastly adhered until he had passed his fortieth year. That resolution was that he would use such economics and also such methods of increasing the revenue as would permit him to carry on the work of the nation without exceptional and precarious aid. The regular work of government should no longer be dependent upon those rich men who proposed to withhold or grant their money at will with the object of taking into their own hands the power of the Throne. It was a resolution which demanded fixed and continuous determination and an unwavering plan, a resolution remarkable in so young a man, and still more remarkable in his long adherence to it. For Charles was only twenty-eight when he thus fixed the goal which he had before him, and during all those years which turn the vigour of youth into the circumspection of middle age, on till he was in his forty-second year, he maintained that even course. He would be King indeed and represent the people against a faction; he *was* King, and his kingship brought peace and increase of wealth, security and well-being throughout England. It was a great achievement.

It has often been said that Charles intended to destroy Parliaments, or at least to call no other during his reign. He is said to have dropped words in anger as he took off his robes on that 10th March after the strain of incipient rebellion and to have cried that he would never put them on again for a like ceremony. But it is not possible that any such real intention can have lain in Charles's mind and that for two very good reasons. The whole machinery and tradition of government demanded that for any considerable change in positive laws, for any fundamental enactment to meet new circumstances, a Parliament must be called. It would have been impossible to carry on permanently without it, unless the King were prepared to carry through an open revolution of his own, counter to the revolution which had been brought against himself. But of this Charles not only gave no sign – and it would have been in the nature of things

MATURITY

impossible. There must, in the nature of things, arise circumstances in which some new laws would have to be made, and these could only be made by the King in Parliament. But the second reason was the more immediate and important. He could not have intended to reign permanently without Parliaments because though he might live (as his ancestors had lived) upon his own revenue when he should have sufficiently settled that, even so he world have had to call a Parliament under any exceptional strain such as a war: and no government can be certain it will not have to meet a war of aggression. One could carry on for a very long time by proclamations in the place of new laws, but not for ever; and one could not carry on without exceptional grants save in years when there was no exceptional strain. Moreover, a Parliament would be summoned of necessity with each new reign.

Meanwhile in order to carry out his plan of a sufficient revenue which should make him independent of the revolutionaries, all was prepared. Maritime trade was rising, and the Customs rising with it, but there was a necessity for obtaining more, because there was still a gap between the necessary expenditure of Government as the modern state developed and the existing national revenue. With this object the King and his advisers, working strictly by precedent and within the law, took three courses. First, they proceeded to grant monopolies, that is, through patents to individuals (but more often to corporations) giving to such the right to deal exclusively in a great number of goods. For such privileges the beneficiaries paid. Secondly, the Government also put into practice the existing law upon the taking up of Knighthood. Thirdly, what might have been a most fruitful source of revenue, what was most excellent in principle but what proved in practice subject to the strongest opposition from the most powerful men in the nation – he proposed to recover the Royal lands from encroachments made upon them in the past.

These three sources of revenue led naturally and inevitably to friction, as taxation always must when it is novel and imposed in time of peace; and it is essential to the comprehension of the time that we should grasp that air of innovation against which such feeling was aroused.

The Parliamentary leaders who proposed to bring down the Crown were Revolutionaries. But the King, on his side, could not carry on with the old revenue alone. He was compelled to make demands for which there was ancient precedent, but which were new to his time.

The Modern State was being born and would not work on the lines of the mediæval. Therefore the King also had to be revolutionary in practice if he were to hold his own.

The monopolies established by patents were in some things (that of soap is a notorious example) obnoxious to the generality of the people and particularly in London, upon the opinion of whose growing populace so much turned. The taking up of Knighthood affected only the substantial landowners, it meant a lump sum in payment to compound for one's knighthood if one had rents in land amounting to what we should call today £240 a year or thereabouts. It fell, therefore, not only upon the squires, but also upon the fairly well-to-do rentiers – the men with dues from some hundreds of acres. It was not a very heavy impost, but it was unaccustomed, and therefore a further irritation. It was the law, but a law long disused and one which the change in the value of money had rendered an anachronism.

That most commendable of all policies – the recovery of encroachments upon the Royal demesne – unfortunately, in the main, misfired. It was not only the most equitable of all the efforts made, not only the one which, if it could have been pushed through, would have produced most revenue – it might have made possible the abrogation of the most burdensome patents – but it was also in the full spirit of the recovery of the monarchy. Royal lands had been filched outrageously in England and Wales through the weakness of the Crown during the last hundred years. They had gone in grants to favourites, in sales at half-price to those whom it was desired to placate or from whom ready-money could be got in a crisis; that is how, for instance, two-thirds of Henry VIII's Crown land derived from the suppressed monasteries and colleges and hospitals disappeared. It had been mainly taken by the harpies who looted at large when the boy Edward VI was on the throne; and the courtiers of Elizabeth had enriched themselves on all sides in the same way.

But it was not easy to go back on such a long acquired wealth. The titles were there; the cases in which encroachment could be proved illegal were but a fraction of the whole, the Crown had been despoiled through its own lack of power much more than by direct

MATURITY

theft. Efforts were made to reaffirm the old boundaries of the forests as they had been centuries before, but they came to very little practical result. All that the King got from this policy was not one-tenth of the difference between the old regular revenue before the reforms were undertaken and the present necessities of the Government. It did not furnish five per cent. of the whole revenue aimed at.

Meanwhile every other form of income was pressed, and – what was a dangerous but perhaps unavoidable expedient – Royal leases were turned into cash by changing them into fee-farms: that is, into permanent freeholds subject to a small regular annual payment. Thus a man paying £100 a year rent to the Crown on a lease of say 60 years, would provide £500 in cash (ten years' purchase) on condition that in future he should hold the land as freehold with a £10 a year ground-rent – what is still called in the north of England a *feu*. Such sales were perhaps unavoidable, but they were a pity, for there was a loss of capital to the Crown. The fines for recusancy – that is, the revenue obtainable from Catholic landowners who compounded for the right, not of practising their religion (that was forbidden under terrible penalties) but only of *not* practising a religion which they abhorred – were strictly gathered.

There is a negative side to all this, for the greatest economy of all was a policy of wise peace. The wars were ended; subsidies to the Protestant cause abroad were no longer made; this peace and retrenchment constituted the prime condition without which Charles's reforms would have been impossible. Yet, by an unhappy fatality, that wisest part of the whole scheme could be used to diminish the prestige of the Crown. There was a strong popular sympathy throughout the whole nation, not only confined to the Protestant majority, for the suffering of the Princess Palatine, whose misfortunes were still vivid in the public mind. The Protestant cause in the Germanies was in part restored by Gustavus Adolphus during these very years just following upon the dissolution of the last Parliament, but that did not cause the Palatine to be restored to its hereditary Lord, for Charles had not paid the subsidy to the Protestant armies from the North and Gustavus Adolphus refused to arrange for the restoration of Charles's sister and her husband. All that work of weakening Catholic Austria had been the work of Richelieu, and what was noted in England was that Charles had played no part in it. Still more was it noted that the English Princess Palatine and her husband and, after his death, her son remained unsuccoured.

And there was another handicap. The great, very greatest of the great, families were of doubtful loyalty; at least, many of them were. We may take as an example the Percies. When the old pro-Catholic Northumberland was dead a young anti-Catholic Northumberland succeeded to him. It was to men of such social status that the higher posts of command had always been given in the society of that day, and Northumberland had been made by Charles Lord High Admiral. We shall see later how he betrayed the King by letting his enemies take the ships. Even in the best of days there was no real loyalty on his part, and with Wentworth at the head of Government in the north the strain was increased. The younger brother was loyal enough, but the head of the family was shaky to the end and at last openly a rebel.

More important however than that head of the family of Northumberland or his brother was their sister Lucy. Upon her, as we shall see later, the failure of the King in face of his last Parliament turned, for at the critical moment of the whole struggle when he might have used his power to coerce the Parliamentarians it was she who betrayed the Court. She shall be considered in that place; but for the moment we may note that this very capable, intriguing and unscrupulous woman was the closest friend of the Queen, Henrietta Maria. She had married the genial spendthrift Hay, one of James's Scottish creations, whom he had made Earl of Carlisle, she was therefore fully in the Court, in the heart of it, and she had become everything to the young Frenchwoman who in her turn was beginning to mean so much to the King.

For Henrietta Maria was now becoming, after those first few years of indifference and coldness from which she had so much suffered, the second great affection of Charles's life. The phrase has been used that Charles thus "fell in love with her" nearly four years after the marriage – that is, when, from the still growing girl who came to England in 1625 she had become the vivacious and active young woman of nineteen.

Henrietta Maria's influence upon her husband, I mean her political influence, has been greatly exaggerated. The error is natural enough. Charles was a man who would never look elsewhere and

MATURITY

who, so far as that relation went, would think of none other but his wife. All women in such a situation have power over a faithful man. His affection grew with the years and the birth of the children; the Queen was pregnant in the first few months after Buckingham's death and though this first child did not live the second did, born in the year after the Parliament was got rid of. He was christened Charles, after his father. It was he in babyhood who made a perfect woman of Henrietta Maria; the baby with the large dark eyes, ugly as sin and deeply adored.

The exaggeration of the Queen's political influence is also due to Clarendon, whose excellent book has done so much to misinterpret the history of the time — for good writing always tells, and the man was contemporary, judicious and of very wide range. But he disliked the Queen, he hated her nation, and he still more thoroughly hated her religion. He could not but believe that she was intriguing and that her intrigues were successful. Yet all that view is not consonant with the woman's nature nor with Charles's either. His decisions, in all matters of religion especially, we know were not influenced by her. He also hated the Queen's religion heartily; it was a sentiment in which he never wavered — and in foreign policy she did not perceptibly interfere. She would not, with her character, have cared to do so — save of course, when the life and death crisis had come and all and any aid must be sought.

So Charles stood at the opening of the year 1633, when it was decided that he should go north for his long-delayed coronation as King of Scotland. He had peace and a sufficient revenue at home; his task was in process of successful accomplishment; he suffered from such opposition as we have seen but he also had strong support and it was taking root. Nor did anyone imagine that in the word "Scotland" there lay the menace of what was to come.

SCOTLAND

CHARLES STARTED IN THE EARLY SUMMER OF 1633 FOR SCOTLAND, where he was to be crowned King of that country. He crossed the border in the second week of June, he was back in London before the end of August – it was but a matter of a few weeks and the time in which the essential things were done was but a matter of a few days – yet that brief interval was more important in the story of Charles and of his three kingdoms – and especially of England – than all the rest of his reign. For it was Scotland, Scottish energy and power of organisation, that gave the first shock, starting the train of events. The things that were done in this summer of 1633 in Scotland led four years later to resistance – resistance led to armed action – war – and war to the necessity imposed upon Charles of demanding aid over and above the regular revenue which he had so wisely and successfully built up.

It was the Scottish war, the seeds of which were sown in this summer of 1633, which compelled the King once more to summon a Parliament – the one thing which could not but be fatal to him, for it was summoning his enemies in array. That done, there must needs follow the Great Rebellion and in The Great Rebellion the defeat, betrayal and death of the man himself and of that ancient sacred monarchy which he was the last to exercise – for in his death it died.

That Scotland should have been the origin and agent of all this is one of those recurrent examples appearing all through the history of mankind in which we see that potential is of more value than mass, decision and courage of more value than numbers, and energy the deciding thing. For Scotland was not of a stature with England. I have said it might be one-fifth in numbers – hardly that; it was not one-tenth in wealth; it lay remote from Europe; it seemed unequipped for action; and yet Scotland was the author of all that followed.

Throughout the story of the seventeenth century we have to be constantly alive to the changed meaning of words. We have kept

SCOTLAND

all the names, we have quite changed the things; but because we have kept the names these always carry with them a false modern flavour. Thus when we read of "The Commons" we cannot but think of that House of Commons which held the mastery in the generation before our own time and which even in its pitiful modern decay is nominally master still. But the word "Commons" in Charles's time meant nothing of the sort; it meant a gathering of the wealthier men of the kingdom specially and only occasionally summoned to see what they might be good enough to grant in the way of supply for the Government in some critical and exceptional case. The word "Lord Chancellor" means for us a lawyer who has gone in for professional politics and has thereby attained to £10,000 a year with a pension of £5,000. But the word "Chancellor" in the days of Charles Stuart meant the chief officer of the kingdom, who might be chosen from any profession or from none, who was chosen personally by the King as all other Ministers were chosen, and who could be, and was, unmade by the King at will. It meant also one whose income was vastly greater in proportion than the income of his modern namesake. So with a whole host of words – "Admiral" has a different meaning – "Fleet," "Army" – and so in especial has the word "Scotland" a different meaning.

Scotland in 1633 meant a small, intensely vital, poor nation of less than a million souls; one that had lived independent of England, alien to England, and, by tradition, for centuries hostile to England. It meant a place off beyond the extremity of England, most of it covered by mountains unknown, but the Lowlands also foreign to their neighbours across the border. It meant a place which a man could not reach from London in less than three weeks' normal travel; a place, an event in which was not heard in Westminster, even by the more rapid transport of news, for the better part of a week; a place from which the reply to a message sent up to the southern and nearest part from the seat of Government on the Thames would not be received for something like a fortnight. It was barely thirty years since Scotland had been a quite separate kingdom with a resident King of its own, the last of a long line going right back to the heart of the Middle Ages.

That King had inherited the English throne and had hastened to occupy it, but for the Scottish people he was still the King of

CHARLES I

Scotland. He – James, Charles's father – had been *their* King from his babyhood, for 36 years, more continuously resident among them than any of their Kings had been within living memory and for long beyond living memory. Scotland could make war on England as really and as fully as France could make war on England. Both Crowns were now united in one person, but they were in the minds of men quite distinct and stood for two nationalities which might well be under separate rulers again if fate should so serve – which were suspicious and prone to anger one against the other.

Even in that which is the strongest bond of culture, religion, there was a quite different air in those days from what there is now. Today in all essentials of religion, that is, in the general cultural atmosphere, in the attitude of men towards the universe, in the philosophy which governs our society, Great Britain is one. It is true that Scotland by 1633 was Protestant. The Reformation had made a novel bond between what had been enemy nations. But all depends on proportion, and the proportions of the religions north of the border were very different from those to the south of it. Scotland had not now, in 1633, any large Catholic minority, England had. There was a difference in intensity also. Scottish Protestantism was not only mainly Calvinist, but especially was it intensely so. All the driving power came from the inspiration of Calvin, and outside the remaining districts which were either isolated, or sparse groups of mountaineers, where certain governing families were too strong to be beaten down, the religious life was that of the Presbytery and the full Presbyterian spirit was at high tide.

Bishops there still were in Scotland, and an Archbishop at St. Andrews; but a bishop in Scotland was hardly a bishop. What ruled was the enthusiastic organisation of the Kirk by congregations and by assemblies. The Establishment, which had now taken full form in England and was the mechanism of English religion, meant to the Scottish Protestant something which he suspected and of which he desired to have no experience. To those who governed in England, and especially to the King, the Establishment was an essential framework for the nation.

Moreover, this must be remembered, that to Englishmen and to the English Court, to Charles himself in spite of his Scottish traditions, Scottish accent, and remaining Scottish national sentiment,

SCOTLAND

Scotland was a thing hardly known. The affairs of Scotland formed no part of conversation at Westminster and were of no interest to the Court; they were hardly heard. Charles dealt with Scotland apart from all the rest of government, treating its business as a private thing, dealing with it directly through a special secretary and relying mainly upon young Hamilton, who was his adviser and spokesman and the rest of it where that distant little-considered province was concerned. Yet the province was not a province, it was a kingdom; and jealous of its own quite separate life.

Charles went north in great pomp, marking this reunion between himself and the land and kingship of his ancestors as something specially to be remembered.

In his progress through the Midlands and the north the splendour of his equipage had been enhanced by the voluntary action of all the landowners, great and small, on his way; they had outdone themselves in hospitality and pageant, and even in his hunting, when he paused for this in Sherwood Forest, there was a grandeur of circumstance.

When he came to the border every care was taken to mark the occasion. All offices hitherto held around the King in his Court by those who had accompanied him were given over to Scottish gentlemen, and on reaching his capital at Edinburgh he was received with enthusiasm and acclamation. The ceremony of his passage down the long street from the Castle to Holyrood was splendid; there was nothing outward to show that any danger lurked. The dirty town had been reasonably cleaned, by a pretty piece of decency the rotting heads of criminals, stuck on spikes over the gates, were taken down and the gallows, on which swung a man recently hanged, were with equal decency removed.

Charles spent the vigil of his coronation alone and in meditation. On the morning of his crowning day, at eight o'clock, he met his nobles of Scotland, proceeded to the sacramental function, which was performed with all the rites which sacramental kingship had inherited, sanctified by centuries since the transformation of the Roman monarchy under the Gaulish Kings. So was Charles anointed and crowned in the country of his birth. It was Tuesday, the 18th of June, 1633.

CHARLES I

On the next day, the 19th of June, he met that group of magnates called the Parliament, but a Parliament not after the English model, not a great host of squires large and small, not a great concourse of landlords assembled in hundreds, but a restricted group of men representing the country by hereditary power and by nomination, and, by nomination also, the Church.

For the Church there were the bishops; and the sixteen Lords of the Articles chose eight from among the landlords, eight to stand for the towns, while the King himself added eight officers of the Crown. Among the lords chosen were two young men who were counted as Charles's own, the Duke of Lennox and that Marquess of Hamilton upon whom we have seen that he had persistently relied for Scottish affairs.

It is worth noting at this point that Hamilton's treasonable temper was already suspected by those who could see clearest. Two years before, when he had been away on the Continent, giving such tiny aid as his country could give to Gustavus Adolphus, one of his fellow-nobles had accused him; but Charles suspected nothing. He was strongly attached to Hamilton, thought him simple (which he certainly was not) and loyal (which he would not long be). He trusted him – and his trust was as usual betrayed.

This Scottish Parliament did its official work, it ratified the old "Revocation" of 1625, it imposed a small tax – but there was also an opposition. The King had his majority safe in hand, but it was questioned.

When in those days, by some accident, there was an explosion of gunpowder and the cause of it was sought, two questions had to be answered. First, one on the presence of the explosive, how did it get there?; second, one on the putting of the match to it, who fired it? There was to come of these early days in Scotland in 1633 an explosion most formidable; becoming at last no less than open war between Scotland and her King. The presence of the explosive, the gunpowder, was due to the greedy discontent of the great landowners angered by the Revocation. The slow match which in time was to touch that gunpowder off was the religious indignation of the masses and particularly of Edinburgh.

I have said that the original point on which attention must be fixed, the starting point of all that was to follow, was the Revocation

SCOTLAND

at the opening of Charles's reign. He had declared his intention to reassume, in some degree, properties alienated by the encroachment of the wealthy families from the Crown and the Church. The enactment of the Revocation had roused excitement in Scotland six years before; the Royal letters had arrived on the 11th of July, 1626, already expected. All that was proposed was to take back so much of the looted Church goods as would decently endow what had become a starved ministry. There was at the same time a proposal, slowly and imperfectly carried out, of ending those hereditary jurisdictions which were among the chief cause of weakness in the Scottish Crown. Both proposals were distasteful to the men without whom nothing could be done, and with whom everything could be done, the Scottish nobility – the great landowners. These great nobles had had everything their own way for a lifetime, quarrelling violently among themselves, murdering and counter-murdering, conspiring in shifting groups but still, always, the masters of the country.

Had *they* not felt themselves to be in peril from the vigour of the new reign, the religious quarrel would never have achieved what it did. It is *they* who are the real direct motive force behind what came to seem upon the surface a religious enthusiasm. It was by *their* permission and by *their* aid that the revolt against the Crown was possible, just as, a long lifetime before, it had been *their* permission and *their* aid which made successful the revolt against the old religion.

The Revocation, even in the very limited form which was attempted, was furiously resisted and on the whole successfully resisted. When Commissioners were named to arrange terms for those who should voluntarily surrender their ill-gotten gains before the 1st of January 1627, there was no response; not one owner of them all surrendered. Actions followed in the ensuing summer and by 1628 the plan – the very limited plan – of re-establishing the Kirk with some part of the monies which it had owned by right was politically accomplished – but morally it was not. Those who had actually lost, small as the sums were, bore an undying grudge; all their class (including many who had retained most or all of what they should have disgorged) were on their side, and – let this be particularly noted – *the Kirk itself felt no gratitude for the relief which the King proposed*. Their ministry might be raised from starvation to a tolerable livelihood, but the action came from without, it was alien to the nation, it was almost as distasteful to the Presbytery in such a form as it was to those who had lost by it.

We must remember, however, that all this feeling was slow to grow. There could be no question of the King's right. The Crown of Scotland had full right by custom (as the Crown of England had not) by tradition and by law to reassume public properties looted during royal minorities. Moreover, the effect of the King's presence among them – a man of Scottish birth and name and a truer incarnation of themselves than ever he was of England – had, for the moment, its effect. The anger of the great landowners was as yet only smouldering, but would ultimately burst into flame – and particularly upon this account. The sums demanded were not large, the amount of the restoration was restricted, but the principle was there – there was not an owner of land north of the border who did not feel himself to be imperilled. They felt, as the English beneficiaries by the religious Reformation had felt under Mary Tudor nearly eighty years before, that all their new fortunes were at stake.

To this explosive matter was set the match of the religious quarrel. Charles had committed an error against which he could not have been warned, the nature of which he could not have understood, one which was not indeed understood by any of those about him nor even fully by those who were most aggrieved by it. He had taken north with him as his confidant, his friend, his principal adviser in all affairs of religion, the Bishop of London, Laud, who was also in possession by promise of the reversion to Canterbury. Now, that Laud's name stood for uniformity in Church matters throughout the Kingdom for an organised ritual, for liturgy as opposed to prophecy and individual prayers, was not the chief trouble. The chief trouble was that he was not *national*. He was a foreigner. His presence meant to the Scottish Presbyterians, and for the matter of that to the bishops, the presence of English interference among them. The strongest, though not the most evident, of Scottish feelings was touched. It would have been easy to have left Laud behind in the south in his bishopric, to have consulted with him before starting, to have reported to him on return. It was his physical presence at Charles's side that had this irritant effect.

There had been certain signs already which might have warned the King. A group of the Edinburgh Presbyters, through the mouth

SCOTLAND

of their spokesman, had presented a list of grievances even before the King had ridden through the town. The most important of these grievances was a demand to restrain still further the shadowy power of the bishops. But the presentation of grievances to a King when he approached his capital was the common form of the time, and it did not represent any organised movement. Charles was given the list of religious grievances at Dalkeith, the day before he came into the capital; he read it, but did nothing more.

For the moment there was no violent reaction; and it was the opinion (perhaps erroneous) of careful contemporary observers, that if an attempt had been made at that time to ask for the acceptance of the English Prayer Book and its official Liturgy in Scotland, the thing would have gone through. Even if that view was erroneous (and it was widely held by men on the spot and well able to judge) it is almost certain that with some compromise the thing could have been carried. The more learned of the divines who were consulted disagreed not with the English Prayer Book as a whole but only with details in it.

There might have been opportunity for extempory prayer side by side with the ritual. Episcopacy already existed and had been accepted, and it would have been enough to have left it where it was with the bishops something much less than they were in England but still bishops in name, or slowly and imperceptibly to have increased their influence and jurisdiction. But the error having been made of presenting everything as an alien innovation, a second error was made of not acting while it was still possible to act. The founding of a Liturgy more or less the same on both sides of the border, that effort for unity under the Crown which was part of the whole general effort for unity Charles and his chief servants were engaged upon – it was the great task of those years – was postponed. It was thought that such resistance as there was would diminish with time, and it was decided not to attempt the thing for four years.

But the calculation was quite wrong. Time inflamed resistance here just as it inflamed the anger of the landowners who had been forced to make their partial restitution. What the King and Laud did between them was not to effect the compromise which might have been effected, but to introduce certain personal changes which were the cause at first for grumbling and later for anger.

CHARLES I

Thus Edinburgh itself had never been a city, it was, ecclesiastically, only a borough within the Archbishopric of St. Andrews. The King, or rather Laud and the King, proposed to make it the seat of a bishopric, with the principal church of the town for a cathedral; and they carried their proposal into effect.

Again, while delaying to give further spiritual power to those ghosts of bishops – a thing which might cautiously have been started – there was given to them political power, and this seemed at once anomalous to the Kirk and hateful to the nobles, in whose eyes all political office was theirs of right. Charles gave to the Archbishop of St. Andrews the Chancellorship, the highest office of the kingdom, and the Chancellor had never been a member of the clergy since the Reformation. He put a certain number of bishops into the Privy Council, making them Lords of Session – something hitherto unknown. All this work had been done in the short space of five weeks; and on the 18th of July Charles turned his face southward for England.

Henrietta Maria was again pregnant, he was anxious to meet her, but the Royal progress could not be hurried; it was a month before he was in the neighbourhood of London and the Queen, who lay at Greenwich. The King would have been well-advised to have made some show of his return and to have ridden through the streets of the capital, but whether from fatigue or negligence or from a wrong advice of disaffection, he went east of the city and crossed the Thames at Blackwall to find the Queen in the Palace. He did not know what seed had been sown in those brief days north of the border – and as for the harvest that would be gathered, neither he nor any other man dreamed of it. He was glad indeed to be again with his wife, hoping that the child to be born might be a second son; and so it proved, when on the 12th of October following the boy was born who was to be James II, and the last Stuart to wear a crown in England.

THE EFFORT FOR UNITY

I. The Central Effort

CHARLES'S YEARS OF PEACEFUL RULE MEAN IN THE HISTORY OF England the great effort for unity. The opportunity came between the violent ending, of the confused Parliament of 1629 and the calling of the Short Parliament in 1640.

This is a period of over eleven (nearly twelve) years; from the first days of March, 1629, to the first days of November, 1640. During all those years under the action of kingship, under the direct monarchy, careful of precedent, always appealing to the tradition of the law, but free from a rival or supplanting power, the common aim of those in authority was to make of all the British Dominions one state: one, not by the destruction of local cultures, but one in the essential of morals, religion, foreign policy and prestige; and one because authority was in one hand.

While this was the inspiring idea of the whole period, it was only fully at work after the King's return from Scotland in the summer of 1633. Until then the headship of the Church held by Abbot made a reduction to order therein impossible; until then there was no one carrying out the policy fully in Ireland; until then there had been no beginning of it in Scotland. But from the summer of 1633 onwards the machine was in working order: the headship of the Church was in the hands of Laud; Wentworth acted with Royal power as deputy for the King in Ireland; a Navy was created; a continuous revenue, sufficient for the needs of Government, was supplied; and a strict repression of whatever might bring central authority into contempt was practised.

There was lacking to this great experiment one necessary element – an army, or police force. It had not the physical power which is the first requisite to an ordered unity. Today such a power is taken for granted. Without it, the modern unified state could not exist. But

CHARLES I

in the England of the mid-seventeenth century Government had no such power nor the means of creating one. It had not that power because the revenue which could regularly be raised, however carefully administered, however rigorously collected, barely sufficed for the civilian activities of the State and for the creation of that new Navy which was necessary to the position of England among her rivals. Therefore, when there came a trial of strength and when the effort to impose unity upon Scotland had led to an armed rebellion, the general effort at unity broke down. There was no method of obtaining money for the creation of a Royal force for the defence of England from Scottish invasion save by an appeal for voluntary grants-in-aid and thus a necessity of calling upon the wealthier classes to appear, again organised in Parliament, and beg for their aid. But that aid their most active leaders would refuse to give save at the price of destroying the Crown. For they were determined to rule, and to put an end to the rule of the King.

This effort at unity was in the true spirit of the time, for it meant the enhancement of the nation. Nationalism for good or evil (but mainly for evil) had arisen in Christendom before the end of the Middle Ages. It had grown strong during the Renaissance and the Reformation in the previous century; by this century (the seventeenth) it rivalled everywhere the other great enthusiasm, that of religion.

Every new national culture struggled to expand and to develop as great a strength as might be, and everywhere this could be done only by unity under the Crown.

In the Germanies the attempt had failed, through religious causes and through the avarice of the lesser Princes, who opposed the general interests of the Empire; also through the jealous independence of the Free Cities and the smaller States. Even in the Germanies, however, the cause of unity would have succeeded had there not been pitted against it the genius of Richelieu. It was his power of intrigue, his exact calculation, his knowledge of where to purchase support and how to raise up difficulties against the Austrian rival, which determined the issue. He it was that hired the best soldier of the day, Gustavus Adolphus, to come in and turn the tide at the critical moment.

Heavily did the Germans pay for this failure to achieve unity; they fell into the welter and horrors of the Thirty Years' War – nor has any effort at unity succeeded with them since, for in every case

THE EFFORT FOR UNITY

when an attempt has been made to achieve it the two divergent ideals – Catholic and Protestant – have been pitted each against the other.

But in Spain the thing had been triumphantly achieved. Throughout the Peninsula, including Portugal, one rule had been established, a true monarchy, one culture depending upon one religion had been compacted. It extended beyond the seas, covering the Americas – in a sense it covers them still – and though that mighty body was failing from within, unity preserved it from fall. The example was before the eyes of all Europe, showing how a nation could be strengthened by central control.

In France a similar and even stronger result had been obtained – the stronger because allowance was there made for diversity, without which there is no life. France lived by diversity within unity. Richelieu had raised the national monarchy and with it the nation itself; it was in future to be one thing and attempts at division within it were to fail. But the provincial assemblies and local laws remained. The whole of the century after Richelieu's time was filled with the new strength of France, which lasted on for more than a hundred years and was yet another example of what unity could do. With such examples everywhere in Christendom the thing was now to be attempted here in England. France had achieved unity after almost succumbing to anarchy in the religious wars which had hitherto been spared to England; but the forces of disruption were at work here and it was the task of this effort at unity to master them – a task in which Charles, in spite of devoted and loyal service from men of high ability, failed.

Externally the mark of this new movement was to be the power of England at sea. That leading idea of the Stuart dynasty outlasted the misfortunes of the Throne which had launched it. Buckingham was the originator, Charles's government was the creator, James II, his son, was the final organiser of, a permanent and increasing naval power. England was to take up the weapon which made her progressively greater and greater and at last invincible; until modern conditions, even in our own time – the change in weapons and transport – were to make invincibility at sea no longer possible, nor, even if it were possible, of decisive utility. Through this instrument, a strong and permanent Navy, the government of Charles set out to make England what she had never been under Elizabeth or even in the more prosperous times of James – a great European Power.

CHARLES I

This effort at unity England owed to the King himself. The basis of it was the exercise of his authority, the centralising of it, the strengthening of it to resist attack. But there were three subsidiary efforts at unity proceeding from, surrounding, and supporting this central effort in the kingship. These were first, an attempt at religious unity: the unity of the Church and the making of that Church the form of religion for all the subjects of the Crown; secondly, the reduction into the Royal unity of Ireland, religious and political; thirdly, the similar reduction of Scotland. We shall understand the great experiment best if we take each of these separately.

As to the power of the King, the first thing was to obtain the economic basis without which he could not carry on. The next thing was to repress (what was difficult to repress) the contempt of authority expressed mainly through religious fanaticism. The policy obviously required authority in one centre. The distribution of authority among the more powerful subjects was, in the eyes of those who thus strove for unity, anarchy and chaos. Rule by the wealthy seemed to them to create disruption, the weakening of the State, the lowering of England's power among the nations and the breakdown of prosperity at home. No one foresaw what actually happened when the revolt of the wealthier classes in Parliament was successful. It led to a brief period first of hopeless civil confusion in rebellion under arms, then to a brief despotism violently opposed to tradition and contemptuous of law, then to an illusive verbal restoration of a nominal King who after what had passed could never really govern – no one could suppose, I say, that out of such a welter would arise that principle of Aristocracy under which England rose to be greater and greater, stronger and stronger, through more than two centuries. Least of all could anyone then dream that this very character of national unity which had so nearly been imposed by the kingship would at last, after a century of violent divisions, be re-established more permanently, and more thoroughly here than in any other country through the action of a governing class and their ruin of the Crown. So true is it that a State grows otherwise than by plan.

The obtaining of revenue – the very first consideration – was successful. That success was remarkable because it was necessary to keep all within the bounds of precedent, that is, of law. Law meant for England, as in general for the rest of Christendom (but particu-

THE EFFORT FOR UNITY

larly for England), precedent. It meant not what it means nowadays, a great mass of ever-increasing positive enactment: it meant that which those who were the guardians of the law, the judges, should declare to have been custom. Charles perhaps could not, certainly would not, act outside those limits; but the lawyers, of whom the judges formed a part, were not to be allowed to act as a power independent of the Crown. They already formed part of that which was to be in future the governing class; the young squires studied their law, and such few lawyers as were not of their rank rose into that rank and felt themselves to have a common interest with it. The judges in Charles's plan were not to be allowed to destroy the approaching unity of the State by setting up an absolute power of their own; but such new revenue as was acquired, and such methods as were devised for rigorously collecting the old dues, must be within the law. Charles would not outstep those limits. He and his would argue the legal case as lengthily as did their opponents. Like their opponents they would use the chicanery of the law for their purposes as continuously as the rebels would desire to use it for theirs.

The Customs were levied as they had always been levied, uninterruptedly, and as the judges had decided it was lawful to levy them, by the King's authority; and the rates of duties were decreed from the same source. Trade continued to expand, partly because all civilisation was expanding, partly because England was feeling the benefit of her Atlantic position now that the Americas had developed, but most of all because the security which strong and good government provided brought its natural consequence of an increasing commerce. Throughout this Stuart century the Customs continued to be the one steadily rising source of revenue.

I have said that, unfortunately, the wise policy of preserving and restoring the national lands called Forests partially failed. Though great fines and compensations for encroachment were imposed it was always difficult and often impossible to collect them against the opposition of the great. What the principle of restoring public land to public use might have done had it been given a proper chance and kept in being long enough, we cannot tell: all we know is that when the King's power was broken, the national lands (what was left of them) were nearly all swallowed up, and the private landlords became all-powerful. That is why you do not find in England, Scotland or Ireland, as you do in all the rest of Christendom, great areas, especially of mountain, heath and woodland, belonging to the State, village or town.

The comparatively small sums, also demanded upon precedent (but not upon *recent* custom) as composition for Knighthood, added to the revenue. The Patents and Monopolies further swelled the income but, as we have also seen, at the risk of considerable friction, especially in London.

Taken as a whole this financial part of the new policy was safe; there was a sufficient income arranged for Government to carry on; and the good administration which central authority secured, the absence of corruption, the reduction of perquisites and of raiding by wealthy interests, gave, on the negative side, the same advantages which strict collection of revenue gave on the positive side. As we should put it today, "The Budget was balanced" – and balanced for the first time within living memory. English Government under Charles acquired for the first time a secure economic basis.

Even for the special necessities of the fleet, the building up of a permanent naval power and the founding of England's international position thereby, money was found. But it was only found after a difficult struggle and at the expense of a legend created, not only among the wealthy but among all the mass of owners of land, large and small, which appeared later among the causes of the King's failure.

There had always been the right and custom in England of impressing ships from the ports, and, from very early times, of demanding money in lieu of such ships as were too large for the lesser harbour-towns to provide. But under the simple conditions of older days the pressing of ships or the demand for them from the seaport towns was solely a maritime custom. It had naturally begun as asking for nothing more than a concrete thing, a ship. Then, when the development of arms forced the Government to ask, say, Lyme Regis, for something much bigger than Lyme Regis could launch, Lyme Regis would be asked to pay money for building such a ship elsewhere.

All that custom went without saying. But now France was building a great fleet, and England, if she would support her foreign policy with any instrument at all, must support it with a permanent fleet also. And what had been Buckingham's attempt, and ideal, a strong continuous English Navy, became now Charles's achievement.

THE EFFORT FOR UNITY

Noy suggested the form of the writ in the year after the King's return from Scotland. And in 1634, that year, but after his death, the first moneys were demanded from the coast districts alone. They produced just over £100,000; say, in modern values, some two-thirds of a million. It is to be remarked that the levy on London was especially noted and challenged that powerful sub-nation. In mere size London was by far the largest port, accounting for at least two-thirds of all the English shipping. London was perhaps eight times larger than its next rival and in wealth twenty- or thirty-fold any rival. It had three times more seaborne traffic than all the rest of England put together.

Now the merchants of London, with their apprentices for support, the craftsmen, all the mass of ownership (then widely distributed) which was affected by such new taxation formed a body of opinion collected in one place, the members of which were all in touch with, and surrounding as it were, the Court.

This ship-money, then, even in its first form of 1634 as a maritime levy, moved London; but the very effort to relieve what was clearly, under the conditions of the day, the injustice of a special tax, on seaports alone, for a policy which concerned the whole country gave, as did all the Government's efforts at the time, a handle to their opponents.

In the next year, 1635, it was determined to raise about double the amount, but to raise it by extending the impost to the whole country – inland as well as maritime. It was no great burden. It came to no more than two and a half per cent. It raised not much more than £200,000. Its expenditure (like everything else during this period of sound government) was strictly and honestly administered. Every penny of the levy was spent upon the building of the new national fleet. But the impost was novel and gave ample opportunity for legal argument.

The judges were duly consulted, though the Lord Chief Justice was changed, and Finch, who had been the Speaker of the House of Commons at the moment of the riot therein, replaced Heath. Finch, acting for the King, sought the opinion of each of his colleagues, and their reply was unanimous. Though their sympathies were already veering to the support of their own social class against the King, they could not deny the plain rights of the case. A written decision was

CHARLES I

given by each judge; only one, Croke, gave a modified answer; while another, Hutton, did not sign. But there was no contrary opinion recorded. The writs for money for the Navy – ship money – charge was, "according to precedent of former times a levy laid" (for the maritime parts) "so by parity of reason when the good and safety of the Kingdom is concerned the charge of it [ought] to be borne by the whole Realm."

This legal decision was given in November, 1635. About a year later (October, 1636) the third writ for ship-money went out; the fleet had already been constituted and was affirming the supremacy of England in the narrow seas, and supplied with men and munitions; thanks to this third levy, a larger armament went out in 1637, with the doubtful Northumberland as Admiral. But this was not before the judges had again been consulted, of whom ten answered as before. With these Croke and Hutton agreed, but under the reservation that they only did so in order to secure unanimity. With this third writ and second general levy it was apparent that the impost might be indefinitely continued – but that it should be extended to any other thing than the maintenance and creation of a new navy there was no ground whatsoever to fear. That pretended peril was a mere factious complaint, and a false one. That a tax for the navy might have come to stay if England were to be maintained as a great naval power was true enough.

At this point, some months after the issue of the third writ but before the new fleet under Northumberland had gone to sea, John Hampden, one of those immensely rich landowners who had formed a fitful but recurrent opposition to government in the Parliaments of James and Charles brought an action which was to make a turning point in the slow swinging away of the lawyers from the authority of the King and their ultimate adhesion to class government by the landed interests.

The Hampdens were an old family. They had been squires for centuries and were of that sort which gradually accumulates; also there seems to have been an unbroken succession from father to son for many generations. By the time of Charles's accession they had property all over the place – in Essex, in Berkshire, Oxfordshire and elsewhere. They had long and steadily bought parcels of land and married into other wealthy families and so by purchase and inheritance perpetually increased. In Buckinghamshire alone they had no less than eight manors and this, their native county, only held a fraction of their very great patrimony.

John Hampden, the somewhat older contemporary of the King (he was six years senior) was the wealthier from having enjoyed a long minority under the careful administration of his Cromwell mother. What with his immense fortune, his long lineage, his purely territorial associations, he was the very man to stand out as an example of that class who, as yet unconsciously, proposed to substitute their government for that of the King, and soon was consciously to do so and to succeed in establishing itself as the ruling aristocracy for more than two hundred years.

The man was also suited to the part he had to play in other ways than through his vast landed interest: from lack of temperament more than from calculation he was one of those who make no enemies, he would therefore have been useless as a leader, but was excellent as a figurehead and type. He could well afford to challenge the Government on account of his ample resources, and also because he was devoid of any ambition for place. He was still further suited by his deserved reputation for seriousness; he had studied law more thoroughly than most of his equals, the young gentlemen who were set to do a stage of that learning, and he had read a passable amount of history; he also had the reputation of being something of a scholar. Lastly, what was perhaps the most important of all and was to secure his reputation among those who took him for a symbol, he leant – without exaggeration but strongly – to the Puritan side in religion. He had steeped himself in the story of the Huguenot movement in France, and always remembered it as a model of how an aristocratic attack upon a national Crown should be conducted. Indeed, to his generation it must have looked as though that French Puritan rebellion had been successful, for his boyhood was passed in the years only just later than those in which the men whom Henry of Navarre had led in battle saw their hero crowned. It is true that the new dynasty in France had accepted the Mass, it was also true that the great Huguenots continued in high places and that during all John Hampden's young manhood something like half the similar young squires across the Channel were strongly and consistently Calvinist. Richelieu's toleration for the Protestants could not but confirm Hampden in the view that a wealthy class could impress its will on government.

CHARLES I

His features had little of dignity in them and nothing of command, but something of that quiet which comes of great wealth soberly enjoyed; and since he was without ambition his motives were known to be single enough.

Though, of course, like all those whom he resembled and of whom he became the type, his motive was not confined to resisting the Crown but – more or less consciously – to supplanting it.

This great magnate protested against a particular part of the assessment on his immense property (an item of a few shillings) and made of his refusal to pay a test case.

He now obtained from the lawyers so large a measure of the success as justifies us in the opinion just given that it forms one of the turning points in the story of the change in the Lawyers' Guild, from its hitherto immemorial support of kingship to its new support of the great landlords.

But Hampden's success was not complete. The arguments were very full; the judges took days in giving their decisions, each at great length, and spread out those days over the next three terms; at the end of the long dragging business seven – the smallest possible majority – decided for the Crown, but five gave their support to Hampden. Of these five, three relied on technical points without denying the right claim by the Crown to levy such an impost – but they intended to oppose the King and their opposition was remarked. The other two, Hutton and Croke, the same who had always stood apart, now openly denied the right of claim by the Crown. This decision was not, in its final form, before the landowners of England, great and small, until the summer of the next year, 1638; and by that time the effort at unity was beginning to suffer for the troubles in Scotland had begun.

Meanwhile the energetic political affirmation of authority was being carried on as well as the all-necessary fiscal policy.

The chief instrument for the affirmation of central authority against the more powerful subjects was the Court which the Tudors had set up with the special object of protecting the Crown and public from the menace of the great landowners, who could often, in effect, override the authority of the ordinary judges. This Court was called from the place in which it met "the Court of the Star Chamber." It was designed to be of special strength morally and politically; two or three of the great officers of State, a Spiritual and a Temporal Lord,

THE EFFORT FOR UNITY

two of the judges, members of the Privy Council (which was in those days the organ of Government) were collected together to form the tribunal. Their assembly on the great days was a thing of splendour which powerfully impressed the imagination of the time. Naturally the lawyers of the Common Courts were jealous, and equally naturally were the House of Lords, and the House of Commons (when they were sitting in Parliament as a Court), jealous of this superior Court. The Star Chamber was still, though it only dealt with a particular kind of case – those affecting the dignity and authority of the Crown – the most awful of the various tribunals.

There had come to be judged by this Court, before the King had gone to Scotland, a case which became famous and the excitement in which played directly into the hands of the revolutionary opposition, because, though it was a case of sedition and therefore proper matter for the Court, it did not affect one of the great landowners but a humbler individual who could be made a popular martyr. A certain fanatically Puritan lawyer, by name Prynne, had written a violent diatribe against play-acting. This effusion had in the previous year been duly licensed by the authority of Abbot, the Puritan Archbishop. Prynne therein attacked the plays which were given at Court, but he also attacked the common amusements of the people; dancing drove him mad and he called every step in a dance a pace towards Hell.

Now the King and the Queen danced. That Prynne could not bear maypoles may be taken for granted, and putting up of greenstuff at Christmas excited him unduly also, as did chanting in Church, which he called "bellowing." The man, like so many of his sort, was hardly sane. But he clearly aimed at the King and Queen. Therefore was the prosecution of him ordered in the winter before the King had gone to Scotland. It was more than a year before he was condemned, but when the sentence came it was severe. He had to stand in the pillory to have his ears cut off (they were sewn on again), he was deprived of his profession at the Bar, and he was imprisoned. It was but the most striking of the many and general repressions undertaken now by Authority in its own defence against revolution; and in connection with it we come to the second part of the effort at unity, the effort at a united religion.

163

CHARLES I

II. The Effort in the Church

We shall see later on that Prynne, in the days when the word "imprisonment" did not mean what it means now, had been free to write from his place of confinement and to join with others in a second attack – this time upon the attempted ordering of the Church.

This effort at unity through religion was made principally by Laud, and his full power to act came when, immediately after the King's return from Scotland, the Puritan Archbishop Abbot died and he was given the Archbishopric of Canterbury. Laud's aims were essentially national and Protestant. They were Protestant in their strong rejection of Catholic claims, they were national in their main reason for rejecting those claims – the independence from all alien jurisdiction whatsoever, spiritual or lay, of the subjects of the King of England. They were national also in their determination to be rid of dissensions within the body of the Church of England.

Laud, as we have seen, was a man not mainly interested in theological debate, but passionate for unity – for a unity which was the very opposite of the old Catholic unity of Christendom, for a *British* unity of religious order under the *British* Crown in these realms alone.

We must remember that Calvinism was cosmopolitan just as much as Catholicism was; a Calvinist sufficiently extreme was ready to call in the alien aid of Scotchmen in arms against his own country. The Calvinist spirit desired foreign policy to turn upon support of fellow Calvinists abroad, and Calvinism was in necessary antagonism to that framework of unity which we call "hierarchy." It was for the sake of national unity as well as from historical conviction that Laud was so determined upon the strengthening the authority of the bishops in England, and Scotland, too; but bishops, even when they were accepted at all by the Calvinist type of Churchman, had in his eyes little or no spiritual position; they were at best a political necessity.

Under Laud the Church of England may be said to have reached conscious personality. It had hitherto been openly torn between tendencies neither of them thoroughly national. On the same bench of bishops you could find Goodman, who spoke of the Catholic Church as the Mother-Church of Christendom and who ended by accept-

THE EFFORT FOR UNITY

ing her; and Abbot, who called the same Catholic Church "the old Whore." This is not to say that the Church of England as an institution had not already that unity by which alone a thing can be a thing at all; and Hooker with his arguments, which Charles knew by heart (those writings were among his favourite books), was a forerunner of Laud in this respect. But it was in Laud's time and under Laud's influence that this institution, the Church of England, attained what may be called full self-hood, and Laud would have made it, had he succeeded, a body united in teaching, discipline and ritual, expressing throughout its being the unity of the nation and acting with authority in every part of these islands wherever the King's writ could run.

Such an ideal as Laud's was necessarily indifferent to, and by implication contrary to, the conception of a universal visible Church: what he did feel, and what has indeed always been a living principle of the Church of England was that that Church should be the expression of the nation.

His policy appeared in prosecutions – which is the same word, and has the same effect, as "persecutions" – and by this we return to the name of Prynne; for among others the names of Prynne, Burton and Bastwick exemplified, though their cases were taken not before a Church Court but before the Star Chamber, this effort at ecclesiastical unity, and the whole spirit of the prosecution was Laud's. Like all men who are determined on unity through authority in government, he pushed far the boundaries of severity.

Prynne, from his prison, had poured out his spirit in ink before the public, telling the bishops that they were "of Lucifer," that they were "wolves," that they were "execrable tyrants." Bastwick, also a prisoner at the time, a Doctor of Medicine, had had one fling after another at the hierarchy, that last of which writings (he called it his "litany") was the maddest, talking of Hell broken loose, devils in surplices, and carrying on with words which even the licence of our times does not permit me to print – though I wish I could do so, for they are as funny as they are disgusting. Burton was a clergyman who had preached sermons of the same order, telling the public at large that the bishops were "dumb dogs," "wolves," "mushrooms," "robbers," "limbs of the beast," "factors of anti-Christ," etc.; words which, from a priest in Holy Orders, possessed of a benefice, once Chaplain to the King, one who had preached publicly in London, were strong.

CHARLES I

They were sentenced, Prynne for the second time, in the summer of 1637; but things were already moving, and the men in the pillory with their shorn ears were martyrs and, for many of the mob, heroes, as they went their way to their distant imprisonments. The Puritan faction was already powerful, but Laud faced it unflinchingly: it was in this, as in every other department of the effort at unity, a trial as to which of these two opposed energies would win.

Apart from this most famous case there was a mass of executive action through the Ecclesiastical Court of High Commission, which fined, imprisoned and imposed costs. The Ecclesiastical Courts inquired into cases of private immorality even among the wealthy and powerful, and – what was perhaps the most dangerous challenge of all – thereby excited the enmity of the lawyers; for the revived activities of the Church Courts appeared as a power rivalling their own.

Laud, nick-named "The Shrimp," was a sharp-edged little man, saying openly what he felt and saying it to whom he would; he shirked no quarrel. He had to encounter many foes in his own immediate surroundings, and even upon the Council. Weston (later Portland), the Lord Treasurer, who had done so much for Charles's finances, was his opponent till he died. On his death, in the second year of Laud's tenure of the Archbishopric, the Treasury was put in commission and Laud was, unfortunately for himself, made one of that Commission. It brought him directly into political and civil matters outside his clerical profession, and added to the hostility he had to meet. But he had a supporter in a man of very different temper – equable, popular enough, fond of field-sports, one who had been a colleague of his at Oxford, Juxon. Laud had already caused Charles to give the Bishopric of London to Juxon when he himself vacated it and that Bishopric Juxon held to the end of the reign.

In the matter of Liturgy again, Laud's whole business was unity. He was not so indifferent to Liturgy as he was to theory, but it is a misreading of him, due to modern quarrels and to the absurd exaggerations of his contemporary enemies, to think of him as principally devoted to ritual. What he had at heart was regularity and decency, and above all a common standard.

When he came into power the Calvinist spirit in the Church had left many buildings haphazard and their furniture more haphazard still; there were cases of incumbents who broke stained-glass win-

THE EFFORT FOR UNITY

dows, and it was common to find the Communion Table treated as a table indeed, set up anywhere in the nave and perhaps with a man's hat and cloak lying upon it, and men smoked in church at their ease. On the simplest items of clerical dress and of dress special to the performance of the Liturgy there was dispute, and, what was perhaps more important, extreme diversity. All this Laud set out to standardise, but to standardise with some violence. It was thought extreme in him to have permitted or even to have renewed statues, such as that of Our Lady and the Holy Child at Oxford; his opponents called him "Papistical," and would have it that he nourished some design for reconciliation with Rome. We have seen the falsity of that accusation. His nationalism (what many would call his patriotism), his devotion to the Church as Church of *England* and to the English Crown was sincere, single, and limited to its object.

It is true that foreigners also misunderstood the position, as foreigners were already beginning to misunderstand most new English developments: it is true that the King, desiring to have the Pope's influence on the side of his nephew of the Palatinate, was in political negotiation with Rome: it is true that individual Catholics, especially those surrounding the Queen, also misjudged the situation. But it is not true that Laud – who thought with the King, who in Church matters inspired the King, and with whom the King was agreed – was other than the King in his devotion to the Church as an English thing. The particular acts into which Laud threw the busy energy of his little body should be sufficient to show what he was at. His activity was all administrative – not a whit of what is called (rather inaccurately) mystical.

He revived the full authority of Canterbury, setting up metropolitan visitations so that he could supervise the whole working of the Church; he extended the custom of railing off the Chancel (a great scandal to the extremists of the other side) and on the reverent use of the Communion Table he insisted. He had it placed where it now universally stands (and is now, almost as universally, called the altar). If he was the most hated by the Puritans of all those supporting the King's effort at unity it was not so much because he differed from them in social morals; it was because he was the most active and the most successful in the prosecution of the general design of the time. Had his effort been carried on long enough and so succeeded, had that effort been carried on throughout the century and descended to our own time, men would not have before them a Church of England after the fashion today called Anglo-Catholic; they would not even have a Church of England of which the practices were, to use the common adjective, as "advanced" as its practices are today. But they would have, what they do not have today, uniformity.

III. The Effort in Ireland

The third department of this effort at unity was the business of Ireland, which also begins at much the same time. Laud became Archbishop of Canterbury immediately upon Charles's return from Scotland in 1633, and Thomas Wentworth (now an earl), already nominated some months past to the Viceroyalty of Ireland, took up his duties there the month before, in July, 1633. His arrival opened a chapter in the story of Ireland which stands out separate from all the rest – a singular experiment, and one on which we must use every effort of the imagination if we are not to fall into the error of regarding it as merely fantastic.

He was wrong; events have proved him to be wrong; any Irishman could have told him he was wrong (and most Irishmen did tell him he was wrong); any widely travelled, well-instructed intelligent Irishman could have told him where and why he was wrong, why and where the thing at which he aimed was impossible and the methods which he used ephemeral and doomed to failure. But all this did not appear to him nor to most of his contemporaries; they were not out of the spirit of the time. That is what we must grasp, for Wentworth like Buckingham (and carrying heavier metal than Buckingham) had genius. It was a proportioned and reasoned genius, and it was not his fault if the major elements of the problem escaped him.

He came new to Ireland with a well-earned reputation for strength, and, what was more important, an internal conviction of his own that he was right. As President of the Council of the North he had shown that strength by acting with artillery against a rebel magnate, and he had not feared to tell the colleagues of that magnate in session that they would have to obey the King.

THE EFFORT FOR UNITY

He had always been for unity even when he had stood in opposition as a magnate himself – the very wealthy member for Yorkshire in Parliament.

It was as a man of his own class that he had led the early resistance of the squires in Parliament, but when the quarrel threatened disloyalty he proposed moderation; when it threatened disunion and chaos he saw clearly the duty of supporting authority.

For there were two passions in Wentworth's soul, apart from his pride (which was too great – pride of lineage, pride of standing, pride of strength and intelligence); the one was the passion of patriotism and the other the passion for order, that is, for efficiency in administration.

It was because he was a patriot first, intensely national, that he was disgusted by the religious extravagances on which his colleagues of the opposition in Parliament had come more and more to depend as their unworthy ally. It was his sense of efficiency and order which had disgusted him with their reliance upon rhetoric and their perpetual proposals to destroy an authority which, so far as he or any man could then see, they had no means to replace. He was now a man of forty in the fullness of his powers, impressive with his tall broad frame, often stooping somewhat, as is the way of men who ruminate, and impressive: his dark, manly but troubled face alive with energy.

What he inherited in Ireland was mainly the failure of his predecessors to deal with corruption among the fortune-hunters who had the alien English power in their hands. He also inherited, though he did not know it – and none of these aliens in authority knew it – the much more dreadful, indeed the insoluble, problem of attempting to overcome two of the strongest things on earth – the Irish feeling of nationhood and the Irish attachment to the Catholic Church. What he saw was that the whole place had been mismanaged and exploited by men who were all of them at heart and some of them in open practice, adventurers and unscrupulous.

The Ireland to which he came bore the aspect of a conquered country; and in Wentworth's mind it *was* a conquered country – Irishmen themselves complained that it was a conquered country (and still complain that it was so); but it is a far too simple reading of history to regard it thus.

CHARLES I

The first who had come over from England five centuries before were men interfering in an Irish quarrel and supported by Irishmen who fought one side in that quarrel; the feudal, French-speaking leader of those new-comers from England, or rather Wales, had married into, and by feudal law was the rightful inheritor of, one of the Irish princedoms. There had been clash and friction, from that day in the twelfth century onwards, between the Irish tribal organisation which was as old as time and the feudal system, which then seemed to Plantagenet society and indeed to all western Christendom the only conceivably true and just one. The attempt to impose feudal law in the place of tribal custom had led to continued and increasing injustice, to what was often in practice (though not as yet in theory) confiscation for the benefit of the new-comers from overseas.

But the active hold of England upon Ireland was slight: the King's† writ ran only through a belt of the eastern sea-board, the Pale. Richard II, more than a century before the Reformation, might have accommodated the two nations one to the other; but his cousin's usurpation of the Throne put an end to all that. England under the Lancastrian usurpation and the consequent "Wars of the Roses" all but let Ireland go. The Tudors, and especially Henry VIII, increased the power of the English Crown by the use of artillery, and when Henry had broken with Rome he assumed the title of "King of Ireland"; but still, in the main, the land, and therefore the economic power, was in the hands of men who were either of aboriginal Irish blood or long descended from Plantagenet nobles intermarried with Irish blood. Not even the first plantations in the reign of Mary Tudor nor the treacherous massacres of Irishmen under Elizabeth formed anything that could fully be called a conquest of Ireland. The real change began under the father of Charles, in the first years of his reign. After a rebellion of the great lords in the north, land was confiscated wholesale and began to be planted by adventurers, who were now the more abhorrent for being of an alien religion as well as speaking an alien language – for nearly all the Irish race still talked their native Celtic.

---

† I.e., The King of England's Writ. But he was not King of Ireland: he was only "Lord" of Ireland. That is, Feudal Superior by international papal grant, until the sixteenth century, when Henry VIII's new papal power made him king.

THE EFFORT FOR UNITY

This is the main thing to grasp in any attempt at understanding Wentworth's government and its result; that the ruthless seizing of native land and the beginning of alien plantation wholesale was not further removed from the memories of men than is the South African War from our own time. Indeed the "Flight of the Earls" (as this first main defeat of the Irish was called), was nearer still. Tyrone had not left his native country until 1607, the confiscation to the English Crown of the Six Counties was later still, and the first general plantation – the wholesale robbery of native land and its transfer to foreigners – came after that again. A man of fifty when Wentworth came to Ireland would have been already a young man exercising rights over his own land, when he had seen it torn from him only twenty-five years before.

Two things were essential to Wentworth in Ireland, the second depending upon the first: revenue, and an army that should be well equipped and paid. Otherwise the country could not be held.

For revenue it had been attempted to get voluntary grants from the landowners by a compromise. In legal theory it should have been impossible for any Catholic, no matter how great his descent and possessions, to retain ownership of land in Ireland – in other words in legal theory all the nation except the small alien Protestant body was dispossessed. For a man could not take up the land he had inherited unless he took the Oath of Allegiance. But in practice, of course, such a universal theft could not be achieved. Trusts and Uses were arranged so that the business of taking up an inheritance was escaped (much as men escape death duties today by giving their land to their sons before they die). When, therefore, in 1628, before Wentworth's day, a gathering of the main landowners had been asked to give money to the King, two-thirds of them were still Catholic, and of the nation as a whole, of course, a very much higher proportion.

Now there had been obtained from these main landowners a grant to the King of £40,000 for three years; but it had been obtained as the result of a bargain. Charles was to grant certain "Graces," over fifty in number, some of them relieving the Catholics of many disabilities, and in particular this difficulty of legally owning and transmitting land. For the Oath of Allegiance was to be substituted an Oath of Loyalty which did not include any repudiation of their religion, and the professions (notably the Law) were to be thrown open to Catholics, that is, to the mass of the nation. There then took place what you find perpetually in the story of such compromises (we had first-class examples of it at the end of the Great War) the repudiation of a promise on the plea, that, technically, it was never made. What one side accepted as a solemn engagement the other interpreted as mere proposition yet to be ratified. Meanwhile the solid money had been paid.

Wentworth on his arrival dealt with the situation in a way which he believed to be politic. He got the Assembly to give him a further sum of money for the Crown by playing upon their divided interests – frightening the Protestants and cajoling the Catholics. But the "Graces" were not confirmed and the Catholics were embittered by such breach of faith. It might be pleaded that to confirm them would be impossible without raising such a storm in England as would have destroyed the effort at unity; but it was grave injustice nonetheless.

Wentworth himself believed that the religious difficulty could be overcome after a fashion of which he gave examples, with chapter and verse to prove that it was feasible.

He restored to its full strength of action the Court of Wards; the Catholic landowner who was under age would be educated as a Protestant, if he was over age he should not have his land until he had taken the Oath of Supremacy; and to prevent the avoidance of this Wentworth openly attacked, and in part destroyed, the Uses and the Trusts. His idea was that if the wealthier men were thus gradually changed in religion the mass of the nation would follow. Also he did not fear to call a regular Parliament, dangerous though the King thought it.

The Irish House of Lords meant in Ireland men for the most part English or Scotch who had got their titles recently enough in the last two reigns, and from these Wentworth collected proxies: for the Commons he sent letters creating official candidates specially recommended. From a Parliament so formed he got, at the end of the first year of his administration, the largest grant yet given by subsidies. The Commons and Lords between them paid over £46,000 and from the clergy of the official Protestant Irish Church Wentworth collected £24,000.

It was a very large revenue of a new sort, and if he obtained so much it was largely through the hope which the Catholic majority of

THE EFFORT FOR UNITY

the landowners still entertained that the "Graces" would be granted. The landowners of Connaught put up a very strong resistance, but surrendered after strongly disputed pleadings. Those who surrendered were of course to receive much or the great part of the land back again as tenants under the Crown; yet in the case of Galway, where the resistance had been particularly strong, it was proposed that only half should be returned and the remaining land thus seized by the Government should be planted with Englishmen.

These plans were never completed, for Wentworth was recalled by the new troubles in England before he could carry them out, and the continued and grave injustice done to the mass of the Irish people was not the main difficulty he had to meet: that main opposition came from the official Protestant clergy and from the old possessors of office and power. The corrupt politicians he offended by his insistence upon accuracy in accounts and upon the supreme power of the Crown, by the guard with which he surrounded himself and the armed state which he kept in Dublin Castle. The anger of the Irish Church against him came through his acting in alliance with Laud. That again was an effort at unity, and the most unpopular of all; for the parsons of Ireland, living in the midst of a hostile religion, leant towards Calvinism by way of reaction. They had canons of their own; and when it was proposed to reduce their professed doctrines to the model of the Church of England, as Laud saw it, there was vehement protest. The Irish Protestant Convocation submitted at length, though reluctantly and remaining as indignant as ever; but Wentworth had carried his point, and he might hope, if his power continued, to see unity established, on Laud's model, for the official English-speaking Protestant Church.

In the third year after his appointment Wentworth came back to England to look after his own lands in Yorkshire for a moment, and also to confer with the King. Charles supported him in all he had done; he especially defended the rigour with which he had treated subordinates who thought themselves free to rebel, and his use of martial law and the rest. Wentworth had raised a large and regular revenue such as had never yet been received from Ireland; he had enrolled altogether 20,000 men, of whom nearly half were a true army, well equipped and could be used as an expeditionary force; he had cleared the Irish seas of piracy, and had started a further source of prosperity in the flax and linen industry. The impossible but vigorous effort was continuing, and Wentworth might have expected that it would be ultimately successful, when the last stage in the effort at unity – that which concerned Scotland – made the whole scheme break down.

IV. The Abortive Effort in Scotland

It will be remembered that the King, and Laud too, for that matter, had postponed what they still intended, the extension of the English Liturgy to Scotland. They had thought that to let a few years go by after the coronation in 1633 would make the task easier – and that judgment proved quite wrong. Not only time, but also certain incidents had increased the spirit of resistance. Lord Balmerino, one of the original opposition when Charles was crowned, had been prosecuted for a document offensive to the King which he had never intended to publish; it was only traced to him through a betrayal of confidence. He was tried and, by a majority of only one in a jury of fifteen, found guilty of slander against the Royal Government and estate and even the King's person.

That made him liable to death; but the people began to stir, the mass of the great landowners would have supported them, and Charles signed Balmerino's pardon, but signed it very late.

In the same year as that of this belated and therefore abortive act, the bringing into Scotland of a new Liturgy modelled upon the English, was carefully being considered. This new Liturgy admitted certain acts of the Scottish Assemblies, but the base of it was the English Prayer Book, and the men who were going over it to prepare it for publication were Laud himself and those of his school, Juxon and the Bishop of Norwich. A book of canons was issued which was not so objectionable to the feelings of the Kirk as the Liturgy, but was enough to warn every Presbyterian north of the border of what might be coming.

The new Liturgy was announced in the autumn of that year, and at once condemnation of it arose from pulpit after pulpit.

The legal position of Laud and the King in this matter was weak. Charles was not at the head of the Scottish Church as he was

THE EFFORT FOR UNITY

at the head of the English; he was not "Supreme Governor" thereof; the whole spirit of the Presbytery was to dissociate (as, in a totally different fashion, Catholicism dissociates) the civil power from the spiritual. The English effort at unity was told that its authors were dethroning Jesus Christ and betraying the Kirk to the lay power.

Things were in this state when on Sunday, the 23rd of July, 1637, the Bishop of Edinburgh and the Dean of what had now become his new Cathedral proceeded to obey the perilous order and to conduct the service upon the new model.

From that moment begins the crisis in the reign, and the breakdown of the effort at unity after just four brief years of its highest exercise. The final effects did not mature for two years more. Kingship still seemed secure for yet another, third, year, though in jeopardy; but then was to come, from this tumult in Scotland, war, the necessity for an army, therefore for extra money, over and above regular revenue, therefore for a Parliament, and thence at last the Great Rebellion, wherein the King fell, defeated, and was killed.

Speaker Lenthall Asserting the Privileges of the Commons
A FRESCO BY C.W. COPE IN THE PALACE OF WESTMINSTER, 1866

THE MENACE

THE TRAIN OF THE SLOW-MATCH WHICH LED AT LAST TO THE explosion of the Great Rebellion, having been lit in Scotland, ran thus:—

In the process from the first of the troubles to the summoning of that Long Parliament which was the author of armed revolt against the King and at last of his death there were six phases: the first phase was that which led up to the Calvinist Covenant in Scotland; and from that to the proposed invasion of England by a strong Scottish army. The second phase was a beginning of war which came to nothing. The third phase was the beginning of new pressure from Scotland and the danger of the Scotch getting French help. The fourth was Strafford's insistence on meeting this threat by a new war. The fifth was the summoning of the Short Parliament; and the sixth was a renewed Scotch war and the fatal summoning of the Long Parliament under which the English monarchy fell down.

When on this 23rd of July, 1637, the new Liturgy was about to be first performed in what was now called the Cathedral of Edinburgh, there was a considerable congregation in the Church, much the most of them women. Upon the opening of the service there were murmurs which grew, became violent and at last turned into a riot, wherein the legend of a woman called Geddes has become famous, in that she threw a stool at the Celebrant's head. A contemporary witness has told us that the thing was organised by the great territorial magnates, and this is likely enough, for nothing of this kind happens (or at least happens successfully) without organisation. But popular enthusiasm was also present, and without it no organisation could have done what was done. The tumult grew so great that the clergy fled for their lives, there was a danger of the Bishop being stoned as the mob howled after him; he had to be given sanctuary and refuge. The Council whose duty it was to act for the distant King and his

CHARLES I

Government, were frightened and compromised; they proposed to take measures against ministers not for refusing to use the Liturgy but only for refusing to buy it. But the flame spread rapidly, and to nourish that torrent of excitement there were four sources.

Looked at superficially, these four sources were, first (and least apparent) the long-nourished resentment of the lords against their loss of income by the Revocation; second (a more powerful motive), their dread that the policy of restoring to the public and to the King what the nobles had looted might be extended indefinitely; third (most apparent) was the national feeling, which you may say all shared. There had been direct interference from England, not like the infiltration of English intrigue in the previous century which had undermined the old independence of Scotland, but immediate and overt orders proceeding from English sources and presuming to impose themselves upon Scottish life. That Laud had come, and stood there side by side with the King, was never forgotten.

But of the four sources from whence those torrents poured which converged to form the flood, the fourth and much the most evident (so vivid that historians long lost sight of all else) was the intense Calvinist enthusiasm of the Lowlanders.

It is a waste of time in this as in all other political convulsions to argue too closely upon numbers; the more violent enthusiasts were of course a minority, as they always are, but if we include all those who had sympathised with the tradition flowing from Knox before any but the very oldest men alive were born, then certainly the great mass of Scottish men and women were affiliated to *that*. We can get plenty of cases of those who were lukewarm, even of those who had to be coerced, but the Scottish Calvinist movement south of the Highlands was that of a whole society.

All this is true; yet there is one essential point to remember if we are to understand the thing: the apparent relative importance of these four causes is the reverse of their real importance.

The violent religious enthusiasm, though a powerful factor, was not the chief factor; the less conscious national feeling underlying it was more profound and formed the chief common bond; but the necessary motive force, the commanding thing, was the power of the magnates and their dread of losing income by the recovery of what

THE MENACE

had been looted during the religious upheaval of the last lifetime. This economic menace was the solid thing behind it all. The recovery of stolen public – i.e., Royal and Church – property was a menace only to the landowners, and severe only to the greatest of these; it was actually an advantage to the ministers of the Church, and indirectly to the mass of the people; yet it provided the power by which all was moved. Had not the great lords been behind the revolt it would never have come to what it did.

Charles again commanded the use of the Liturgy; young Lennox rode down south with solemn ranks of clergy and nobles, lairds, burgesses and clergy and common people waiting on either side of the way as he left Edinburgh bearing the Petition for Charles. The King's answer was not expected till somewhere about the middle of November – a lunar month at least after that riding forth of the messenger, so distant was Scotland then, so much apart. But meanwhile that quality in which the Scottish people so closely resemble the French, a quality of spontaneous organisation, set to work, under the influence of political excitement and with the countenance of the great lords.

That which we call today in England a "Board" was then called in Scotland, by a similar metaphor, a "Table." Four "Boards" or "Tables" were set up; one for the nobles, one for the bishops, one for the lairds and one for the clergy; and the mass of the people also were in sympathy. Each of these "Tables" was composed of four members. The whole body thus numbered sixteen, and this Committee (which has been well compared to the French Committee of Public Safety) virtually took over government from the time when the first excitement spread.

The King's answer, dealt with in early December, had no effect in lowering the heat of the furnace. He protested his hatred of the Catholic Church, under the title of "Popery"; he protested with equal sincerity his determination to do nothing against the law – and that determination had been apparent in all he had done. But the current was set, and flowing more and more fiercely with the passing days of that winter. Traquair negotiated between the infuriated people and the Court. On his return to his own country he was told by his fellow noble, Rothes, that they would insist upon all they had had; they would reject any innovation of Liturgy. A proclamation from the King, in which he took all the responsibility upon himself and denied that the fourteen bishops of the Scottish hierarchy had been responsible for the new proposals, was without effect. So was his denunciation of meetings as treasonable in the same proclamation. The days were filled with more and more violent popular emotion, and at last, with the opening of the month of March, 1638, there was done that which henceforward gave a name to the movement and stamped it with a special character. This was the taking of the "Covenant."

The name was an old one familiar to the Scottish Reformation, but that which was now taken was of so great effect and was the beginning of so many things that it is remembered as "The" Covenant in especial, and its adherents, down to the last of those who were martyred in defence of its ideas, are remembered as "Covenanters."

The Covenant was, in theory at least, a renewal of the confession of faith of the Kirk of Scotland which had appeared nearly sixty years before. But there was this peculiar and (to us) whimsical character about it, that it took on legal form: a contract between the Chosen People (Scotch this time) and their God, to be appealed to as an instrument and learnedly argued whenever occasion served; a solemn instrument and bond with Jehovah "while sun and moon shall endure." In the churchyard of what had been in the old days of idolatry the Franciscan Church the thousands poured in to sign the document upon a flat stone; the date was the 2nd of March, 1638.

All conditions signed, all ages, and signatures were demanded throughout the country, save of those mountaineers to whom these quarrels were indifferent.

One effect of this new and all-powerful organisation of "The Covenant" was to make Scotland a place of terror not only for those who opposed it but for those who were suspected of indifference. Therefore did those political magnates whose place was with the King and the English Court but who were of the Scottish nobility fear their fellow-countrymen and, henceforward, thought twice before they would openly stand against their people in that quarrel.

This is the true explanation of Hamilton' double dealings. No doubt there was something natively treasonable about him, but he had no far-fetched plan; what diverted him, what warped him in the service of the King, who had ever treated him as the one adviser on Scottish affairs, was fear.

THE MENACE

Charles took counsel with him and with Spottiswoode, the head of the Scottish hierarchy. Spottiswoode was too terrified to go north, but Hamilton went as Charles's envoy – not, however, until he was empowered to forgo the demand that the Covenant should be dropped. Such a demand would never have been obeyed. In the mood which had been aroused men were much more willing to die than were any soldiery which could be brought against them.

Such a mood was necessarily urging towards arms. The Government, the King of the nation, himself a Scottish King, could only successfully be met in arms. If it be wondered how a nation so few in numbers compared with the English even of that day (one man to five) and so very much poorer in proportion could hope to succeed – and they did succeed – in arms, the answer lies in two things: first, that the one requisite to the small unprofessional forces of those days, rapidly raised and soon dispersed, was money for their sudden equipment, food and pay; secondly, what all armies need and without which they are not armies at all, *cadres*, the framework of officers, the hierarchy of command, was, for these new Scottish forces, readily provided: Scottish gentlemen had fought all over Europe and were ready to officer any force. The very poverty of Scotland was here to her advantage; for many of the Scottish gentry, and lesser men, had adventured themselves in the Continental wars, under Gustavus Adolphus, in Holland, and throughout the religious struggles. There were enough, it was said, to provide with officers an army of 50,000 men, and officering was only needed for half such a force. As to money, enthusiasm would answer for that; whereas on the side of the King there was nothing to be had beyond the regular revenue, save by the dread experiment of summoning yet another Parliament.

So ended the first phase of the increasing menace which was to bring to ruin that long and hitherto successful effort at unity. In Scotland it had broken down altogether. In 1638 and the early days of 1639 the armed forces of the Covenant were raised, organised, drilled, and officered; and with the opening of the summer it would come inevitably to conflict. For the Crown could not without abdication admit that an unauthorised body should take over the function of government or that its own orders should be directly disobeyed.

The second phase saw this conflict initiated – and broken off. Charles had gathered an army in England, with difficulty. It was made up of most disparate forces, much of them half-trained, some of them untrained, their natural leaders – the nobility of England – for the most part disinclined for war and lukewarm in supporting the power of the King.

Of this English army's three generals, the Lords Arundel, Essex and Holland, the first two had no great appetite for fighting, and it has been asked whether the King really desired it to come to a fight at all; whether he did not think perhaps that his mere presence on the border with a large force would lead to an acceptance of his authority in Scotland beyond.

He lay in camp by Berwick in the field of Birks within a few miles of the border, a day's march from Duns, the first place in Scotland on the main road. The Scottish forces had been put under the leadership of a man who had grown elderly in foreign war, crooked in body, courageous, Leslie by name. The forces were not as yet considerable, and the advance body with which Leslie lay upon the North Road was formed of only 3,000 men, on that round hill near Duns. Holland set out in the dark hours of the morning of the 1st of June, or just after midnight of the 31st of May, to cross the border. Of such poor quality were his infantry that a march of ten miles in what they complained of as "heat intolerable" found them exhausted. They lay there immobile ten miles upon the road with the guns, while Holland rode forward with his cavalry another four miles. He both over-estimated the force in front of him, and also clearly could not trust his own infantry behind him: he did not engage, he returned to the King and Berwick – and this curious simulacrum of war was over. But it had already swallowed up in cost as much as half a year of the regular revenue.

I have said that the noble commanders on the English side were lukewarm enough, but apart from this most of the great English nobles present had an excellent motive for breaking off the war. Much of what they commanded was at their own charges, and every week under arms was an additional diminution of their wealth. Arundel certainly wanted to get away, and the pithy thing said about Pembroke was that he preferred hunting to battles. The Scotch had sent letters separately to each of the three English generals, addressing each by what was thought to be the best approach for conciliation, protesting their devo-

THE MENACE

tion to the King himself and to his office, and saying that they were but defending their religion and the lawful rights of their country.

It has been asked why Charles gave way. There are four answers, each of them true in parts: his torturing sense of duty, which never left him; the lack of money with which to continue; the policy of playing for delay; and the very low standard of the troops under his command.

It is true that he had every desire to avoid bloodshed, and in this, as in every other contest into which he had been thrown, he had been fair-spoken and conciliatory. It is true also that the lack of all funds for continuing was an imperative motive; it is true that delay might have served his purpose; but the cause there was no getting over was the wretched quality of his troops – a function of the lack of cash.

This is the answer to those who ask, as so many have asked, why Charles did not in this critical moment go forward. If he had won his battle against Scotland in the summer of 1639 he had the country at his mercy; if he lost it, it might yet be possible to rouse English opinion against the traditional Scottish enemy, though in a very few months it would be too late. It has even been said that if Charles had not only been defeated but killed in action it would so have roused national feeling south of the border that a real effort would have been made, and against such an effort by a power five times the population of Scotland, the Scottish forces could not have stood. But the army as it was would have been defeated.

For all these reasons Charles gave way and accepted what was called a Treaty, but was really a Truce.

The requests of the Scotch were that he would ratify, in a Parliament to be held next month, all that the Kirk had done, including the excommunication of the bishops; that he would permit all ecclesiastical matters to be dealt with by the Presbyterian Assembly; and that he would withdraw his army.

Neither body agreed in the interpretation or even in the words of the truce which masqueraded as a treaty; yet it bore a date, and there may have been some (though few) who expected it to be final. Charles throughout the negotiations had increasingly won the respect and even the affection of his opponents; it was probably in these first months that Montrose was first moved to what became later the service of the King, though the mood did not develop at once. Charles's patience in discussion, the clarity of his reasoning, were as conspicuous then as ever; but the end of it was – and necessarily – retreat. And after such an ending the King fell into a melancholy which lasted many days. He knew what was now before him.

The third phase of the advancing menace began with a meeting of the Scottish Parliament on the last day of August. The fourteen bishops were excluded, their office was declared unlawful, a term which when it was submitted to the King he did not accept though it now mattered little whether he accepted it or not. The Covenanters demanded that the custody of the Royal castles in Scotland should be in the hands of natives – a demand most agreeable to the magnates. They sent one of those magnates, Lord Loudon, down to the King to lay their conclusions before him, they were prorogued until the month of June of the next year, but while Loudon was at Court, Traquair gave the King a piece of news which Charles imagined might turn the tide in his favour, at least so far as English support for further hostilities was concerned. What Traquair had to tell the King was that Loudon was one of those who had secretly approached the Court of France with a request for an alliance against his sovereign.

Loudon's reply was weak enough. He pleaded that the letter had never been sent; even if it had been, he claimed the amnesty which had been granted; lastly, he could only be tried in Scotland. That did not prevent his being imprisoned. It is almost certain that the letter was never sent; it is quite certain that another such letter was sent later. In the latter, which had been intercepted and shown to Charles the phrase addressed to the French king was "*au roy.*" It was pointed out that this was the ritual phrase of subjects addressing their monarch, and that in using it the Scottish rebels were not only calling in foreign aid but accepting a foreign King.

But it was too late – it was becoming too late – for even this to be used by Charles as a lever for his cause. He thought he could use it; it was not unreasonable that he should so think; but in what was to follow his opponents so manœuvred that the thing fell flat. For what was to follow in the coming year, 1640, was that very disastrous thing, the renewed experiment of a Parliament.

Early in that year 1640 an accident apparently small, a mere slight change at Court, but actually of determining importance to the

THE MENACE

history of England, took place. The King's Secretary, the man whom he most constantly dealt with, had been for fifteen years the loyal but now octogenarian Sir John Coke. It was natural that he should be replaced; he had always been slow, though methodical and certainly devoted; and there was ready to hand a man who, though not really energetic was always busy, mixing in affairs, ready of tongue, Sir Harry Vane, the Controller of the Household. Both the Queen and Hamilton favoured his appointment. He replaced Coke, he became that voice which the King most frequently heard, never absent from his Council, and he was a thoroughly untrustworthy man. One of those traitors who have the more effect from their lack of character and weight: a man smooth and sly, who could do things without appearing to do them. It is with his appointment that the fourth phase of the menace begins.

Wentworth had been given the superior title of Lord Lieutenant and made Earl of Strafford,† he had come over from Ireland, he dominated the Council with his strength of mind and, though he was suffering grievously, of body as well. He pressed the necessity of a new offensive. A rival and enemy of his from of old, Saville, was playing traitor. Saville had been Strafford's opponent when, as Wentworth, they had shared the first territorial influence in the County of Yorkshire. Wentworth had defeated Saville in the claim to represent that county in the Commons, and now Saville was secretly intriguing with the Scotch, conspiring with London and corresponding with those north of the border.

Strafford not only urged the necessity of taking the offensive again against the forces of the Covenant, now greatly increased and better trained, but before the end of the year 1639 he had urged the King to call a Parliament. This of all things was what Charles most dreaded, but such was the force of Strafford's personality, coupled with the crying necessity for money if an army was to be formed, that he had his way. Strafford was persuaded that the national hatred of the English for the Scotch was now sufficiently inflamed to support him; he remembered the growing prosperity of those eleven years of peace, of swelling trade and of general well-being, he judged (wrongly) that the time which had passed and the effect of wealth

---

† January 12th, 1640.

proceeding from good government would prevent any great opposition when this Parliament should meet.

So it would have, had not those who were managing for the other side shown the tenacity they did and under a leadership of genius (that of Pym) a power of using every occasion and of moulding things to their end. Strafford wrongly imagined that the immediate danger of invasion would move the squires to support the Crown. He had been long out of England. He had formed and easily controlled his own Irish Parliament as an instrument pliable to his hand. Strafford was right in the judgment that the country as a whole would have supported the King in a renewed effort against invasion. But Parliament did not in this stand for the country as a whole, it stood for the landed interest, the squires, and as things turned out, though even these were at first amenable enough, the landowners, the country gentlemen coming up to London and most of them hitherto out of touch with central affairs, could be worked by the more astute and more determined of their colleagues.

At the meeting of that Parliament on the 13th of April, 1640, the fifth phase opens. Charles showed to the Houses at once the incriminating letter and the incriminating phrase, *"au roy."* Those who heard him were not unmoved. But when four days later the Commons met for business it was clear that those among them who had determined upon a plan of action, unchanged from the old opposition years before, would know how to direct the fluctuating minds of those around them. This large unwieldy body of half a thousand at their full complement, voting often in a strength of close on four hundred, were open to capture by any determined and organised group which knew what it desired – and at the head of these who thus captured them was the supreme ability of Pym.

While these squires, new to Parliament, the very memory of which was only the memory of their boyhood to the younger men, looked about them not knowing what next should be done, Hyde, a contemporary and one of their number, noted their attitude. Pym rose and spoke for two hours. His square, solid face, rather full-fleshed, his fixed regard, his ponderated careful tones, had their full effect upon the House. They had been asked for supply. It was for supply that they had been summoned. But Pym deflected them to the consideration of three points in their order, all of which captured the attention of his audience. First, before they considered supply – and it would be a long business – let them consider their grievances in the matter of revenue. Next, in the matter of imposts (which meant chiefly ship-money, and they had all felt the burden of this); lastly, for their own rights as an assembly, their right – which he claimed, though the claim was revolutionary – to fix their own dates of adjournment at will, not by order of the Crown.

When they came to talk of ship-money, the concrete point which all of them could understand, for all of them had felt it – and no one desires to pay a novel tax indefinitely – the House was not as yet irreconcilable even in its majority. There was always, in any case, a large minority which would support the King.†

When Herbert the lawyer, whose business it was as a Royal officer to put forward the King's case, spoke on ship-money with calm and exactitude, saying exactly what had happened, praising the popular Hampden, though disagreeing with his claim, reminding all those country gentlemen how the King had studiously sought the advice of the judges and how the judges had decided the case in favour of the Crown, the sense of the House was with him. Had the opposition not been organised, had that organisation not been strengthened by the special talents of Pym, the King's case, so ably argued, might have won the day.

But here a blunder was made. The need for supply was most urgent. Haste is a bad counsellor. The Court appealed to the Peers. The Peers suggested that supplies should be voted before the grievances were considered, and at once the question of privilege arose, that point on which the House of Commons was most sensitive. Here indeed was innovation, they said it was no business of the Peers what the Commons should do about supply. For centuries the exceptional and voluntary grants had been the business of the Commons and of the Commons alone. Indeed it was for the purpose of deciding upon those grants that the Commons had originally been summoned, and it still remained in theory their chief business. Just at the moment when

---

† In one test case although religion was brought in to confuse the issue, this minority was five to nine.

CHARLES I

Pym was using this new point with all his dexterity and all his weight, Strafford in the last days of April returned from Ireland.

He was a man of great tenacity as well as of great courage; he was dreadfully ill with gout and dysentery as well, yet he crossed in a bad storm not waiting for the weather, and, after almost dying at Chester on landing, had himself brought up to London in a litter. On arrival, though he was still suffering grievously, he dominated the Council. At that table he seems to have used a certain phrase – whether he really used it or not we can never be certain. Of those present, as we shall see in a moment, all save one seem not to have heard the words. *But the one who did note them down in a brief memorandum of what passed was the new Secretary, Sir Harry Vane.* If he *had* heard those words – and as he probably had – they ran thus:—

"You have," said Strafford to the King, "an army in Ireland." (It was an excellent, well-trained force, one of Strafford's many successes in the administration, 9,000 men ready for the field.) "You may employ them here" (that is, in Britain) "to reduce this kingdom" (that is, Scotland, rebellious and under arms).

That such words were used, I say, is probable enough though not certain; but Sir Harry Vane who noted them down and upon whose testimony so much was to turn, nourished in his heart against Strafford all the hatred which a character made for mean hatreds could feel. And that hatred arose from a petty source. Strafford had strongly opposed Vane's appointment to the Secretaryship. He had delayed it by a month. Poor old Coke was a particular friend of his and he wanted him to carry on as long as possible. In this Strafford misjudged, for Coke was getting past his work, but in opposing the appointment of Vane he judged extremely well, and Charles, on the advice of Hamilton (and somewhat of the Queen) judged ill. But there was another cause for Sir Harry Vane's hatred. Strafford had taken among his titles that of "Raby," and Vane had coveted it for his own, when he should be raised to the Peerage, because it was the name of a house in his possession.

Strafford still hoped, indeed it still appeared probable, that when it came to the voting of supply the Commons would prove amenable. Pym had been careful to speak with respect of the King, and indeed at that moment no other language would have been tolerated; our

THE MENACE

best contemporary witness, Edward Hyde, testifies to the loyalty of their mood. Upon Sunday, the 3rd of May, at a Council which was held with Strafford present, it was decided upon his advice to abandon ship-money. It was a daring but a fruitful policy. Let the House be asked for twelve, or even for eight, subsidies spread over three years: twelve would be rather more than the ship-money for those three years, eight almost their equivalent. Let the King ask for so much aid as was absolutely necessary to find pay for the army and the renewal of the war, lest England should let Scotland go and the kingdoms be torn apart. The demand was to be made through the mouth of the Secretary, Sir Harry Vane.

When on Monday, the 4th of May, the thing was debated, a lawyer of no great eminence, Lenthall, was Chairman of the Committee. No anger was displayed, all passed in the right temper; the Speaker, Granville, who, as they were in Committee, sat among the other members, spoke in favour of the King's demand – an exceptional thing, for the man who was Speaker never spoke from the Chair, of course, and only very rarely in Committee when he was not in the Chair. He sincerely intended to plead for the necessities of the Government, but he launched an unfortunate phrase, saying that ship-money was indeed illegal. He meant it as an argument to be advanced for the replacement of ship-money by subsidies, but it at once reminded all his hearers of that old grievance perpetually discussed and kept green for six years past.

Hyde proposed that they should first make a general declaration of their willingness to grant supply, and later determine the amount. Hampden, whose name carried so much weight, said that there was only one question before the House – whether they should vote twelve subsidies or not. That statement was false but very cunning; it was sufficient to confuse the unpractised and unorganised individuals who confronted him.

They were largely a body of new members, many of them young. The true question before the House was *how much* they would grant. It might be twelve subsidies or less. Hampden, by suggesting that Charles must have twelve *or nothing* put forth a falsehood which the weight of his reputation and experience allowed to pass. It made the King's demand extreme and provocative. How the House was divided on this we cannot tell; there were cries for Hyde and cries for Hampden, and the debate did not halt till late in the afternoon, though the House had been sitting since nine in the morning.

Nor was it concluded; the House adjourned until the following day, when Vane, with a malignant intention (he is the true villain of the piece and this was his first great villainy before the second, which was still to come), speaking as though with the Royal authority, opposed the moderate and wise suggestion of Hyde, which would have gained time and done all that was needed. He did worse, he gave the King a false report of what had happened, representing the Commons as unwilling to consider supply at all and as refusing to help. Whereupon on the next day, Tuesday, the 5th of May, Charles came down in the morning to the House of Lords, and summoning the Commons dissolved what came to be known as "The Short Parliament."

It had sat three weeks.

Then opens the last phase. When Charles found out how he had been tricked he was angry enough with Vane, but anger could now do no good. There were riots in the town directed principally against Laud, whom in their ignorance the rioters thought to be the author of the dissolution. The riots were easily put down, though only two of the worst offenders were executed.†

For the immediate necessities of the army a warranty loan was demanded of the wealthier subjects, and upon the whole cheerfully paid. But it did little more than recoup the expenses which had already been undertaken in the first abortive expedition and carry on for a few weeks. Even so, there was resistance on the part of those who represented the organised money power of the City of London.

The army was to concentrate at York; in that summer they counted upon a force of 20,000 men with 60 guns; but opinion against the Scottish war was rising behind it and its own discipline was weak enough. The King had proposed Strafford, whose health was still deplorable, to command; he had preferred to let Newcastle lead, but it was his advice and his judgment that was followed, he told the King, when he saw what task the army had before it that the forces were not equal to that task.

---

† It was on this occasion that torture was used to discover the conspirators, though the lawyers had declared it illegal twelve years before in the Felton case in order to oppose the King.

THE MENACE

At last, on the 20th of August, 1640, the Scottish army of the Covenant, now fully trained and with enthusiastically subscribed money behind it, prepared to invade. There had been formed a grandiose plan of convergence against it – a loyal Scottish body to come down from Aberdeen by the east coast, a force from Ireland to act on the west, the King's main army from the south. But such plans of convergence even with superior numbers are always very risky, because they demand exact timing – a thing in those days almost impossible of achievement over such distances. But apart from that there was no chance of the plan's success. The movement from the north came to nothing, as did the attack from the west; and as for the movement from the south, that of the main army which the King had gathered at York, it was not prepared. On the 20th of August Leslie, who had concentrated at Duns, crossed the Tweed with 23,000 foot and 3,000 horse (let it be remarked that Montrose was the first to put his foot in the water). The Covenanters issued a proclamation that they were not fighting England but only the "Canterburian faction of Papistical atheists, Arminians and Prelates" at the head of which stood Laud – a man certainly a Prelate, hardly Arminian, as little Papist as could be, and most emphatically not atheist.

An advance body of horse under Conway attempted to meet the invading flood, was hopelessly outnumbered, and apart from that in such poor shape that with next to no losses it broke. All Durham and Northumberland were overrun by the invaders; Strafford coming up with the retreat at Darlington returned to York and told the King that the army was still quite unfitted to meet the better training, the larger numbers and the superior officering of the enemy.

The four northern counties were abandoned to the invasion, and, what is more, a levy of what would be in our money nearly £40,000 a week was paid to support these alien occupiers of England; over and above that they looted at will and confiscated all that they found on the numerous estates belonging to Catholics as well as on the estates of many Protestants whom they regarded as their opponents.

As a last desperate expedient to obtain supply Charles summoned a Council of Peers which met him at York on the 2nd of October. It counselled peace with Scotland – since he could not fight – and the summoning of yet another Parliament, though the Covenanters were in active correspondence with those who were preparing rebellion at home and were clamouring for the blood of Strafford and of Laud even before that cry was heard in London.

The King accepted the inevitable. The writs went out, and on the 3rd of November there met at Westminster the last of the King's Parliaments, that in the name of which, and through the action of many members in which, the Great Rebellion was raised; that which began by putting to death the greatest and most loyal of Englishmen, Strafford, and of which a little remnant, before it was dispersed, put to death the Master whom Strafford had served.

Oliver Cromwell
BUST ATTRIBUTED TO BERNINI, NOW IN THE HOUSE OF COMMONS

THE CRISIS

THE STARTLING THING IN READING CONTEMPORARY EVIDENCE on the opening of Charles's last Parliament on Tuesday, the 3rd of November, 1640, is the complete change of spirit we discover between its temper and the temper of the Short Parliament, dissolved little more than six months before. In that brief interval the mood had wholly changed.

No longer were the wealthy country gentlemen and lawyers, many of whom had at first been new to debate, amenable to compromise; the revolutionary spirit hitherto concentrated in a few determined men had spread through such great numbers of them that the tone, of the majority at least, was becoming fervid in favour of catastrophic innovation.

There is a line (or phrase) most illustrative of this turnover in sentiment, "Hostile indifference, a mote can move." When our attitude towards a man or a policy is hostile, but not active, it may be regarded as indifferent; but it has an indifference which a very slight impetus may convert to activity. Indifference not hostile may be compared to a vehicle still on the further side of a pass before it has reached the summit; the work is against the collar and it is difficult to drive up hill; but when the summit is passed, although no pace has been gathered, the conditions have changed; down hill a small increase in power will work a very great increase in pace, and one which gathers momentum rapidly.

And indeed that is what had happened. Between April, 1640, and November revolutionary feeling had been kindled. The leaders had passed from having to do heavy uphill work in urging rebellion, to easy downhill work: a summit had been crossed.

Why was this? What were the new factors? In the first place, much the most important of the causes, the second breakdown in the face of a Scottish army (and this time an army invading and triumphant) had powerfully affected the squires and their lawyer allies.

THE CRISIS

It was illogical; it was their own fault; their failure to grant supplies had produced the disaster; but the disaster had caused a profound irritation. It was the more unreasonable because the more reckless of the revolutionaries were actively corresponding with the Scotch and supporting their rebellion – but so it was. The large sum of over £800 a day (something like £5,000 in our money) had to be found for the invaders, who absorbed it over and above the loot in which they indulged, and in such a position the prestige of the Crown, standing there impotent in the face of invaders, lacking funds, with an army half mutinous and with no resources for its proper pay, equipment and training, sank away like water falling in a lock.

Now all this played indirectly into the hands of that small highly organised clique of which the Russells, with Bedford at their head, were a chief money power, and Pym – who had risen as their hanger-on – the great strategist. Pym and Hampden and St. John and the rest (with Pym in control) had the strategic situation ready-made to their hands.

Clarendon, who knew his fellow-countrymen well, has justly said that in great affairs Englishmen love to leave decision in the hands of a few. It is perhaps their first characteristic, as opposed to those nations (or cultures) which lend themselves easily to the combination of great numbers; to the principle of the "swarm." It is part of that characteristic which the Englishman's friends call his appetite for the practical, and his enemies lethargy. The managers, if they led well, would have all in their hands, few though they were; and Pym led them with supreme ability. Had it been a campaign in arms instead of a campaign by words Pym would have remained as one of the great generals of history – he had all the qualities of one.

We must remember that these leaders were no longer what they had been eleven years before. They had passed through eleven years of maturing and amalgamation, of thinking out their problems, of growing familiar with the task which they had to face. Hampden in the old Parliaments had been a young man beginning his public life just after coming of age; he was not over thirty-six when the third of Charles's Parliaments in the early part of the reign had broken down in tumult. He was now approaching fifty. Pym had the weight of what was felt in those days to be age; he was nearly sixty, and he was of the greater importance because, to his undiminished strength of will

CHARLES I

and if anything increased mental powers, was added the fact that he seemed to them venerable. The young men, either new or bewildered, were ready to be led for the most part; and those who were not bewildered were fanatical.

It must also be remembered how many of them had come from contact with the army, underpaid, underfed, mutinous and disappointed, the source of exasperation – for the squires were many of them officers over the soldiers. Pym to this art of management had added, during the interval since the Short Parliament, the policy of "open house"; he entertained largely and lavishly. It is a feature you will find in all the movements of that age, from the French Ambassador's entertainments before the Lady Jane Grey business eighty odd years earlier, on to the meetings in Bloomsbury at Southampton House in the last conspiracies against the Stuarts half a lifetime later. Pym was able thus to act perhaps with the use of Russell money, perhaps no more than its support; he had spent the eleven years in commercial adventure, wherein doubtless his talents for intrigue and organisation would have reaped their reward.

Next it must be remembered as a cause of the great difference between the new House and the old that the Short Parliament had ended in a quarrel between itself and the King, a quarrel which had been deliberately fostered by Sir Harry Vane. Next there was the strengthening of that very large Catholic-minded group which the rest of the landed interest particularly feared, and on which their sentiment varied from dislike to detestation. That the actual numbers in sympathy with Catholicism (for the full practice of Catholicism was another matter) had increased in the eleven years is probable, though it has been denied. That their freedom and sense of security had increased cannot be denied, and a subscription which the principal Catholic landowners had made as a free gift for the Government in its military difficulties had exasperated the feeling.

Then there was their annoyance, or to put it more strongly and more truthfully their anger against Cottington as Treasurer, which was but a continuation of the old anger against Weston as Treasurer, he who had worked so well for the Crown and who was now dead. The Minister responsible for the gathering of monies not voted by the squires themselves in Parliament was the natural target of their hostility; and on top of that Cottington, like Weston, was more than

THE CRISIS

suspected of sympathy with the Catholic Church: and justly so suspected. He died a Catholic.

To the prestige of Parliament the King had himself added weight by summoning it on the advice of Hamilton and in some degree of the Queen, but especially through a false judgment of his own – thinking thereby to forestall the action of the Peers whom he had gathered at York and who were, as a body, strongly for having this Parliament called. It was at the first plenary meeting of the Peers that Charles had announced his intention of calling it.

Then there was the fact that the clergy in Convocation had continued sitting after the Short Parliament at the end of the year had been dissolved, and acting against precedent and tradition had voted their own supplies to the King after the Commons had ceased from sitting. All these things converged to harden the opposition and to aid the change.

There was yet another factor of greater weight than anything except the new position and power of the managers (the small organised clique) which gave the essential character of organisation to the whole Movement. This other factor was the presence of the Scotch in London, and notably of their chief preacher, Henderson.

They inflamed the current of opinion already setting so strongly in the capital, supported as it was by the money power of the City. Henderson's sermons, delivered in a foreign accent, and to our taste, as to the more cultivated of his contemporaries, dull enough, had prodigious effect; he preached to packed congregations, the women of which had waited sometimes for hours to obtain good seats while men overflowed the buildings, and even hung on at the windows from outside to hear the "Word of God"; which Divine Message was always directed against the counsellors of the King.

Lastly there was – a determining thing – the great opportunity offered by the special position of Strafford.

He stood isolated, a towering mark, cut off altogether from those who were about to destroy him. He was to them the great apostate. He – one of the very richest men in the Kingdom – had in the eyes of the other great landlords betrayed the cause of the opulent. His own character in every way lent itself to that fatal opposition, even his continued increasing breakdown in health made things worse for him; he was abrupt, he had the disdain of strong intelligence for weak and of clear thought for confused. He had collected personal enemies of every kind. He was careless of his words, disdainfully incautious; for instance, he had once said hotly that Holland would be better with his head off – and Holland always remembered it. He had bitterly offended Essex, and that poor and doubtful leader in arms, bad speaker and peevish soul felt for Strafford all the hatred of fear in the presence of open strength. All the intriguers and all the straightforward revolutionaries knew Strafford to be their enemy; and as for the Scots, he had determined to destroy them "root and branch," so the Scottish temper – ever avid of challenge – had grown fixed in its determination to destroy *him*.

Throughout the body of the Lords there was a feeling of a somewhat different kind from, but almost equally strong as, that which pervaded the squires and lawyers of the lower House. The Peers received with friendship their Scottish fellows who were present to negotiate; Rothes, the Scottish Lord who from the beginning had most fomented rebellion, and London, whose activities we have seen. And the Scottish Lords as well as their preachers were here in London clamouring for Strafford's blood.

The Houses had barely been sitting a week when the revolutionary torrent had so swollen that the Lords agreed to the arrest and confinement of Strafford. He was to be imprisoned pending his trial under an Impeachment – and it was the Lords thus concurring which gave such overwhelming weight to the attack.

Here we must remember and note of these revolutionary movements that they were of two kinds, following in successive phases. First come the revolutionary acts which were not assumptions of sovereignty as yet but were only revolutionary in procedure; later were to come the revolutionary acts which were a direct usurpation of royal power; orders to garrisons, orders for munitionment, and all that which so rapidly culminated in Civil War. But for the moment the first phase only was at work, that of procedure. It was revolutionary, for Parliament to effect the sudden arrest of a man who was about to be impeached and that seizure of Strafford at four o'clock in the afternoon of Wednesday, the 11th of November, 1640, was the first revolutionary step in the way of procedure.

Now Pym, in some underground way, had obtained knowledge of the note set down by Sir Harry Vane which purported to record

THE CRISIS

Strafford's advice (in the privacy of the Council Meeting) for the use of the Irish army. He kept that decisive weapon hidden and in hand, ready to use it when the moment should come. Young Harry Vane was in the secret, a fanatical hair-brained fellow, the son of the sly and sleek Secretary – young Harry Vane, a member of the House of Commons and of an extreme visionary temper, which the strength and wisdom of Pym must have heartily despised. How Pym kept such a character quiet until the last moment we do not know; but there are ways of doing these things – the commonest is the use of fear, and another is the use of money.

Pym, holding all well in hand, now proceeded to the next revolutionary step. It was proposed that an accusation of treason against Strafford should be lodged, though no treason could be proved, and this was to be done in the following manner. It was to be judged that a number of acts themselves not treasonable might in accumulation be called treason. This was a thing abhorrent to all the legal traditions of England; for treason was so much the gravest accusation that one could bring against a man, and so certainly productive of death if it were proved, that condemnation for it was safeguarded in a special manner. The strongest proof was required, and the most explicit indictment. But Pym carried this second revolutionary step, and it was decided that in the impeachment of Strafford for treason an accumulation of non-treasonable acts might be deemed, as a whole, an act of treason.

But the third revolutionary step was the masterpiece. Pym procured a declaration of the principle that Privy Councillors might be examined in the coming trial, and called upon for evidence of what had happened in the privacy of the King's Council.

This was not only a violation of all custom and a flat contradiction of the Constitution, it was also of its nature the end of the King's Council as the governing power of the country. Let Councillors suspect that what they said at the Council Board could be brought against them publicly outside, and each Councillor would be suspect to each and all of his colleagues: the unity and value of conciliar debate would have disappeared. Therefore this third revolutionary step was the shrewdest blow of all. But though the ultimate effect of it was what it could not fail to be – the destruction of kingly power – for the moment Pym only brought it forward as a platform on which to mount his great gun, kept secretly in hiding, Sir Harry Vane's note upon what he affirmed to have been Strafford's advice for the use of the Irish army in support of the King.

The King agreed to that fatal move: he allowed members of his Council to give evidence. Whether he could do so constitutionally or not was doubtful; the Councillors were bound by a personal oath to divulge nothing of what had passed at the Council Board save by special leave of the King in exceptional and particular instances. The King's right to absolve from oaths was not an accepted part of the English Constitution; but as things were now going men cared less and less for precedent, law or right; and the revolutionaries were determined to neglect all three. It was indeed a necessity of their programme so to do, and that the King himself should do it also in this or that was hardly noticed. And the Councillors agreed with the King in this decision – ignorant as they were of what a weapon Pym held ready to use.

Land's name had been coupled with Straffords throughout this attack, but he was for the moment left on one side. It was hoped that his age and infirmity of health would, under the rigours of imprisonment, rid them of his presence, and that death would come to him before there should be any need of the axe. Against Strafford all was directed, and for the destruction of Strafford the whole phalanx moved.

At the opening of the fourth week of November, 1641, on Monday, the 22nd of that month, Strafford, imprisoned for High Treason, was brought after more than three months of confinement to the Bar of the House of Lords assembled for his trial in Westminster Hall: but that which stood at the Bar of the House upon this fatal date was not Strafford alone – it was the ancient monarchy of England.

It was not Strafford's blood alone, though for that the Scottish Commissioners, all his enemies among his fellow Peers whom he had offended in this way and that, all the revolutionaries for whom he had become a symbol of resistance to revolution, were athirst. Much more largely, more permanently, in a greater manner, was there an implacable spirit working for the ending of kingship. A spirit which ran in varying degrees throughout that class which the Reformation had so permanently enriched – the masters of the villages of England, the great territorial body, the younger members of which now present in

THE CRISIS

the two Houses were to see themselves enthroned in power, before they died, where once had sat the majesty and authority of the King.

A lad of twenty-one coming into this Parliament soon after his majority, as so many of the young squires did, would live to see before his seventieth year the flight of James II, and the end of that long process during which the remaining remnant of monarchy under the two last of the Stuarts was to disappear and its mere name to be left contemptuously surviving, with the gentry ruling all.

While Strafford and Laud had lain in prison the great change in the temper of the Commons and the acquiescence of the Lords had produced something like terror. Some fled, others went into hiding. All Catholic officers were cashiered. In six short weeks the King had been deprived of a Secretary and of his two chief Ministers – the one by exile, the other by imprisonment and under the threat of death.

A strange effort had been made to save Strafford, a proposal that the worst enemies of the King should be admitted to his Council and should form a sort of compromise ministry with Bedford at the head, Pym himself at the Exchequer, and even Hampden occupying the extraordinary post of Governor to the Prince of Wales. The reason generally given for the breakdown of that effort is that Bedford, now very near death, refused for this reason or for that. The real reason is that to accept (and Pym was on the point of accepting) would have saved Strafford's life – so nothing came of it.

Strafford then must stand his trial. The three months' delay he had already had in which to prepare his defence had been chafed at; anything that could give the quarry of that hunt a chance was obnoxious to the to the leaders of the Great Change, for whom the killing of Strafford would mark their initial victory and the mortal wounding of kingship. The first day of the great proceedings was taken up in formalities, the setting down of questions and the answers thereto. On the morrow Pym opened the attack. He spoke with deliberation, weight and skill, and the modern reader smiles, perhaps too broadly, at reading in his opening passage the phrase that "truth and goodness are the beauty of the soul."

Other men of Pym's calibre have not found it necessary to emphasise good morals; but the spirit of the time required something of the kind, and we may be grateful that no texts of Scripture were

CHARLES I

introduced at the beginning of the speech, nor even (as would have been the fashion of Elliot) a spate of Latin tags. No, Pym was worthy of himself, save for that little passage on truth and goodness in which he sacrificed to the fashion of the day.

What he said was well thought out. His case was bad; perhaps he knew in his heart already that it would fail, but he went at it with resolution, with great invention, with tenacity and a continuous effort – all of which were characteristic of the man even in these his later years.

For nearly a fortnight the thing dragged on, with the King listening in the Royal Box (he had refused to occupy the throne which had been set up in Westminster Hall), with the public thronging the great open building, and the Peers more and more impressed by the weakness of the pleas which were being put before them – for all the while Strafford was winning.

For a strong-tempered and dominating man he held himself well in hand. He found the best line of attack – he ridiculed this novel conception that executive acts *in favour* of the King even though they should be thought excessive could, by mere accumulation, be called treason. The public, for what that was worth, gradually turned to be on his side. His judges the Peers grew more and more doubtful. They desired his fall, but they had to decide a definite point and it was obvious that Strafford's case was sound. By the twelfth day it was clear that the impeachment would fail.

But Pym was not so easily defeated. The conviction borne in upon him, and indeed upon all who had been in Westminster Hall, that the effort was doomed and that Strafford would be acquitted was reached on Saturday, the 3rd of April, but the state of affairs was already clear a day or two before that, and it was upon the Friday that a secret plan had been made to proceed by Attainder.

The point was of the first importance. Impeachment – though the revival of it in the last twenty years was an anachronism, the resurrection of an old mediaeval thing which had lost its meaning – was at least a trial; evidence had to be brought, arguments had to be used, a man could defend his life and might save it, however powerful his enemies. Process by Attainder was a very different thing. It had been the favourite method of Henry VIII and his minister Cromwell when they wanted to get rid of a man or woman: it consisted simply in passing a law in the ordinary way by the King in Parliament – that is

THE CRISIS

by a majority vote of the two Houses and the assent of the Crown – which law condemned its victim to death. There was no trial under it, no calling of witnesses, no pleading; you could kill anyone by a Bill of Attainder just in the same fashion as you could, by the same procedure, add a new law to the Statute Book.

It should be carefully noted that Pym was too clever to bring in the Bill of Attainder himself; the thing was worked by others, and in so confused and skilful a fashion that to this day no one is quite certain how it was done. Pym actually appeared in the character of the virtuous man who must keep his word, and having promised to carry through the Impeachment must go on with it – but the Bill was Pym's all the same, it was his law, and it is he who stands forever responsible to England for Strafford's blood.

This Bill of Attainder was brought in suddenly after Pym had as suddenly produced before the astonished House at the opening of the third week, Monday, the 5th of April, the paper on which was jotted down the sentence Strafford was affirmed to have spoken in the secrecy of the Council when he offered the Irish army to the King for the subjection of Scotland. But Pym so read the thing and so emphasised it that he gave his audience to understand that if the words had been said at all they applied to *England* – that Strafford had proposed to use the Irish army for the subjugation of the English – as though the phrase "this kingdom" meant England.

Put simply it would have been a bold and resolute lie but quite unconvincing – almost ludicrous – but Pym understood the art of lying as do all men possessing his sort of genius; it is one half of their strength. Moreover, he had used this weapon not only with secrecy, concealing it all this time and even imposing silence upon the featherheaded younger Vane, but he had skilfully prepared his approaches in bringing it forward. He was ready with evidence, true or false, but at any rate a document, and it would be attested by the younger Vane. He would show that he (the younger Vane) had got hold of his father's keys, unlocked the box in which his father's notes were contained and copied the original minute some time after it was made.

The King had ordered the original minutes to be burnt, but the younger Vane's "copy" of them remained. We can be morally certain that the younger Vane would not have made and kept that "copy" without the complicity of his father, the Secretary and writer of the original memorandum. But Pym already knew what would be the answer to that; obviously the elder Vane was not going to give himself away; he would have the pleasure of seeing his enemy Strafford – the man who had tried to prevent his getting the Secretaryship and who had taken the coveted title of Raby – destroyed, but he would not destroy *himself* by admitting that he had betrayed the secrets of the Council to which he was Secretary. When the thing was put before the Lords, his Judges, Strafford called as witnesses the Privy Councillors who had been present. Not one of them had any recollection of the words. Windebank, the other Secretary, had been driven out of the country, but in a letter he testified that he had not heard any such words, though listening carefully. Harry Vane, the elder, hypocritically pretended that he did not know whether the words "this country" referred to England or to Scotland. But the thing was too clear. They *could* only have referred to Scotland – if, indeed they had ever been spoken – and all the world knew it.

The Impeachment went on, but all the life had been taken from it, for the Bill of Attainder was going on side by side with it in the lower House while the regular trial proceeded in Westminster Hall.

At the end of the week, on Saturday, the 10th of April, Strafford was recapitulating his defence, the thing was drawing to an end and all in his favour, when Pym asked to be allowed to bring forward new evidence. Young Harry Vane's copy (or supposed copy) of his father's memorandum (or supposed memorandum) was to be solemnly brought forward. The Lords adjourned, consulted the Judges, and decided that if the attack was to be begun all over again so also might the defence be – as was common sense. This gave Pym exactly the opportunity he wanted, the accusations had to be withdrawn, Pym came back to the House of Commons, had the doors locked, brought out the paper, and then those who had to bring in the Bill of Attainder did so in spite of Pym's own virtuous protests.

There was strong opposition to so odious a course as the sudden dropping of an open trial and the substitution for it of a mere command to put to death by law; eleven days passed before the vote was taken and even so half the House was ashamed to abet the deed; attendance was poor, and there were only 263 members present and of these 59, including many of the greatest weight, voted in the negative.

THE CRISIS

Meanwhile many merchants of the city of London, the chief centre of wealth in the kingdom, and, in their general direction and as to their main body, mainly with the revolutionaries, presented a huge Petition that the Bill for killing Strafford should go through. They claimed 20,000 signatures. The Second Reading came before the House in the middle of the last week of April, on the 27th. It was by no means certain that the Lords would pass the Bill, yet the King tried to save Strafford by force. One idea was to enlarge and change the garrison of the Tower of London, where Strafford was confined, but the Governor of the Tower (so low had the King's power sunk in London) sided with the Commons and refused entry to the soldiers. There was also at the time an obscure plan afoot for using the Army, as yet not disbanded, and it is fairly certain that the King intended to secure himself in Portsmouth.

A plan to use the Army there was, though how far it went it is difficult to say; at any rate Pym used it for all it was worth, and this peril to the Parliamentarians, which was not wholly imaginary, helped to determine the voting.

On Saturday, the 1st of May, the King met the two Houses in person and promised as a last resort not to employ Strafford any further, if the Bill should be dropped. His action was at once made, as might have been expected, a ground for protest of privilege, and the constitutional purity of men who had acted throughout in violation of all constitutional precedent inflamed part of opinion in the upper House against Charles, so intermixed were the debates of the Houses. On Sunday the Puritan preachers roused their hearers in the churches to fury, and on the following day Pym resumed his battering speeches in the Commons.

It was a week later, on Saturday, the 8th of May, that the House of Lords came to the vote. All London was aflame in those days, great mobs had gathered, and anyone who voted for saving the life of a man whose regular trial had thus been denied him went in some fear of attack from hired ruffians.

Already the walls of the capital had been placarded with the names of those who had voted in the Commons against the Bill of Attainder. The fear of the mob kept most of the Peers away, and on that day, when their responsibility was most heavily engaged, when

205

only their vote in full numbers could have had moral weight, there were not fifty present – there were only forty-five.

Of those forty-five, nineteen only were brave enough to vote for the acquittal of the man who had been condemned by no tribunal and upon no evidence. It was therefore by a majority of seven among his equals of the House of Lords, that Thomas Wentworth, Earl of Strafford was condemned to death. Only twenty-six of his peers – not a sixth of the full number – such was the work of that Saturday.

And the day following, the Sunday, Charles in his Palace wrestled in agony between his duty to save his loyal servant, who had governed so well and had been the last strong prop of the Crown, his duty to his people at large to avoid civil war, and his duty (for that was his duty also) to save from the mobs raised by Pym and his allies, and howling outside his palace windows, the lives of his Consort and his children.

To duty Charles had all his life been bound, but especially since Buckingham's murder: and here was divided duty indeed! Three calls, each imperative, all divergent.

He took counsel. The laymen were for sacrificing Lord Strafford as a matter of necessity, and that great man had written a noble letter to his King offering his own life for the safety of the Royal Family and the peace of the kingdom. The bishops also gave their judgment, and perhaps had they been united as their ministry should have determined them to be, Charles, torn between these duties, would have decided for Strafford's life and for the inevitable catastrophe which would have followed such a decision. But Williams, Archbishop of York, at heart Strafford's bitter enemy, urged the King to sacrifice his greatest servant. He put it in the highest of moral grounds and determined the issue. By Williams was the King, in his reverence for prelates, doubtfully persuaded to that duty which was to destroy him. Charles thought to save the nation from civil war: he was making it certain and with it the destruction of the Crown.

A Commission was named for the signature and the Bill of Attainder was passed into law: so Strafford must die. And it is said that when he heard that things had so passed, he so far in the sudden bitterness of his heart neglected his own action as to cry out, with Holy Writ, "Put not your trust in Princes!"

THE CRISIS

So Charles acted: and it cost him dear.

When a man of sensitive conscience and high honour is torn between various imperative duties, he will bear remorse till death for whatever course he has taken; for thus abandoning Strafford and securing a brief precarious peace among his people Charles bled inward tears of blood to the day of his own death by the same violence.

It was law then, on Monday, the 10th of May, that Strafford should die. The day after the morrow was appointed, and on that Wednesday, the 12th, he was led out from his prison in the Tower to the scaffold. He died with that same contempt of the base, with that same confidence in the justice of the cause he had served, and the same courage as he had shown throughout all these years. The aged Laud blessed him from his window as he passed below and fainted after doing so. Pym and those who were with him, all the great monied interests of the City of London, the main part of the territorial body, the main part of the lawyers, had won what was not only their first victory but in a sense the decisive and final one. It was still early in the morning.

*****

The eight months which followed the destruction of Strafford and the triumph of Pym's organisation are a welter full of picturesque incidents which have filled legend, but not one of which was capital in the history of England or of Charles himself. They were an interregnum during which a simulacrum of the King's power remained, but during which also the revolutionaries under Pym's strict organisation and supported by his widespread secret service of spies were at least equally strong. Each party was watching the other prior to the final ordeal by battle. Charles was willing to sign and sign, knowing well that if when the fighting came he should win, all could be undone again. How heavy the chances were against his success when it came to arms he could not guess; for he – and most other men for that matter – were still under the influence of the past, and that kingship should be finally defeated, was a thing hitherto unknown in the history of England.

In that interval of eight months all manner of unreal things were done – unreal because Charles would accept one thing after another which could not be maintained if he were to be ultimately successful – and yet most of these unreal things the ultimate victory of the Parliament rendered permanent in English life.

For instance, the lawyers insisted upon a clean sweep of everything which had hitherto challenged their claim to be the arbiters of justice. By all the traditions of England, and indeed of every other Christian country, the source of justice was not the Lawyers' Guild but the Government – that is, in England, the King. But on account of the growing complexity of the law the King had, as the Middle Ages advanced, to use the lawyers (even after they had formed themselves into a strong body with traditions of their own) as advisers in matters of dispute, and largely as the executive officers of his justice. However, not only had the principle that justice was not the monopoly of the lawyers been maintained, but it had been given very active and vigorous life in practice. The House of Lords was the highest Court in the kingdom below the King, and that meant, not a few lawyers deemed to be the House of Lords as it means now, by a fiction, but the actual collection of the Peers – laymen with no technical knowledge of the law. Then there was the Star Chamber, the most valuable institution for the maintenance of authority, especially against the great men who lived at a distance from Court and could be supported by armed retainers. It was signed away. There was the Council of the North, with a jurisdiction of its own; there was the Court of High Commission which dealt with Ecclesiastical affairs. Now, in this interregnum before actual hostilities began these two also were swept away, and the lawyers began to assume that complete monopoly of justice which has, by this time, endured for so long that people take it for granted, without considering its lack of moral basis.

It is significant that all this should have come after the death of Strafford; for his fine intellect had discovered and expressed in the clearest manner the peril which the future held of seeing the lawyers' organisation thus omnipotent, and his known hostility to their claims was no small part of the converging forces that brought him to the scaffold.

Later in the summer Charles grasped at the illusion that a certain reaction in his favour which was taking place in Scotland might be used. He went thither, but all to no purpose. He found nothing to his hand, and in the last arrangements there, which he had to accept, the

THE CRISIS

one solid result was that the lands of the dispossessed bishops should go to swell the fortunes of his enemies. He started back on the 18th of November, after entertaining the Scottish Estates with a show of friendship.

Meanwhile there had begun out in Ireland a serious rebellion, because the revolutionary party in England had succeeded in obtaining from the King the disbanding of the Irish army and there was no force with which to hold down the conquered people. It was a rebellion mismanaged and haphazard, sporadic fighting of the dispossessed against the new usurpers of their ancestral lands, numerous murders of the alien or half-alien oppressors, the deaths of many more who were driven out starving, the re-taking of the fields that within living memory had been their own and the restoration of the national religion. An attempt to carry Dublin failed but land was recovered and the national religion returned.

The rebellion and its cruelties had a prodigious echo in England. How many of the aliens in Ireland and their sympathisers were actually put to death or died of destitution during the troubles we do not know. Modern anti-Irish scholarship has been compelled to reduce the total to 5,000 at the most, but the wild rumours at the time in London talked of 100,000, 200,000 and even 300,000. The apologists for the excesses of the rising have argued that not 2,000, if as many, actually lost their lives – at any rate the thing only half recovered Ireland for the Irish; but it did intensely inflame such opinion as was already excited in England against the Royal House, and added to the numbers of those who were ready to take arms against it.

Nevertheless when Charles returned to his capital he was entertained with splendour by the City of London and cheered by the populace, to his great content (the 25th of November). These cheers only meant that those of the City who were with him took the streets for the occasion: those who were against him (and they were more numerous) would take the streets to demonstrate wildly on the other side as they had already done with such success in the immediate past, and the revolutionaries in Parliament were at it again with yet another of their documents – called this time "The Grand Remonstrance" and memorable for one phrase in which, alluding to the martyred, artistic and temperamental Elliot, it protested that his blood "called for vengeance." Now if his death was at anybody's door it was at the King's door and the meaning was obvious. This verbiage was memorable for the test it afforded of the true situation in the House of Commons. Warped history has represented the House as though it were unanimous, and even identical with the nation. They talked and talked upon it, and talked and talked for twelve hours, from the middle of the day to the middle of the night while Charles was on his way down from the north on the 22nd of November. But they only got a majority of eleven in a House of over 300 present, and the feeling on the Royalist side ran so high that swords were drawn and there was a worse tumult even than there had been all those years ago when the young King had got rid of his third Parliament in 1629. There was a desperate attempt by the insignificant majority to have the thing printed and distributed to the people, but though they still talked and talked on for three more hours till they were beaten by fatigue, nothing came of it.

All was in chaos. On New Year's Day, 1642, Charles actually approached that other King, Pym, with one last effort for compromise, offering him to be a sort of First Minister as Chancellor of the Exchequer. Whether Charles repented of that offer or whether Pym refused it is still uncertain.

In those same days, Charles, hearing some rumour that an attack was to be made upon the Queen, possibly by Impeachment, proposed in his turn to impeach the leaders, and Pym, whom he had approached but a few hours before, was among the five members of the Commons whom he selected for his vengeance.

The New Year was but four days old when after a long discussion in his palace whether the thing should be done or no, he went down to the House in person followed by a great number of his gentlemen and not a few soldiers under arms. It was a rambling, ill-arranged affair, which has become too famous because it was picturesque. It has come to be called "The Five Members."

It seems certain that the Queen in her indignation urged her husband to go. It is possible or probable that she used violent language in so urging him. It matters little. He went and failed. But if he had succeeded it would not have greatly changed the current of events, which were making in a strong and steady tide for war.

When he entered the Chamber, some few of those under arms followed while through the open doors the greater number outside

THE CRISIS

could easily be seen by the members. Within all rose to salute him and stood bare-headed. The speaker, a timid second-rate man called Lenthall whose appointment Charles had himself secured or admitted, thought it safer to tell his sovereign that he had no power save as the servant of the House – which constitutionally was nonsense. The King looked around him from where he sat and found that Pym and the four others (Hampden was one) were not in their places: and he said that the birds had flown. What was of some significance about this incident was that Pym had been given ample warning by the French Ambassador, and by that woman whose name has already been emphasised, the Queen's most intimate friend, Lucy Percy, Lady Carlisle.

As for the French Ambassador's action it was but a part of all French policy had been doing since the beginning of the troubles, since Richelieu had secretly sent money to help the covenanting rebellion in Scotland. But Lady Carlisle's action merits a special mention.

She was a woman who might well have been the pivot of the time and in some respects was so. Her delight was to feel that she had power and to exercise it, not so much on this side or on that as for the mere sake of its exercise. Her real passion was to be somebody, to feel that she had influenced men who were in the public eye.

Strafford had perhaps been her lover; at any rate he wrote with less than his usual wisdom of the "noble friendship" which she had deigned to extend to him. But then she had also extended (and she was no longer young) something more than a "noble friendship" to Pym, who was a hearty liver and "indifferent neither to Bacchus nor to Venus." He was possibly her lover, as perhaps Strafford had been.

At any rate her motive in sending Pym word to save him from the King's abortive attack was no other than her motive had been when, quite a short while before, she had betrayed to the Court the conversations Pym was holding with his friends in Chelsea.

It was not that she loved treason for its own sake and would exercise it impartially to the right and the left, but that she loved to feel she was in action and that what she did was of effect. She was certainly intelligent, she was certainly a forcible character – she was even called beautiful. Her portrait (a most living one) in Petworth House does not support that judgment in our modern view, but the standards of beauty differ so much from age to age that no one must dogmatise thereon. In circumstances happier for herself she might

211

have been the very centre of all things: as it was she was not that, but she could at least say that she played a part, and she lived on to play a part in great and small matters one after another for many years. Nor did she lose the friendship of Henrietta Maria. After all what is of the greatest significance about her action and her position is that it fully illustrates the wire-pulling and confusion of this interregnum – this gap of nothingness between the last remnants of regular government and the open appeal to arms.

At the end of that same week, on Saturday, the 9th of January, 1642, Charles thought it no longer safe to leave his wife and children in London. He left his capital for Hampton Court, and he only returned to it seven years later to die by the axe.

There was as yet no open conflict. Towards the end of February (on the 23rd of the month) the King saw his wife off from Dover; she sailed for Holland, whence she might expect aid sooner or later, for her little daughter Mary was legally the wife to the young Prince of Orange, though as yet still a child.

Parliament prepared a militia bill to give them control of the popular forces – a thing which could not become law because the King's assent to *that* would have been abdication and the putting of immediate full force into the hands of his enemies. The thing, therefore, though making much talk, meant in reality nothing. The fighting that was to come would be carried on with such forces as each party could levy through its own strength according to the districts which it controlled and the local magnates who might take sides with it. But the Parliament had not seized the person of the Prince, Charles, a lad now twelve years old. His father after seeing the Queen off, picked him up at Greenwich on his way to the north, and felt some content, some slight mood of half security, in having his heir at his side.

The essential for either party in the coming struggle was to seize the ports, as also to be possessed of the fleet. Therefore the first overt act of usurpation on the part of the rebels was the seizure of a port.

The walled town of Kingston-upon-Hull, capable of standing a siege, stands upon the estuary of the Humber and is therefore the gateway of all sea-borne traffic into the waterways of Yorkshire and the Midlands; it had an arsenal with plenty of munitions and guns. There was in the Parliament one Sir John Hotham, a big squire like most of them and a Yorkshireman whose lands lay in the vicinity of

THE CRISIS

Hull. He was not very keen for the rebellion, but he had like many Yorkshiremen a personal hatred of his fellow-Yorkshireman Strafford, the richest of them all. He had a son who was much keener on the rebellion than himself. Seeing that his attitude on the Strafford matter had put him hitherto on the revolutionary side the Parliament sent this man up to Hull on the very day after Charles had left London for Hampton Court; but as they mistrusted him they sent his son with him as a sort of spy upon his actions. He had instructions to hold Hull for the rebellion against the King. From that action of the 11th of January, 1642, may properly be dated the first overt act of the war.

Charles out of London breathed a better air; in most places he would find loyalty – especially among the common people – and a very large proportion of the landed gentry as well, divided though they were, would actually serve him; nearly all would treat him with full respect. He began going northwards by Newmarket until he reached York on the 24th of March, and he had about him a bodyguard of gentlemen.

Meanwhile the head of the great family of Percy, Northumberland, whom Charles had made Admiral of the Fleet, committed treason. The first step was for the Parliament to ask him to name as his deputy in command over the ships Lord Warwick, who was not only thoroughly in sympathy with the rebellion but an active Puritan. This deputy was in closest touch with the command, and through him Northumberland handed over the armed vessels to the revolutionaries. It was a defection of capital importance. The rebels could now command the sea, and while keeping commerce open to themselves, hamper it for the King and especially interfere with the landing of imports for him.

Not long after his arrival at York Charles, in April, proposed to test the point of Hull.

He sent his nephew and the young Prince, the Duke of York being only eleven years old, in to dine with Hotham, who received them with due ceremony, but when he himself appeared on the 23rd of April before Hull and demanded admission, it was refused. Charles had not the force wherewith to take it: he retired. He was raising troops by commissions sent out to private gentlemen and met also by voluntary offers. On the 11th of July such few peers as had made up their minds to stand by the Rebellion, and the much larger proportion of the House of Commons which was now fixed in the same intention declared the King to have been guilty of the first act of war, because he had begun raising troops. It was a falsehood, they had begun the war. It was but part of that propaganda which continued uninterruptedly now throughout the period of hostilities.

The rebel government in London sent word to Colonel Goring who was in command of the fortified town of Portsmouth, its harbour and arsenal, telling him that they had raised him to the rank of Lieutenant-General, and requiring him to acknowledge their authority. He answered that he could not do this without the King's leave, as he had been commissioned by the King. They replied by sending Lord Essex, whom they had made their General, down to besiege the town and port. And the discharges fired in that siege were the first shots of the Civil War.

On the 2nd of August the King proclaimed Essex and those with him traitors unless they would return to their duty within a specified time. A week later, on the 9th of August, Parliament countered by asserting their right to use such methods and to appoint such a General.

On the 12th, three days later, Charles summoned the gentry of the north and for twenty miles south of Trent to rally to him at Nottingham. And there, ten days later, on a cold grey day with a gale blowing he set up his standard in a big field south of the town, having about him as yet no more than 2,000 men. The gale was from the north and that night his flag was blown down: an omen.

By the time the news of all this reached London Parliament was prepared to move in full force in its turn, and Essex set out by the North Road. By the 16th of September he had concentrated at Northampton and had under his orders altogether some 20,000 men. Charles by that time had prepared 6,000, but he was marching westward with them towards the Welsh Marches – where he knew that most people were on his side and would treble his numbers. He made straight for Shrewsbury. Essex, believing that the King intended to operate on the line of the Severn, marched westward also from Northampton. He left garrisons as he went to hold various posts, particularly Warwick, and reached the Severn at Worcester. The war had fairly begun.

Trial of King Charles I in Westminster Hall
From "True Copy of the Journal of the High Court of Justice for the Tryal of King Charles I," Nelson, 1684

THE GREAT REBELLION

WHAT WERE THE CHANCES OF THE TWO FORCES NOW IN action? As a purely military problem, the chances were heavily in favour of the Rebellion, and this was especially apparent in those material things which can be exactly estimated and measured.

The moral factors were almost evenly balanced. Monarchy still had a high prestige; the King's person was still sacred in the eyes of nearly all men, rebels or loyal; Royal authority was still the air of the time. Even those who were in arms against Charles hesitated to deny some great part of his claims; he was still their King. They had not yet suggested his deposition nor, most of them, more than what they pretended to be a return to their legal rights – which they said he had violated.

Moreover, the King's attitude was unequivocal. A King was a King: he had a right to govern: rebellion against him was treason – that had been a thing taken for granted throughout the whole story of England, while the position of those who led the Rebellion was ambiguous, they were not united in their programme and they varied in the degree to which they would push their claims.

Again, that amputated body which still called itself "Parliament" was not even a Parliament. Of the Peers only a remnant remained; of the Commons more than a third had either absented themselves or openly joined the Royalist Party. And those numbers tended to grow. Soon hardly half the Commons would be left sitting, and of those who were left sitting at Westminster, a certain fluctuating proportion, secretly disapproved, in their varying degrees, of the Rebellion. It was one thing to have talked, it was another thing to have taken up arms – and a risky thing. For the word "treason" had a sort of horrid magic then as the word "murder" has today. Moreover, when it came to fighting the mass of the common people would naturally think their

THE GREAT REBELLION

King to be in the right and rebels against him to be in the wrong; for the simple and immemorial traditions of the populace still held to the sacramental doctrine of kingship.

On the other hand, the moral forces supporting the Rebellion were also great. The mercantile classes furnished a large proportion of the Puritans, especially in the seaport towns, including London. The memory of the novel taxation imposed by the King still rankled, though in the long run it would be forgotten under the far more oppressive levies necessary for the Rebellion to be carried on. Again, the authority of the King had been weakened by his perpetual failures; by his breakdown in Scotland and after that by the Scottish invasion; by his necessary but humiliating concessions to his opponents, by the fact that he was supported throughout by the large Catholic body, which the much larger Protestant numbers of the nation now hated.

Moreover, great violence of feeling (that which its opponents call fanaticism) though it usually applies only to a fraction of any large body of men, is a driving force of high potential. There was plenty of fanaticism on the side of the Rebellion, especially among its leaders; there was no corresponding fanaticism on the side of the King.

The great moral handicap against Charles was that nearly all the landed men of England, not only the great men but the mass of small freeholders – feared a return to the full kingly power of the immediate past. It was connected in their minds with the new, unaccustomed economic burden. This feeling lost the King the wholehearted support of numerous land owners, even among those who followed him. A test case was that of Southampton. He is only one of many, but he is a perfect example. He thought it expected of him to support the Crown when it came to actual fighting, but his heart was the other way, and he admitted it. He was the head of a new family which had become immensely wealthy, principally through the ecclesiastical lands filched at the Reformation, and all his traditions came from that fact. One section of the landowners did wholeheartedly support Charles, the Catholic section. The greatest example of these was the Marquess of Worcester, who handed over his whole revenue to the Royal cause – and he was one of the wealthiest men in England. Save for such support Charles would have had hardly any money to carry on with in the early part of the war.

CHARLES I

So much for the moral forces. But when we consider the measurable forces geographical, of armament and financial, we see how strong were the odds in favour of the Rebellion.

There were four main factors in this superiority.

In the first place that rebel body which called itself the Parliament held most of the ports of any consequence in the kingdom. They had Hull, they had Portsmouth, Plymouth, Bristol (at first), Gloucester at the head of the sea-way of the Severn, and above all they had London which, as a port for receiving supplies and for providing money by trade counted as much as all the rest put together three times over.

Secondly, to make the holding of these ports worthwhile, they had the Navy, and this possession of the Navy (which they owed to the treason of Northumberland earlier in the year) cut both ways. Negatively it prevented the King from getting supplies from overseas; positively it enabled the Rebels to get supplies from overseas themselves. It should further be noted that the ports thus held were those best suited for communication and supply from the neighbouring lands; from Plymouth all the way round to the mouth of the Humber they faced the Continent and its trade. The King held Chester and this gave him a port in communication with Ireland; certain lesser places in the north could also be precariously used, but the great ports of value and best placed for the receipt of material from abroad were all held in opposition to the King.

Thirdly, the Parliament had what the King most conspicuously lacked, a sufficient and regular supply of money. Now that was capital. The armies, though later they were recruited on both sides with pressed men, required pay if they were to be kept from mutiny and wholesale desertion; apart from that (and much more expensive) they required supplies of arms, munitions, food – everything. The Parliament had all the machinery of taxation in its hands and was master of much the richest taxable area – the capital itself – and the fertile lands of the south and east.

But far the most important Point, summing up sea power and money and strategical advantage and all, was the possession of London.

Throughout English history, throughout the whole record of 2,000 years, London – until it ceased in the late nineteenth century to

THE GREAT REBELLION

be a unit – has turned the tide. It has been far more important to the political story of England than has Paris to that of France. Its great size had always made it impossible to seize by a surprise, and equally impossible to secure by a siege. London was the nodal point upon which all the great roads converged from the south and north upon the first crossing of the Thames. It possessed accumulated wealth, vast compared with any other centre of that time. The chief money-dealers were there, and the Customs, with the regular organization for their continuous gathering. And also in London was the equipment of all the machinery for action of every kind, printing and publishing, concentrating the service of messages – and for *recruitment*.

London alone of any district possessed a military force of some efficiency, "The Trained Bands." They were, of course, only a militia, but their organisation existed. Lastly, London, from its geographical position apart from its being a nodal point, was an invaluable asset to the side which held it in any war.

The eastern counties all lay in its grip both north and south of the Thames, and the west also to within a radius of a long day's march from its gates – say, twenty miles. In all that large and wealthy sector of England that which hold London could do what it willed. Further, with such a place behind them a force leaving London had supply all during the beginning of its advance.

When we say that the Parliament and the Rebellion "held" London, the word "held" must be taken literally. London was not unanimous for the Rebellion – far from it. Mobs had easily been raised against the King during the late troubles preparatory to the war but then mobs had also been raised on occasion to cheer the King. Most of the great merchants had been heart and soul with the resistance to Charles's new imposts but no such proportion of them were enthusiastic for the risks and expense of war.

On the other hand, all London was very enthusiastic for preventing the loot of the town, or even an attack on it – it was a tempting object to plunder, had that been possible, and all but the very humblest citizens were here touched in a vital point. Now as the Royalist Operations could only mean, for London, an attack on London, this feeling was a great asset to the Parliamentary Party; and I think it may be said that the war was lost to Charles principally through that source. We shall see it at work in the first days of the active operations.

CHARLES I

The forces being thus balanced, with the scales heavily loaded on the Parliamentary side, there did remain for the King one brief opportunity for success. If he could win a decisive action early in the operations, and having won it, advance directly on the capital, with a proposal ready for some compromise, backed by a conquering army, fresh from the field, but not threatening the security of the citizens or their property, he might have re-established himself: not as a monarch such as he had been, but with a sufficient authority which might increase with time. That decisive victory he did not win; that effect on London he was therefore unable to produce.

From Shrewsbury Charles began a direct march southward and eastward, making towards Oxford and the Thames valley, so as to approach the capital with a sufficient body of men in arms. Essex, who was a thoroughly bad general, slow, timid, and with no heart for soldiering, might have intercepted him: he delayed too long, he allowed the Royalist army to pass right in front of his advance, and by the time he was aware of his errors and tried to put on more pace Charles's army was already to the south of him. It had arrived at the end of the third week of October south of the region of Warwick and lay around Arlescot when Essex had only come up to Kineton, four miles behind the King; the date being Saturday, the 22nd of October, 1642, the weather cool and a strong wind rising from the north.

There lay between the two armies a certain formation aptly termed Edgehill. It is rather the edge of a plateau than a hill, the higher land suddenly falling down in a declivity which faces the north. Essex's advanced body lay in the lower country north of this declivity, Charles in the higher country to the south of it.

The King could not pursue his march with the enemy force so near lest he should be caught in column of route; moreover, it would be to his advantage to run and fight because he had the superior numbers. When hostilities had begun Essex had commanded 20,000 men to the King's 16,000 in the field – apart from garrisons. But Essex had depleted his force by leaving bodies of men who guarded the towns through which he passed, a political necessity to the rebellion especially in the west and the Midlands where the people were mainly with the King: and his organisation and his marching power were bad. His rearguard under Hampden was a day's march behind him when

THE GREAT REBELLION

he arrived at Kineton on this Saturday, the 22nd of October. The men he had with him and could actually put into line were perhaps not more than two thirds of those the King had with him.

The marshalling was slow on both sides during the morning of Sunday, the 23rd, when, under the increasing northerly gale, the King drew up his command with cavalry on either wing (under the accepted rule of the time) and the infantry in the centre. They stood on the first slope to get the advantage of the ground, and Essex's command was similarly drawn up at the foot of the hill or rather a little north of the foot, in the lower land. Charles had the advantage of having with him his nephew Rupert, the third son of his sister, the Queen of Bohemia, the widow of the Elector Palatine whom the King of England had so constantly and so unsuccessfully tried to reinstate. Rupert was a young man of twenty-three, most able all round, intelligent, courageous and a leader who understood military affairs well enough for his age. He had been put at the head of the cavalry and therefore on that day commanded the right wing.

Both the Royalist wings charged, bodies of horse sweeping the plain on the right and on the left. That on the right under the command of Rupert had a complete success; it drove the Parliamentary horse before it, using the tactic of mere shock, which was the main tactic of the time, though Gustavus Adolphus had already given the example of the newer method which Cromwell was to adopt so successfully and later to develop. He got right into Kineton village where Essex's baggage was, and lost time, as cavalry always did lose time after these main charges, in halting to recover formation for the return. There was also a pillaging of the baggage which caused further delay – save for that, there would have been a decision. But when Rupert returned to the field he found not only the infantry of the two centres engaged but that of Essex obtaining some advantage. The King's standard had been captured and the bearers, among them Verney (one of the trimmers, by the way), killed, though the standard was recaptured again. Charles himself, near the standard, had narrowly escaped death from a cannon ball.

The action had not begun before one o'clock, and in the end of October on a stormy day it is getting dark after five. The lines were still confused when the gathering dusk put an end to further opera-

221

tions and either body fell back with the issue still undecided. Next day, after a night particularly cold and dreadful for the wounded who still lay out in the open, the King resumed his march southward.

At this point comes one of the critical discussions of the Civil War: Rupert suggested the sending of an advance body at once, strong in cavalry, to London. The distance could be covered by good troops in five days, and, even by such ill-trained men as were present at Edgehill, in a week. Moreover, Essex had proved himself a bad organiser and unable to get good marching out of his men, he was to show the same disabilities the next year in the march on Gloucester. The dash on London could certainly have been made – but having been made, would it have been successful?

It is doubtful. And the decision went against Rupert's idea. One can almost say that the issue was not doubtful at all, save that in war pretty well anything may happen. The City in its terror of being looted organised a defence. The streets were narrow; chains were stretched to prevent charges down them, and there was still a large half-trained militia remaining within the walls, although many of them had been drafted to fight with Essex.

And now it was the fact that, by all normal calculation, London could not be taken which determined the war.

If Edgehill had been a decision in favour of Charles it would have been another matter: the victory might have moved the fluctuating terrors and passions of London to a tide of opinion which would have mastered the Revolutionaries and compounded with the King – but Edgehill had been a drawn fight. Since it was believed in Charles's camp that an attack on London was impossible, the approach of the Royal army towards the capital was not strategic, but political, and that is what explains its extreme slowness. They might have got near London in a week of easy marching; it was nearly three weeks before the King, after occupying Banbury and setting up his quarters at Oxford and leaving a garrison in Reading, came with his forces to Colnbrook.

There he came not to fight but to treat for peace. In the second week of November the negotiations began between him and the Commissioners of the Parliament. Though the conditions were those of truce the Parliamentarians or someone on their side moved on to Brentford and occupied it, and indignation against this breach of an

THE GREAT REBELLION

implied understanding led on the 13th of November to a Royalist attack on Brentford, which was carried with fifteen cannon and 1,500 prisoners and many of the Parliamentarians drowned in the river.

On the next day, the 14th of November, Essex, who had some time before arrived in London by a march parallel to, and north of, the King's, was at the head of 24,000 men, mainly drawn from the City itself. They stood in order on Turnham Green, and Charles had nothing adequate with which to meet them.

Negotiations for peace dragged on, with the venue changed to Oxford, which was now to become the King's headquarters, but the Parliament knew that London was no longer in fear and were determined against any understanding; so the whole thing was broken off by April, 1643. Pym knew well enough that the King was in a bad way for ammunition, while *his* party and troops could get all they wanted with time. Still, the negotiations for peace had had one effect, which was to create a strong undercurrent of discontent among those who overtly supported the revolutionary cause, and Waller the poet was intriguing. But Pym was too much for them, and the usual absurd propaganda, which is of such value when men are under the influence either of enthusiasm for a cause or of terror, was used. The Londoners were told of Waller's intrigue, told there was a plot, Charles's plot, a Papist plot; that they were fighting a Papist army and a Papist King – and all the rest of it. In the executions which followed in the summer (and we must remember that the Revolutionaries always kept up a certain measure of terror) Waller saved his life; by submission it is said, more probably by an understanding that he would act in future as an informer for Pym.

Meanwhile Henrietta Maria, the Queen, had shown heroism. She was still a woman in the prime of life, she was barely thirty-three; but her health was not what it had been; she had great difficulty in child-bearing and the frequent birth of children had worn her down. Nevertheless she had worked with feverish industry for the King in the Low Countries, raising money on the jewels, buying munitions and guns. In the middle of the February past, while the negotiations were going on she had crossed in a bad storm, landed at Bridlington, just escaped the rebel fleet, which fired on the houses in which she and her company had taken refuge.

She was received in York, helped Newcastle with part of what she had brought, and then went on to meet her husband in the

CHARLES I

Midlands and found him on the 13th of July, 1643, upon the very battlefield of Edgehill, at Kineton. The trouble about ammunition was over, she had sent plenty on before her, guns and stores also; and in that same month, a fortnight after the King and Queen had met, Rupert carried Bristol by assault.

It was a main success for the Royal cause, though there still remained Gloucester (to which sea-borne traffic could reach) in the hands of the Rebellion. Waller, the General, who since his success at Portsmouth and one or two other places bore an exaggerated reputation, was destroyed in the west, the army of Essex went to pieces. London was again alarmed for what might follow, earthworks were thrown round it, there was again a movement for peace: and again the enthusiasm for war was roused principally by the Puritan preachers.

It was a difficult moment for the Rebellion, although looking back on it now we can clearly see that after the failure to obtain a decision at Edgehill the King's chances were diminishing. Charles could be precariously reinforced, as he had been by the courage and energy of his wife, but he had not (as is opponents had) a source of permanent supply, a hold on the ports of the country and the command of the sea. And above all, he lacked money.

It is interesting to note, seeing how often the words "The Nation" and "The People" are used as equivalent of the Revolutionary party, to what Parliament had shrunk. The largest musters it could make in the Commons would prove (as we shall see in the next year) to be much less than half its total numbers – only 220 all told – and while the negotiations for peace at Oxford were in hand the gathering was still smaller.

The figures of three interesting divisions at that time are illuminating. In the first vote on the peace proposals there were, out of a theoretical total of well over 500 (the full muster of the Commons) less than 160; and of these 94 voted for peace and only 65 against. The leaders of the Rebellion worked hard, however, and on another division there seemed to be but a narrow majority for peace, 81 to 79; and when a recount was demanded the there was a majority of eight (89 to 81) for continuing the war. Of the judges only three consented to serve the Revolution. But for that matter the Revolutionaries were prepared to treat as a criminal any judge who had given a decision against their claims. They were actually persecuting those who had affirmed the legality of ship-money.

THE GREAT REBELLION

The total muster of this last and critical vote in the Commons was, then, only 170. The Lords were no more than a ridiculous remnant. There were fourteen of them in the days when that vote was taken, and of these fourteen, seven went off in disgust, Northumberland at their head. So doubtful did the situation seem that Essex threatened to fall out, and was only brought back to what was now his fragment of an army (it had shrunk to less than 3,000 men) by the skilful flattery of Pym.

But the real situation was not either that which the fears of London or the hopes of Oxford made it out to be.

There had been in the minds of the King's commanders, and particularly of Rupert's, another of those grandiose plans of convergence, such as that which had failed years before in the beginning of the Scottish troubles. It is strange how much the men of that time went in for "war by the map," seeing what imperfect things maps then were, and synchrony even more difficult to attain than it is today.

The idea had been that Newcastle from the north and the King's army should advance together, the one southward and the other eastward towards London, with a central body advancing in between them and supporting either as was necessary, until there was a concentration present in front of the capital. Some even thought it possible so to seize the banks of the Thames below the Pool as to starve those who held the City into surrender.

The whole thing was moonshine. There were neither the numbers nor the munitionment nor the capacity in any form for action on that scale. On both sides armies tended to melt away, on both sides there was necessarily a mass of sporadic fighting and small dispersed garrisons; and, on the King's side especially, men soon grew tired of the marching far from their homes. They could get neither the Yorkshiremen nor the men of the West Country to go far or stay long. What *was* possible (and also important) was the capture of Gloucester, the one serious point held by the Rebellion in the Severn valley, where it destroyed the homogeneity of the King's hold on the West.

Siege was laid by the Royalist army to Gloucester on the 10th of August, 1643, and had it been possible to carry the town as Bristol had been carried it might have made some change; but Massey, the Parliamentary commander in Gloucester, held out skilfully with quite a small garrison, not much more than a thousand effective men. An

CHARLES I

new army was raised for Essex by the Revolutionary Government and it started from his camp (one march out from London to the west) on the sixteenth day of the siege, the 26th of August.

I know not why this march to Gloucester should have been represented as anything of a feat. It was the height of summer, Essex covered only a hundred miles of main road, and yet he did not appear in front of the town until the 5th of September – in other words, he covered less than ten miles a day. However, when he did come up, Massey still resisting, Essex's force far outnumbered the besiegers and the siege was raised. It was a serious setback for the Royal cause. As this army marched back towards London the King's army proposed to intercept it, came down south to Newbury, and the advantage of position and effective numbers was on that occasion (three weeks after the raising of the siege) with the Royal forces. The Parliamentary army was badly off for supplies and caught with the enemy between it and its objective, London. If the Royal army had stood on the defensive and the Parliamentary army had been left to attack it would have been defeated and perhaps destroyed.

But the Royal army did not stand on the defensive; therefore the day was undecided, and on the morrow the forces of the Rebellion could resume their march to London. The King's army had nothing to do but go back whence it had come.

Time was now the real anxiety of Pym and his colleagues. They may or may not have seen that, as a purely military problem, all was in their favour; but hostilities were now well on into their second year, the cost was very great, murmurs against the new heavy taxation began to grow loud, and a quick end might be made to the whole thing by an alliance with the Scotch.

Now alliance with the Scotch, as everyone had proved to their cost in the last few tumultuous years, was not an easy matter. There would be hard bargaining and extravagant political demands as well as financial. The Kirk was willing enough to march once more against the hosts of Baal; the torrents of the Old Testament metaphor were ready to be poured out again and Scotland (or at any rate the great Covenanting part of it, which by this time was hardly indistinguishable in its own imagination from Israel) would serve the Lord with the more zeal from its memories of success in the North of England those few years ago.

THE GREAT REBELLION

But what about the money? Well, those who followed Pym were ready to promise anything, a tribute was to be paid the Scotch of £1,000 a day and £100,000 down for equipment. But apart from money, there was Godliness. Would the English revolutionaries bring themselves into the Covenant? Would they make war not only for the reduction of the Man of Blood, but for that reasonable and practical scheme, the imposition of Presbyterianism upon all the Irish, and of course all the English too? The English negotiators worked the thing skilfully enough; they cozened their enthusiastic brethren into accepting an ambiguous phrase; if only the Scotch would send a large force south in aid of the Saints the religion of England should be established "on the model of the best Reformed Churches," and the Kirk, knowing itself to be the best reformed Church, doubtfully accepted, though the conscription for the army (which to the honour of the Scottish nation was vigorous and widespread) was only got fairly under way when the first 60,000 honest English pounds had rung upon the counter.

On the 16th of January, 1644, the Scottish army crossed the Tweed.

Two other things were happening in this beginning of the New Year, while the face of the War was thus being changed by the new Scottish invasion. The King had brought over a force from Ireland; it had got as far as Nantwich, but was there held up by the defences of the town; and he had called a Parliament at Oxford.

The figures are significant. Of the Commons who appeared from first to last the total was 175; of the Peers 83, while the Rebellious fraction of Parliament in London could count of Commons all told but 220 and of Peers (of every shade of opinion) but 22. Nor could the Peers have numbered as much had not the seven who had left in disgust with Northumberland at their head been repelled by the King – rightly enough, with such a name to lead them, the man who had betrayed the fleet. The gathering at Oxford did little. It is interesting chiefly on account of these numbers, which give some index to the pretension of the Rebellion that it alone stood for Parliament, nay, for "the English People" – which even at its best Parliament could hardly be said to represent.

It was in these days also that Charles said good-bye to his wife forever, though neither knew it was forever. It was in the late summer of the year before that they had met again after her heroic journey from overseas. She was now with child and a few weeks only from her time. She was in occasional agonies of rheumatism and would try Bath for a cure – a difficult attempt for her.

Charles went with her as far as Abingdon, and there, on the 3rd of April, said good-bye. What follows helps us to understand her own courage and the passion which then divided England. She took refuge in Exeter just before it was besieged. Thither came the Royal physician, Mayerne – but he so hated her religion that he could not forbear from insult.

There in Exeter she bore her last child with great suffering, in June; a few days later the siege began. She appealed to Essex, who commanded the enemy forces, to let her pass through the lines. He answered by telling her that he would take her to London, that is, to her death. She escaped, lay concealed without food for two days in the countryside and was off to France in a Dutch boat in Plymouth Sound – all this within the fortnight after the baby's birth.

But to return to the war:—

With the Scottish army now in the north, as the fighting season approached, Newcastle and his tired local force were in peril. They were grievously outnumbered. By April the Revolutionaries under Fairfax and their Scottish allies were besieging York. Later Manchester, one of the tiny remnant of the Parliamentary Lords, would be coming up with a further reinforcement for the besiegers of 14,000 men. York must at all costs be relieved; the son of Fairfax had not only defeated the Irish but captured many and incorporated them with his own forces and come and joined his father. With the advance of the summer York might fall, and Rupert was given orders to save it at all costs.

He gathered every man available for the field in the army under his command and marched across the Pennines. Allied Scottish and Revolutionary armies thought to intercept him. He evaded them and effected his junction with Newcastle's command.

This was on Monday, the 1st of July, 1644, during which the Scotch and Parliamentarians, from 24,000 to 25,000 strong, raised the siege and moved somewhat to the south, but left a rearguard to watch the next movements. On the morrow, Tuesday, the 2nd of July, the combined Royal forces, 19,000 strong, marched out westward and

THE GREAT REBELLION

deployed on the open expanse of Marston Moor, between the town of York and the river Nidd. The main enemy army then turned back north to use the advantage of its superior numbers against Rupert and Newcastle, but they were not fully deployed till late, and as it was six o'clock before any attack was made Rupert thought the action was being postponed till the next day.

When it was past six o'clock and the sun already within two hours of its setting Rupert, on the Royalist right, dismounted and ordered supper, taking it for granted that nothing would be done that day. It was perhaps the seeing of this relaxation on the Royalist side which led to what followed.

No battle in the Civil Wars (nor indeed in all the course of English history since the Conquest) is more difficult to follow than Marston Moor, for the simple reason that the contemporary accounts which have come down to us are all at sixes and sevens. One uses the word "right" when the other uses the word "left." The most careful of all modern historians and the man who is at the foundation of all modern political history, Lingard, has it certainly all wrong; and no one can give a picture of it which is, even in the main outline, certainly right.† The nearest one can get to it would seem to be this:—

Each line was set out (as the tactical necessities of the day demanded) with the cavalry on either wing and the infantry in the centre. Rupert, as being the senior in command was at the head of the Royalist cavalry, on the right wing – that is the western end of the Royalist line, and perhaps, at first, in the second rank, behind. Newcastle was at the extreme end of the left wing. Facing Rupert at the head of the allied cavalry on *their* left (that is the western end) was the command of a very remarkable man only lately promoted, though he was the cousin of John Hampden and had sat in both the revolutionary Parliaments, the Short and the Long. This man was Oliver Cromwell, second-in-command of the rebel cavalry. The reader has remarked his attention to the King of Heaven, his indifference to the Kings of this world, on an earlier page. He had risen rapidly to this high command in the Parliamentary cavalry. He was now, on Marston Moor, to enter quite suddenly into great fame. We must pause before the battle to consider him, who he was and why he was there.

---

† Much the best detailed analysis, based on a contemporary map, is that published by Firth in 1908, in the *Transactions of the Royal Historical Society*, New Series, Vol. XII.

CHARLES I

The real name of Oliver Cromwell's family was not Cromwell at all, but Ap-Williams; and in those days, when the assumption of false names was not the matter of course which it is today, they still remained legally Williams, though in their own style and that given them by their neighbours they were called Cromwell.

They were a typical example of the way in which the religious revolution of the previous century had suddenly raised men of the lowest social position into millionaires. It had happened thus:—

In the years just preceding the Reformation the Welshman Ap-Williams had a public house in Putney, and a neighbour of his, by name Cromwell, another public house not far off. Cromwell's *daughter* married Ap-Williams's son. Cromwell's *son* Thomas, the brother of Mrs. Williams, disappeared into a vagrant life. Young Williams and his wife had a boy called Henry, of whom in early youth we hear nothing, because there is nothing to hear. Thomas Cromwell came to have astonishing adventures on the Continent, serving on one occasion at least as a soldier, getting into the employment of money-lenders and himself learning their trade. He became a usurer, amassed wealth, and showed – apart from the base calling he followed – an ability and exactitude which brought him to the notice of Cardinal Wolsey. The Cardinal used him in negotiations for the transference of certain monastic endowments to his new college at Oxford – which is today Christchurch. Cromwell is found for a time astraddle between Wolsey's business and the King's; on Wolsey's fall we find him as a useful and trusted employee of that impulsive man, Henry VIII, just at the moment when he was being driven by what he later called the "witchcraft" of Anne Boleyn into the repudiation of his wife, a marriage with his mistress and the assumption to himself of what had been the Papal power in England, and the spoliation to the profit of his Treasury of the monasteries and all their wealth.

In that last business Thomas Cromwell was supreme. It was he who worked it all, ruthlessly and with his high powers of organisation: he acted as Henry's vice-gerent over the Church of England, he was given a peerage under the title of Essex† – he was the chief man in the kingdom.

---

† Nothing to do with the Earl of Essex in Elizabeth's reign or his son, the general in the wars here described.

THE GREAT REBELLION

Of the monastic wealth he took care to appropriate much to himself, but he also remembered his obscure relations, and particularly his nephew Henry. He sent for this nephew and loaded him with gifts.

Before the affair was over young Henry Williams was possessed of no less than thirteen monastic estates; and formed one of the new rich men created by this sudden economic change.

Thomas Cromwell fell from favour and was put to death, but young Henry Williams with his newly acquired wealth was left unharmed in the possession of his new great fortune. Because his uncle had had such fame and been the first man in the land he thought it convenient to assume in public his uncle's name, at first perhaps tentatively, but by the time of his son, regularly: though the name Williams remained for legal purposes.

The grandson of this Henry Williams (*alias* Cromwell), still in enjoyment of immense wealth, though much had been spent in display, had two sons and a daughter: an elder son, whose principal residence out of so many separate estates had been built from the spoils of the nunnery of Hinchingbrook, just outside Huntingdon; and a younger son who lived in a sort of dower house belonging to the family just in the town at the park gates. There, under the shadow of the great house and as part of the family, this younger son's boy Oliver grew up, familiar under his own roof with an income which we should call today only a few thousands a year, but with all the atmosphere of much greater wealth in his uncle's family close by, with which he naturally mingled.

This lad Oliver, inheriting his father's younger son's portion, had increased it somewhat by trade, and had sat after the fashion of these great territorials in the House of Commons in Charles's Parliament of 1628 (being then just under thirty) for the locality which his great family overshadowed, as member for Huntingdon.† He was silent, and not much remarked. His name was for the first time, though not widely, noted among those country gentlemen, and there among them he had found his close relation John Hampden, a first cousin; for Hampden's mother was the sister of Oliver's father.

---

† Hinchingbrook had been sold the year before but the family influence of the great Cromwell family was still supreme in the town.

CHARLES I

He was not an effective speaker, to begin with at any rate; he had been given the rank of Captain when the armies of the Rebellion were first raised, and very soon was allowed to raise a regiment in his own part of the country and became, therefore, a Colonel. Though he was over forty and had not suspected himself of any military talent he discovered in himself, and others began to discover in him, a singular capacity for the training and leadership of a mounted force. The cavalry unit which he formed became a model one; he had repeated successes with it in skirmishes which drew attention to him and he had been promoted continually till we see him now, on this decisive day, in command of the Parliamentary left at Marston Moor with the rank of Lieutenant-General. He it was who charged Rupert so late on that afternoon, with barely more than two hours of daylight to spare, while the rest of the opposing lines clashed to his right.

Now let this first be noted, Cromwell's charge against Rupert at the extreme western end of the line was not after the model of the great cavalry charges which Rupert himself delivered with such success – the method which as yet only one commander in Europe had abandoned. It was not the delivery of the maximum shock, intended to sweep away the opponents in front and carry them with its momentum a mile or two miles from the field. It seems to have been delivered (so far as we can judge) at a not very fast trot, and to have engaged the opposing cavalry perhaps while it was forming, but at any rate before it had attacked. The thing therefore began with a mêlée or at any rate with the two lines entangled.

It hung doubtful, Cromwell's men had to be disentangled by the help of some Scottish horse and he himself was slightly wounded. But though the numbers were more equal in this part of the field than elsewhere, Cromwell was to triumph, for he had conceived, or copied from the Swedes, a tactic which he was everywhere to carry to success and to which he owed, with other qualities, the career that put him ultimately at the head of the State.

Rupert's men were thrust back and partly dispersed; but while Cromwell was thus weighing on the Royalist horse, pushing further and further from its original line, shouldering them as it were off the field, breaking their cohesion and diminishing their numbers all the time, the Royalist centre and left had already won a victory. The horse

THE GREAT REBELLION

on that allied right had given way, the Royalist left had pursued it, while, in the centre, the Royalist infantry was having its will with the broken, scattered, and (in places) now flying ranks of the Parliamentary and Scottish foot.

Manchester himself fled, or if the word "fled" be thought too violent, "retired," under the certitude that the day had gone against him.

It was at this moment that Cromwell, having done his work against Rupert's horse, and keeping his own command fully in hand, leaving some portion of it to occupy the opponent immediately in front of him, brought his new tactic into play. He detached a portion of his men to hold or pursue Rupert's broken men, but the remainder he checked and reined up. With these he suddenly wheeled round to his right and this time charged home, striking full upon the flank of the victorious Royalist infantry in the centre.

Struck thus unexpectedly in the flank, they could do nothing against the horse; their front was heavily engaged by the enemy foot, their flank was open and unprepared. It was immediately pierced, and pierced with a mortal wound. The defeated army of the Rebellion, with its Scottish allies, was given a breathing space and began to rally, Cromwell's horse was not only into, but behind, Newcastle's men – and in that last half-hour when night was falling the organisation of the Royal army disappeared.

Its fragments were gathered together in the darkness and their retreat secured; but of the 19,000 men which Rupert and Newcastle had marshalled on that day against the opposing 25,000; 1,500 were prisoners, all the artillery was taken, and the greater part of the dead buried after the action (4,150) were of the Royalist side, with some unknown much greater number wounded.

Here at last and for the first time in the story of these wars was a decision. The north was lost to Charles, and (as the quicker minds began to surmise) the whole war was lost as well. That Tuesday evening had settled the affair; it would linger on, but the turning point had been passed.

THE TRIUMPH OF THE GREAT REBELLION

AFTER MARSTON MOOR THE WAR FALLS INTO THAT LAST PHASE which you discover in the stories of nearly all armed conflicts; in each there is a first phase when victory is still possible to the side ultimately defeated; but after a certain turning-point (which contemporaries often miss but which on a general review, long after, can be seen clearly enough) the struggle is decided; after that turning-point it is merely a question of time and postponement of the end.

So it was now with Charles. Not that at Marston Moor a principal army in being had ceased to exist; not that Charles had no more forces in being elsewhere, but that the opportunity had been lost to defeat his enemies, to lower them by defeat, and this had come at a moment when their victory was certain to give them confidence and therefore the power of new organisation.

Two things emerge after Marston Moor most clearly:—

First, numbers in every form were going to be more and more decisive against the cause of the King – numbers in men, in amount of munitions and in regular supply of money. There was now to succeed a period of rapid attrition during which the resources of the one side more and more outweigh those on the other, until the difference between them is out of all proportion and the failing cause is overwhelmed.

Secondly, after Marston Moor appears the personality of Cromwell – a combination of lucidity and will which are the essentials of the great soldier. In the complication of many names and of clashing policies, of innumerable lesser factors, the one thing that stands out is Oliver Cromwell's initiative and the determining effect of that one man upon the victorious side. It is really he who creates the new army, called "The New Model" – the first regular army in English history – which is the chief factor of the new thing; it is he who pushes through the final and successful "Self-Denying Ordinance" (as it was

THE TRIUMPH OF THE GREAT REBELLION

called) which was in reality the getting rid of that bad generalship whose defects were due to hereditary and other claims which should play no part in war. It is he who gathers things more and more, at first gradually, at last rapidly, under that unity of command which is the condition of final success in arms.

But all this, I say, contemporaries did not see; the appreciation of the change came slowly, and even the stunning blow of Marston Moor was under-estimated on either side. The victors remembered how nearly they had lost in spite of their superiority in numbers and how badly their chief leaders had behaved. The defeated felt themselves to be defeated only on that particular field, many other theatres of operation remained. So little was the situation understood that the King's own operations in the west, contemporary with, and continuing after, Marston Moor seemed larger in his own estimation and even in that of his opponents.

Charles showed military skill, in these operations of 1644, and Waller, who was his principal opponent, great lack of it; the latter lost his guns and the bulk of his force in a clash not far from Oxford, at Copredy Bridge on the Cherwell, just north of Banbury. Away in the southwest the army under Essex was destroyed as a fighting force. Charles pinned it down upon the sea near the harbour of Fowey.† Its cavalry got away for the most part through the Royal lines, but Essex himself abandoned the infantry – sailing off in a boat and leaving them to their fate. They surrendered with all their guns, munitions and arms. The renown of that feat was so great at Court, and indeed throughout the Royal forces, as to make men forget what had happened before York.

Charles has been blamed for letting the prisoners at Fowey go off disbanded. There is no reason to blame him. The armies of those days (before the "New Model") were perpetually subject to dissolution by desertion. They were for the most part a militia the men of which would not serve long away from home and were always ready to disperse; the King would have had no particular advantage in keeping these men. There was no lack of man-power on either side momentarily available – the difficulty was to keep it under arms, and, particularly in the case of the King, to feed it and to keep it paid.

---

† It was on this occasion that, for the second time, he narrowly missed being killed, and, as at Edgehill, again by a cannon ball.

CHARLES I

Attrition, attrition, attrition is the note of the whole time. Most of the King's forces were tied down to holding fortified houses and small walled towns with petty garrisons. The inconsiderable forces (and large concentrations such as one had at Marston Moor were rare) were for ever in a state of flux; and on the King's side more and more is there felt the inability to keep sufficient field troops together, and those sufficiently armed and provided – for the lack of money increasingly hampered the Royal cause. On the Rebel side there was the inexhaustible supply of London and the now largely extended area which London directly controlled. One army would disappear, as Essex's had disappeared, or another as Waller's had disappeared, but further troops could always be raised because the Rebellion had a large and regular revenue. The factor of numbers was to be more and more evident on its side and only proper leadership with a fully trained force was required to make that factor decisive.

A good example of the new situation was afforded by the second battle of Newbury, which was fought in that same autumn of 1644 not quite two months after the breakdown of Essex in the southwest.

The Revolutionary Government in London had raised new forces of nearly 20,000 men and had sent them out west, though Essex was too ill to command them. They came upon a Royalist concentration near Newbury on the 27th of October. In numbers the Parliamentarians were about two to one of their foes, yet the King's force got away in the night after an undecided battle, and it was events such as these which led to the great change of which Oliver Cromwell was the inspiring force.

For in that winter of 1644–45 was created for the first time in English history a fully trained standing army, permanent, properly disciplined and properly led, with an exact hierarchy of command. This "New Model" was to be 21,500 strong, 7,000 thereof cavalry. The wages were high; even the foot soldier could count himself better off than the average of the labouring classes from which he was drawn, though against that of course there was the irksomeness and peril of military life. The mounted man was so well paid that the service attracted even the larger yeomen and there were to be found, here and there, impoverished gentlemen serving the Rebellion as private horsemen in the cavalry along with plenty of young well-to-do farmers.

THE TRIUMPH OF THE GREAT REBELLION

Side by side with the creation of this excellent novel instrument, the like of which on the impoverished Royal side could not be dreamed of, went arrangements for a rational form of command.

It had hitherto been taken for granted that the higher command, whenever fighting was toward, must be in the hands of a peer or peers – that is why you see at the head of the Rebellion's armies such names as Manchester and Essex, drawn from the tiny such remnant of the peers who still supported the Rebellion. It was also thought a matter of course that military honours should go to those who were politically in power; nor would Oliver Cromwell originally have had a regiment had he not been a member of the Commons. The so-called "Self-Denying Ordinance," which proposed that in future no member of either House should hold a commission to command troops, cleared the ground for the appointment of competent men. It was suspected and resisted – naturally – by the little group of lords attached to the Rebellion; it was unpalatable to many of the Commons themselves, but upon a second appeal to the members it was successful.

It was on the 15th of February, 1645, that the New Model Ordinance passed the Lords; seven weeks later, at the beginning of April, the second and final Self-Denying Ordinance was also accepted. Essex, Manchester (and Waller) were got rid of.

But what of Oliver Cromwell? Here was the man who had won Marston Moor and – far more important – here was the man who had supplied the ideas and the initiative which were producing a new professional force. Here was the man who, in the nature of things, must lead if there was to be any final victory. But he was a Parliamentarian. Fairfax had been given the supreme command of the New Model precisely because he was not a Parliamentarian: what about Cromwell?

Here is perhaps what is the most remarkable example of this great man's talent for intrigue which should stand second only to his military capacity whenever his historical position is considered. Many excuses have been made and all manner of conjecture based on minute research (for research when it is too microscopic is misleading); it is called an accident, it is called the result of an unexpected and momentary local necessity – but the horrid fact remains that Oliver Cromwell was not affected by the Self-Denying Ordinance: he remained in command, not second to Fairfax, but accepted and even demanded by Fairfax, and in the opinion of his own men and soon of the whole army the leading soldier rather than Fairfax. One may put it crudely and say that the Self-Denying Ordinance had proceeded from Cromwell, had got rid of the less competent rivals of Cromwell, and yet had spared Cromwell because Cromwell desired to be spared: crude, but true.

The making of the New Model was not done without difficulty; more than a third of the men had been enrolled by violence, pressed men; they were not even conscripts – who, after all, are chosen with a certain rough justice by lot – but men taken haphazard by force and compelled to serve. There was plenty of physical resistance, but it was overcome. Thus with the spring of 1645 and the early summer of that year, things were set for a trial between the transformed and renewed Revolutionary army, ready for action, and the still dwindling, and soon to be desperate, forces of the regular Government, commanded from Oxford.

There were but three drawbacks to the plan which Oliver Cromwell had conceived. First, there were the Scots; as they were in alliance with the Revolutionary army, they must be considered, but the friendship between them and their English allies was not what it had been. Next there was the Committee of the Two Kingdoms, the mixed political body which still technically possessed, and still in fact exercised, though not continuously, the right to order the movements of the Revolutionary forces. Thirdly there was still the disturbing factor of a standing quarrel between the politicians and the soldiers

The nature of this quarrel should be seized. It took the outward form – fashions being what they were – of a religious cleavage; it appeared as a struggle between those who would impose the full Calvinist system of Church discipline, the Presbyterian organisation of religion, and those called "Independents," who were of exactly the same morals and much the same creed as the others, but supported the right of congregations and even of individuals to worship at will. It would be ridiculous to pretend that those who supported the Presbyterian cause on the English side were in the main enthusiasts for that particular form of Church government; many of them were indifferent to religion altogether; most of them had been brought up in the general doctrines of the Church of England. The English Presbyterian cause, the effort to impose Presbyterian uniformity upon a

THE TRIUMPH OF THE GREAT REBELLION

nation which as a whole would hardly understand it, of which only a minority were ready to accept it even grudgingly, and of which only a tiny fraction were enthusiastic for it, meant not a religious difference but a political one.

Those who were thus called "The Presbyterian Party" among the Revolutionaries were the maintainers of the old Parliament – the few Revolutionary Lords and the Revolutionary half of the Commons – as against the growing power of the soldiery: the organised army. For permanent armies when they come into being and are exercised in action grow to be a state within a state; they come to regard their victorious leaders as natural political heads and are contemptuous of speechifiers.

Moreover, the so-called Presbyterian faction did not only represent the attempt of the Parliamentarians to maintain their old grasp on the Revolutionary movement as against the soldiers who were soon to replace them; it also represented the Scottish alliance. For the Scottish nation, and its army, solidly established here in England, lavishly hired with English money (but at a wage which had fallen sadly into arrears) was genuinely, not quite sanely, convinced that the Presbyterian system would be imposed throughout Great Britain, and for that matter throughout Ireland as well. They were not only convinced that it *should* be so imposed as a matter of duty, they even thought it *would* be so, and therefore the so-called Presbyterian Party at Westminster could rely upon the support of those alien invaders who had been hitherto the best-organised force on the Revolutionary side.

With the spring of 1645 Charles was tempted, dwindling as were his forces, more and more doubtful his chances, to a certain move. In Scotland Montrose had shown military genius in the cause of the King. He had a year ago in the spring of 1644 set up the King's standard at Dumfries. During the summer he had pitted his Highlanders against the forces of the Covenant; during the autumn he had maintained his position; in the winter and early part of the year 1645 he had continued his victories, destroying the force which Argyll had brought against him; and just before the time when the change to the "New Model" was taking place in the English Revolutionary army he was threatening to become master of Scotland.

Here was, in appearance, a complete transformation of what men had hitherto regarded as inevitable north of the border. It may be imagined how the probability of final and definite Royal success in Scotland was exaggerated among Charles's followers and surroundings. It seemed at last certain that the Scottish Covenanting army in the Midlands of England, already very anxious as to what was happening in their own country, would ultimately be compelled to go home and restore the old state of things – the complete domination of the Kirk – which after all had behind it the great bulk of the population. It was by a calculation of this necessity which the Scotch would be under that Charles proceeded to lead his depleted forces northward, in order to threaten the open country between the Scottish army to the north and left and the Parliamentary army to the south and right. Here the key point was Newark, the fortified town which held the crossing of the Trent, still garrisoned for the King and still holding out. Until that point should fall into the hands of their enemies the supporters of the Crown were able always to threaten, and at moments to interrupt, rebel communications north and south.

Charles as he went northward from Oxford and then eastward might hope to threaten those districts where the Parliament had hitherto been unconquered – everything east of the Great North Road. He had with him to begin with perhaps 10,000 men, of whom perhaps half were cavalry, and he set forth at the end of the first week of May, 1645. The Rebellion was besieging Chester at the time, and at his approach the siege was raised. On the last day of the month, the 31st of May, 1645, he turned eastward, raised the spirits of his small force and unduly raised his own by the capture and sack of Leicester. The capturing of so important a place from the Parliament had a great effect, though of military value it had little and the action depleted Charles's already diminished command, for he had to garrison Leicester, and it moved the Committee of the Two Kingdoms to an act of energy and concentration.

Hitherto they had banked upon the capture of Oxford, calculating that a political success here, the taking of the King's capital, would be of decisive effect; but on hearing he news of Leicester they ordered Fairfax to raise the siege of Oxford and go forward at once north and east to join issue with Charles. Fairfax therefore marched off from Oxford northward in early June at the head of over 17,000 men.

Charles (unconscious of his approach) still hanging on during those days of early June in the country south of Leicester collecting

THE TRIUMPH OF THE GREAT REBELLION

supplies, had with him after his losses and the diminution of his force by the detachment of troops for garrison, little more than 7,000 – at the most 7,500 – men. By Friday, the 13th of June, Fairfax was in the immediate neighbourhood of his enemy and Cromwell had come up with 600 horse. Altogether the Rebellion had 18,000 men ready and concentrated in the neighbourhood of Naseby village, the army lying about seven miles southwest of Market Harboro', and more than an average day's march from Leicester.

Tidings of Fairfax's command reached the King's quarters, at Lubenham, two miles west of Market Harboro', in the middle of the night. He woke and summoned a hasty council which decided to stand on high ground somewhat south of the town on the defensive and await the enemy's arrival. So, in the very early hours of that long daylight, Saturday, the 14th of June, the little force deployed – but no sign of the enemy appeared.

About 8 a.m. scouts went out and reported nothing. Rupert rode forward to find out for himself, and, a little north of Clipston, saw Fairfax's distant host, which had no appearance of advancing. He rode forward to meet it edging to the west as he did so to get drier ground, and the bulk of his army followed, till it all stood deployed again on the slight elevation known as Dust Hill, where still stands "Prince Rupert's farm."

Thence the Royalists saw before them a shallow depression locally called "Broadmoor," a slight slope of half a mile leading down to it and on the opposite southern side a comparatively slight rise, on the summit of which, about a mile and a half north of Naseby village, the Revolutionary army stood in line, its heavily superior numbers (more than five to two) partly concealed behind the brow.

Rupert, always too confident – and that was natural in one who had so often and so brilliantly succeeded in the charge and who was but twenty-five years of age – was ready (in spite of the gross disproportion in strength) to attack. He commanded the cavalry on the right wing, the place of honour, and he charged home across the depression, up the opposing slight slope, crashed against Ireton (Cromwell's son-in-law) on the Parliamentary left and broke the whole of his formation, sweeping it away before him in the characteristic tactic of that age, not yet modified (in England) save by Cromwell. Yet Cromwell had already shown the year before at Marston Moor the newer and

241

better way, "the interrupted charge," of which for that matter Rupert might have remembered the beginnings, from the German campaigns of which older men had spoken to him in his boyhood.

That newer tactic Cromwell was now to try again, as at Marston Moor, but today with all the advantage of two men to his opponent's one.

He, on the other end of the line, came down the slight open slope at the same pace as at Marston Moor – the sharp trot and no more, discharging no pistol from the saddle – and at the end engaged in the mêlée of a push rather than a shock. As at Marston Moor he succeeded; but in such superiority that he did the work more rapidly. There was not the doubtful interval which there had been in the previous year, when the mêlée remained for some time undecided. The overwhelming numbers made sure of that. He was able to detach a sufficient portion of his cavalry for the pursuit, and at once swung round to the left, as the year before he had swung round to the right, and clove into the flank of the King's infantry at the centre – and Rupert coming back to the far end of the line with his exhausted horses witnessed the dissolution of the army which so short a while before he still thought would be victorious. As a fighting force it disappeared.

Of those 7,500 men, or less, a thousand were killed (you may yet see the grave pits upon the field), 5,000 at least were taken prisoner, of the remnant many were wounded; all the guns, with the tents of the camp, and – a grave thing morally for the cause – all the King's papers fell into the hands of the victors. Charles's last army in the field was gone.

The Puritan soldiers completed their victory by a massacre of women.

Leicester fell to Fairfax four days afterwards on the 18th, and then week after week of that summer there was a cleaning up of what remained. There were forces of the King in Somerset still organised; Bridgwater, thought impregnable with its marshy approach and the works erected to defend it and an organised body to take the field under Goring. Bridgwater was carried by the 23rd of August, the troops under Goring having been disposed of at Langport in July; and the Revolutionary armies had invested Bristol – the last port left, and essential to the despairing resistance of the Crown.

Rupert was in the town which he had taken so brilliantly two years before. But his task was hopeless. The walls and lines were near-

THE TRIUMPH OF THE GREAT REBELLION

ly four miles long. The town lay in a hollow, dominated, and Rupert only had 1,500 men, lessened daily by sickness. In little more than a fortnight, on the 11th of September, he was compelled to surrender. Charles showed ill-judgment on hearing the news. He was stunned by it; he seems to have thought it a sort of treason – he should have understood that the thing was inevitable. If any man could have held Bristol Rupert would have held it, but how could it be held with that handful of men? And everywhere the King's forces were handfuls – and handfuls rapidly melting away.

In Scotland Montrose had continued a startling series of victories over the Covenanters during the absence of the main Scottish army in England. For a moment it seemed to Charles that some ray of hope shone from the north and he went to meet it. At Chester he saw the last pitched fight lost under his eyes and learnt, just afterwards, that Montrose had failed. His forces had dispersed; a small group remaining had been surprised near the border, surrendered on terms and then butchered at the special request of the Calvinist clergy. Not only were the men massacred – who had only surrendered upon the express condition that their lives should be spared – but every woman and even every little child found in the place was slaughtered in cold blood. Forty women had got away; that band of wretched fugitives was caught in the neighbourhood and by solemn order of the ministers of Jehovah were thrown over the bridge into the Avon and drowned.

There remained to Charles now nothing military; all his fortunes must depend upon the play of political intrigue. And that was the very thing for which he was least adapted. Concealment, deceit, surprise, the making of men believe one thing while he meant another, the use of ambiguous phrases and trickery thereby, the exact and secret judgment of motive, the inflammation of allies one against the other and the defeat of enemies in such a fashion – all those talents which make for the greatness of a statesman he lacked. Once again, and it is the key of all that happened, he had not the art of lying – most fruitful of human gifts!

There were three elements in the problem before him. He might repose upon Ireland. Ireland would loyally support him. Though it was for the moment three-fourths independent, its religion and the recovered land of its people had all to hope for from the King. For

243

the Irish to follow their natural desire for complete independence would have been politically an error. The idea was flirted with, and the support of Charles Stuart might then have been the final policy of an enfranchised Irish people; but the effort he made there came to nothing, because by the time it had in part succeeded Charles had no ports left through which Irish aid could come. He had sent Herbert to negotiate, to promise concessions on religion which should be kept secret (for if they were published it would shake much of the support which the King had in England). All during the summer the negotiations went on, but of course before the winter they had come to the knowledge of the Revolutionary government. What might have been a strength for Charles some months before had become on the contrary a degradation and a weakness.

With Ireland unable to act for him the second opportunity was the quarrel between the Parliament and the Army. Might he not, by concessions to the Presbyterian plan – not a full surrender, for his conscience would never allow that, he would never destroy the Church of England – but by some compromise leaning towards the older part of his enemies, the remnants of the two Houses at Westminster, separate those enemies? The breach between them was already widening – might he not make it a gulf by negotiating to the right and left, keeping the negotiations with one secret from those of the other? It was a task for which he was ill-fitted, and what was more, the Army now had the ascendant. The Army was coming to see more and more clearly that the politicians at Westminster who so atrociously withheld their pay were in their power.

There remained the third element, the Covenanting army of his fellow-countrymen the Scots. It was this, in the mass of refusal and contemptuous silence, rebuff and counter-deception by his enemies, that opened at last most plainly before Charles. A French agent, Montereul,[†] was in negotiation, but even so late as the spring, even by the last days of April, Charles had not decided between such a tangle of doubtful policies. He might stand siege there in Oxford; he still had a garrison; he could hold out for some months – but if he did that the end was inevitable and he would be doomed.

[†] It is a small matter, but that and not "Montreuil" seems to have been the more usual contemporary spelling.

THE TRIUMPH OF THE GREAT REBELLION

On the 26th of April, 1646, he told his Council that unless they heard from him within three weeks they might surrender the city. Everything else had gone, even Exeter a fortnight before. On the next day, the 27th of April, in the darkness of the early hours, Charles rode out disguised as a servant with Jack Ashburnham, the closest of his friends, and Hudson,† his brave and sporting chaplain.

They made vaguely enough for London, and then turned northward with some thought of King's Lynn, whence a ship might be got for flight overseas. In Stamford on the last day of April, while Charles was still thinking of and enquiring for some ship to which he might ride eastward, Hudson was at Southwell, where Montereul lay with the Scottish commanders in front of Newark, Southwell being rather more than a day's march south of that town. There followed that at which his enemies were so proficient and he himself so lacking – a successful betrayal. The Scottish commander would put nothing into writing; he gave a verbal promise that the King should have complete safety if he came to them, and by them be kept in security from his foes – all the rest was left vague, and in particular the matter of religion. Nor can we even be certain of the terms of this solemn pledge, save in the matter of the King's being safeguarded and all honour and respect paid to him and full security promised to him, if he would put that most valuable of assets – a sacred person, the monarchy of England, the Hostage – into their hands.

He came to Southwell on Tuesday, the 5th of May, 1646, early in the morning, calling at the lodgings of Montereul. It was about midday when a troop of horse came to conduct him (as an honourable guest) to Leslie's headquarters at Kelham.

He had decided his fate.

---

† Hudson's death is worth recalling as a detail of these wars and of the spirit in which they were fought. He was caught in one of the last abortive local risings for the King and chased to the roof of a house. As he hung by his hands to the roof edge the Puritan soldiers hacked through his wrists. He dropped into the moat below and there paddled in the water with his bleeding stumps to keep from drowning. His pursuers rushed down after him and battered in his head. I wish the character of this book had allowed for more details on the atrocities of the New Model. Let the reader turn to the story of Basing House.

THE HOSTAGE

I. Hostage of the Scotch

CHARLES STUART IN THE SCOTTISH CAMP WAS A HOSTAGE. No longer in arms and opposed to an enemy in arms but a hostage; for a hostage is one who remains in an enemy's power, but is there as an asset for bargaining – as the security that this or that shall be done. His advantage lies in this: that he is needed by his enemy as a security for the fulfilment of some policy; his disadvantage is that he is a captive and may be killed.

But Charles had a special advantage compared with one who is the hostage of a single enemy; his enemies were three, and at variance each with the others: the Scotch, the Parliament and the English Revolutionary Army – which now meant Cromwell. Whichever of these three held Charles, it would be to their advantage to keep him alive as a bargaining point against the others. But when at last only *one* was left, and the other two were eliminated, that one would have no interest in keeping him alive.

The immediate issue was between the Scotch and the Parliament, for as yet the Army and the Parliament had not come to open divergence; but he knew well enough already that the opportunity was before him of playing upon three, not two, factors. He knew well enough already (and it would become much clearer later on) that he could play not only the Scotch against the Parliament, but also the Parliament against the Army and the Army against the Parliament.

But in this condition of bargaining he suffered from two very heavy handicaps, of which the second was perhaps the worst. He could only bargain as a captive of whichever one among the three he chose to be his captor; and he was the worst of bargainers from his lack of skill in deception.

He could make all the elementary moves (as can any man, skilled or unskilled, in this exercise); he could spin things out and trust to

THE HOSTAGE

time; he could make simultaneously more or less contradictory propositions privately to one and the other; he could weigh, more or less, the advantages of their competing offers; he could even judge – though with no acute penetration – the alternative duplicity of his three various opponents – which of the three sly watchers was the more likely to keep (perhaps!) some part of the word pledged: but for the essential of such an affair – which is to convince one's opponent to his hurt, to lead him into inwardly accepting a particular course which is to one's own advantage and not to his – Charles had no talent at all.

It was to the good of his soul that he had it not, but the ruin of his person and cause.

Of all those who took part in this sorry game of cozening, from the day when the last Royal force was disbanded to the day when the King was handed over to his death, the one man with supreme talent at the game was Oliver Cromwell. Therefore in the long run the King necessarily "gravitates" to Oliver Cromwell; he ends in the hands of Cromwell: and it was the intention of Cromwell to put him to death. For Cromwell saw more clearly than anyone else that until the King was dead he was himself in jeopardy.

Charles, then, had decided between the Parliament and the Scotch for the Scotch. It has been argued that another decision would have been wiser. It has been said that if he had trusted to Fairfax and surrendered to him (and Fairfax was still thus early in 1646 the servant of the Parliament) he would have been in the best of the bad conditions among which he had to choose. For Fairfax was a reasonably loyal man and had a strong feeling for the dignity of kingship and for chivalry in the treatment of a captive. Yet for Charles to have surrendered to Fairfax would have been an error; it would technically have meant, at that time, surrender to the Politicians. Moreover the will of Cromwell now counted for much more in the Army than the will of Fairfax; while as for the Parliament, all the King's memories of it were memories of treason and vileness.

It is true that the Scotch had begun that chain of troubles which had led him to where he was; but that was long ago, and all his active memories of the immediate past were those of struggle with the Revolutionaries at Westminster. Therefore had Charles surrendered to the Scotch.

CHARLES I

When it was learned at Westminster that Charles had surrendered to the Scotch there was a frenzied hubbub. Those who had been brethren and allies, those whom the Revolutionaries had deliberately called in to the invasion of their country, to help them destroy the Constitution and defeat the King, had grown more and more separate from the English Revolutionary cause. It was partly due to the disruptive effect which victory always has upon an alliance; but it was also due to an increasing divergence of aim.

On the surface the two allies were struggling for the mastery, the Scotch to impose the Covenant and Presbyterianism upon the Three Kingdoms; the Parliament on the surface willing to accept these terms, but determined to retain full power in their hands. Beneath all this, however, there were other forces. The Scotch wanted to go home; and before they went home they wanted very much indeed to be paid.

They were owed by the Parliament for their hire £400,000 – that is, half the full revenue of England at the most prosperous moment of that revenue during the long peace of Charles's middle reign. Even now, in 1646, even under the huge taxation of the moment, those arrears were nearly a quarter of the whole yearly revenue that the Parliament could raise.

The Scotch were really owed much more, but £400,000 was the accepted sum to which the debt had been scaled down. If Charles as a hostage in their hands was valuable for this or for that, he was especially valuable as an article for sale. They could bargain for his possession, and with that trump card they partly won the trick. If they could *both* have got their money *and* taken the King with them back to Scotland, it would have suited them well enough; but they could not take the King back with them save as a Presbyterian King; for the Calvinist Kirk which governed Scotland (and indeed the bulk of the Scottish people) would have been fierce to render any other arrangement impossible.

A King who had taken the Covenant and who should be ruling in Scotland would indeed have been a possession! On the Scottish decision would *then* have depended English policy and the Restoration of Monarchy which was certain to be demanded, sooner or later. But the King must first be converted. He must accept the Presbytery and take the Calvinist oath – and that is what Charles refused to do.

THE HOSTAGE

When they saw how strong the feeling at Westminster was against them the Scottish precipitately left Newark and made for the north; it was from the safer distance of Newcastle that they bargained with the little remnant of the House of Lords and that Revolutionary half of the Commons which remained in power. And while they were so bargaining they set out to convert the King.

It was in order to gain time that Charles consented to the long debates on theology; but it is not true to say, as has been said – as was once almost universally said – that his resistance to the Presbyterian arguments was due to nothing but his desire to spin things out and to prolong the opportunity for some favourable accident. Charles was fixed in his opinion of the English Church, which he retained unmoved from his first adoption of it in early youth until his death; its Holy Orders were to him a spiritual reality. A Church without the Apostolic Hierarchy of Bishops, and without a priesthood, was not a Church; on that doctrine not only his conscience but his honour stood, and for that doctrine he was willing to die.

He did compromise so far as to attempt a sort of *condominium*, thinking it possible to make an experiment in Presbyterian Church government while retaining the Hierarchy; that after all was the compromise which his father had made in his native kingdom during years which Charles could remember. He even went so far in this policy as to suggest a three years' experiment; but to subscribe himself, personally, to the Presbyterian denial of Episcopacy he steadfastly refused to do, as he also refused to destroy the institution by law.

Without their money the Scotch would not return over the neighbouring border to their own place. With an Uncovenanted King they could not return. In the bargaining of the Scotch with the Parliament the King had helped by saying that he desired to hear what the Revolutionaries at Westminster might have to say, and to see whether he could not accept their terms. He was the more moved to do so because he was finding his condition amid the Scottish soldiery impossible. "He had never been so bated in his life," he said; their ministers pestered him, and their commanding officers would not give him his due dignity.

The wrangle went on through the summer of 1646 and on into the winter; it was settled at last by a formal promise of payment. The Parliament would hand over half the stipulated sum (that is, £200,000) in cash; for the remaining half they would give bonds – and on those terms by the end of January, 1647, the thing was concluded. Thirty-six carts, full of coin, were the solid proof that this time at least the Parliament at Westminster had kept its word; and as those carts lumbered up towards the border the King, on the 3rd of February, 1647, was handed over to his new masters, the Commissioners of the Parliament.

Here again is another debate on which men will still wrangle indefinitely, because their emotions are – even today! – more engaged than their reason. Had the Scotch played the part of Judas? Was the King "sold"?

The facts are plain and known, and every man can judge for himself. Charles was not sold in the sense that his captors merely took new money for him; it was rather as though Judas had already been owed sixty pieces of silver by the party of the High Priest, and had consented to take thirty. Further, Charles was not sold from a position of freedom and security, with friends, to a position of servitude under an enemy; the Parliament might well prove to be easier masters than the Scotch, and Charles himself had envisaged making terms with them. Lastly, the Scotch could say that they would have kept Charles and given him all the security he wished, and even all the liberty, had he but taken the Covenant – but he had refused.

With all these reservations and making all these allowances, it is nonetheless true that Charles was sold in the sense that the Scottish handed him over for money, and that, but for the money, he would not have been handed over. The money was the decisive factor.

II. Hostage of the Parliament

The Revolutionaries at Westminster had decided that Charles's place of captivity under them should be Holdenby, a fine house now half a century old, near Northampton.

It was his private property; it had been built for Hatton by an Italian architect (although it is usually ascribed to an Englishman). Hatton was that dancing fellow who had been absurdly made Chancellor under Elizabeth, and got a fortune enormous even for those who battened off the revenue in that unfortunate woman's reign.

THE HOSTAGE

Anne of Denmark, with her husband's aid, had bought it for her second son, to have as a present for himself and a private house of his own after it had been used during his boyhood by James and herself; and under that roof (the name was shortened in conversation to Holmby) he had at least the dignity of being at home, though the home was in reality a prison. It was a situation just suited to the policy of the Parliament, far enough from London, and yet not too far for easy communications, with no danger from over the distant border from that rising reaction in favour of the King which the Revolutionaries increasingly dreaded.

Moreover, the neighbourhood was under the influence of Northampton, which had always been hitherto strongly Puritan and Parliamentarian. Holmby was a place within a day's posting of London; the distance was three days' easy riding on ordinary occasions, some seventy miles. It is some six and a quarter miles north-east of Northampton, close to Althorp.

The cavalcade started out from Newcastle on Wednesday, the 3rd of February, where Charles had been lodged at Andersen's Place, a fine house, then fairly new.

Two regiments of horse formed the escort, and the whole of the slow journey down south (nearly a fortnight of it, of which Sundays only were free from travelling) showed how strong was the popular feeling for the King. It was like a great progress of triumph, most alarming to the three peers who had been sent to take over their purchased prisoner. The villages and towns through which they passed cheered the King continually, the bells were rung in the churches and crowds assembled to welcome him. The passage through Leeds was particularly remarkable – for two miles into the town the people lined the road on either side, and there were ceaseless cries of "A King! A King!"

Three days before Holmby was reached Fairfax came up from the south, met the King at Nottingham and paid his homage, going on one knee and kissing his hand; and it was then that Charles made the very true remark that Fairfax was a man of honour. So he was: but not a man of backbone – he was wax in the hands of Oliver Cromwell. The King looked on Fairfax long and earnestly, with those melancholy eyes of his, but he did not see what was in his heart. Had he no hope? Those who could would not, those who would could not

251

CHARLES I

— or at any rate dared not; and as for Fairfax, nominally at the head of the Army, he was neither of those who could nor of those who would.

Holmby was reached on Wednesday, the 16th of February, and it was the residence of the King, closely watched by the Commissioners, for four months.†

Charles, now the prisoner of the Parliamentary Commissioners, as he had been the prisoner of the Scotch, was, during these four months at Holmby, made to suffer more restraint than he had suffered at Newcastle. They would not allow him his Chaplains, and during his time there he never heard the service of the Church of England (which was his solace) in the chapel of the house. He had asked for any two out of a list of twelve, of whom Juxon was one. All were refused.

Also there was some care taken to prevent anyone's approaching him without permits. He could go about, however, and he played bowls in the neighbourhood, at Althorp itself and elsewhere, and of course the ordinary courtesy due to Royalty was still extended to him — the ceremonial meals and the announcement of them by sound of a trumpet; but he felt himself to be more of a prisoner than with the Scotch, and what was perhaps worse (in his eyes more onerous) the Parliament was silent; they would not discuss terms.

For most of the months at Holmby that silence continued, until he himself was constrained to break it by writing, repeating the offers he had made before: a Presbyterian experiment to last three years, the Army to be controlled by Parliament ten years and then to revert to the Crown, and the Parliament to have its own way in Ireland.

These overtures came to nothing, the remnant of the Lords, no more than 22, voted that Charles should be allowed to come to Outlands,‡ his house near London, and as for the Commons, they neglected the whole affair.

For indeed the interest of the moment in the eyes of the anxious group of original Revolutionaries who still called themselves

---

† It suffered the fate of so many of the Royal houses:— most of it was pulled down that the land might be sold, and much of the materials also, in the panic of the Parliamentarians, when they feared a revolt of the Army in demand of its arrears of pay.

‡ Also pulled down by Parliament later to pay the Army.

THE HOSTAGE

"Parliament" was directed to something else. That something else was the menace of the Army.

The army of a revolution, and especially a victorious army, when it has been in existence a certain time, comes to form a State within a State. Men who have suffered the same burdens and enjoyed the same triumphs become comrades, and by a paradox which everyone has experienced who has ever seen the thing at work, an army in being after a certain length of such experiences has about it a certain egalitarian feeling, in no way contradictory to the strict discipline of its hierarchy.

Still more does such an army come to despise the civilian. It is ready to support its officers, and especially men whose names are famous throughout all ranks for having led them to victory. Hence the emergence of Oliver Cromwell.

For now two years Cromwell's name had become something very special among these 20,000 men of the Parliamentary Army – for two years, that is, if you count from the New Model and Naseby; for three years if you count from Marston Moor.

Cromwell now begins to appear as the man who will guide events; Fairfax, his nominal commander, was (by persuasion at any rate) at his orders, for Cromwell was not only the elder man by thirteen years, nor only the man who had shown himself on the field to possess that high individual talent which raised him beyond all others, he had also the stronger will and the greater tenacity and, what was more important, the greater clarity of mind. He knew what he wanted and why he wanted it. He could see many things at once. He could make and carry out his plans.

There had arisen a strong additional force making for the antagonism between Parliament and Army under the mask of a religious quarrel: this additional force was class feeling.

The Parliamentarians were most of them gentlemen. The colonels of the Army regiments were some of them, by this time, men risen by talent or brutality from the lower ranks of society, and the subaltern officers were often of such origin.

It is an interesting paradox that the Great Rebellion which was essentially a rising of the rich against the Crown, should have been served in its last decisive victory by an army grown largely infected with the doctrines of equality. However, that spirit did not survive the Civil War.

Moreover, the Presbyterian Party, as it is called, that is, the original Revolutionaries of the Parliament, were morally insecure. They knew well enough that they had no comradeship behind them. The mass of England was obviously not with them, it had become pitiful for the persecuted King, and an increasing minority was already enthusiastic for him. But the Parliament still nominally governed.

Now the Army had one driving force behind its demand for power, which force was decisive. Like everything else in all this struggle, from the Revocation of the Ecclesiastical Grants in Scotland all those years ago, the capital factor was money. Before the end of March, 1647, the arrears of pay to the Army had become intolerable. Eighteen months' pay was due to the infantry and to the horse and dragoons no less than forty-three weeks' pay – the total amount being half as much again as had been paid to the Scotch. There was no provision of pensions to the widows of those who had fallen, there was no provision for the keeping of the soldiers in food and lodging, and they complained of the friction due to their being billeted on the inhabitants; and while all this was owing to the men who had fought for the Revolutionary cause and suffered in that struggle, they had seen the Scotch bought off before their eyes, while they themselves were left neglected.

There was only one remedy, if the Parliamentary leaders would save themselves. The Army must be disbanded.

Already it had moved to the neighbourhood of London, coming to Essex, within striking distance of the capital. It had petitioned the Houses, sending up a Remonstrance, and in the course of the next month, during April, a last desperate effort was made by the Parliamentarians to get rid of the soldiers. At the end of the month Parliament ordered the officers to allay, as best they could, the rising ferment.

All this quarrel played directly into Cromwell's hands. With the talent which was so wholly lacking to the man whose fate he was to decide, the King, Cromwell thoroughly succeeded in deceiving. He was suspected, of course; there was even talk of arresting him; but in the main he persuaded the Revolutionary remainder of the House

THE HOSTAGE

of Commons that he would support their authority over the Army, while at the same time letting it be felt in the Army that he was supporting the new movement among the soldiery, for many of whom he was already an idol. To play a double game of this sort drew out all Cromwell's best talents.

There seems to have been a sort of passion about the speech he made to deceive his fellow Parliamentarians. It was blunt and carefully rough. It burnt into his hearers. When he affirmed – calling God, of course, to witness to his sincerity – that he would rather allow himself to be burnt with all his family than see sedition in the Army against Parliament, those words had their full weight. So deceived, the Houses in the last week of May decided to do what hitherto they had only talked of, and to compel, on their authority (which had no physical force behind it), the disbanding of the Army. It ordered the guns at Oxford to be secured and the stores there; Fairfax was ordered to set to work, from the 25th to the 29th of May, at dissolving the Army, and put an end to their fears.

Then Cromwell moved. On the night between the 30th and the 31st of May, just after these orders had gone out (Fairfax was so far from obeying them that he had concentrated the Army instead of disbanding it – and remember that Fairfax always did what Cromwell wanted), Cromwell, unknown to Fairfax, summoned secretly some few to meet him at his house in Drury Lane.

There under his own roof and by night did he make that plan which was to change all; he would secure the person of the King.

It was arranged that a certain Cornet Joyce (a tailor in civilian life – a young man, energetic, not ill-looking, determined – an exceedingly good choice, for Cromwell, like all men of high military talent, understood the choice of subordinates) should ride to Oxford with 500 men, secure the artillery, and do something more.

The arrangements Cromwell made for this stroke are illuminating. In the first place Fairfax was told nothing about it. Cromwell felt he could safely leave aside his nominal superior; and what further emphasises this neglect was the fact that Joyce was an officer in the very bodyguard of the General-in-Chief, who was thus left ignorant of the plot. Next let it be noted that the 500 troopers were picked from various regiments, so that suitable men could be selected; a method which combined two advantages: it allowed Cromwell to pick men chosen for their reliability, and it guaranteed him against conspiracy or hesitation among these men, such as might have taken place had they belonged to one unit.

Joyce also was well chosen, not only for his opinions and character but for his energy. He did the whole thing in remarkably quick time. He was in Oxford early on the second day, having covered, with the 500 of his command, some fifty miles; there he secured the guns, presumably warned the men of the garrison (who were half mutinous and clamouring for pay) to stand fast against any Parliamentary orders, and then rode off at once north-eastward for the country round about Northampton.

This second move was again a distance of about fifty miles, and it was again covered in part of one day, the night, and the next day.

Joyce himself at some point on the march rode on ahead of the main body to ascertain for himself the ground and conditions. He must have learnt that the small garrison at Holmby House (not more than fifty men) would be favourable to Cromwell's audacious stroke. By ten o'clock in the evening of Wednesday, the 2nd of June (the night was clear and the moon nearly full), news reached the Commissioners at Holmby House that there was a rendezvous of mounted troops gathering in the dusk about three and a half miles away from the doors and two miles from the south lodge of the Park.

As you go out of Northampton by the Rugby road you come, a little before the village of Harsleden, upon a plantation, but in those days the land was open and there were no trees upon it, it had not yet been enclosed and was known as Harsleden Heath. It was there Joyce assembled his command. Four hours later, at two o'clock in the morning on Thursday, the 3rd of June, Joyce's troop were all round the house at Holmby, and by dawn he and his men were entering the place, the small garrison of which at once fraternised with them.

At six o'clock Charles himself came out on to the lawn in front of the house and spoke with Joyce under the early sun.† Charles asked by what orders Joyce had come; under whose commission. Now Joyce had no commission; he had no writing to show. He point-

---

† There is a tradition that Joyce had already seen him in the night, rudely interrupting his sleep, but this is not certain.

THE HOSTAGE

ed to his 500 drawn up in rank and said, "These are my commission." Charles's smiling answer is famous; he said that he had never seen any commission more plainly set forth. On the next day, an ominous Friday, about mid-morning, Joyce and his men went off with their capture and the King was once more, and for the last time, to change masters. He conceived that it might be slightly for the better. As for the Parliamentary Commissioners, Joyce had given them a rigmarole of a document, unsigned and saying nothing in particular except that it behoved the Army to save the King from danger.

Fairfax sent out Colonel Whalley to meet the cavalcade, and imagined that they would obey his orders to take the King back to Holmby. If we are to believe Whalley the King preferred not to return. Now who was Whalley? Whalley was Cromwell's first cousin and right-hand man; he was the "dear cousin Whalley" of Cromwell's correspondence, and though he went on this errand under the nominal orders of Fairfax, it was Cromwell who sent him. Most certainly he had no intention of restoring the King to the Commissioners of the Parliament, even if the King had desired to go.

On the fourth day, Monday, the 7th of June, Cromwell and Fairfax and others of the Army leaders rode up to Childerley Hall, where Charles had stopped over the week-end, and spoke with the King; and there Cromwell gave the solemn assurance that he was not responsible for Joyce's action – in which he lied: nor did the King believe a word he said.

There had been in this further ride southward from Holmby the same demonstrations of loyalty, the same tide of reaction, as in that first journey down from the north four months before. So strong was the popular feeling that they dared not take the King through Cambridge, where a great reception had been prepared for him, but went round south of the city; and Charles, after staying in a little palace of his own at Newmarket, went on by further stages, still in the hands of the Army. He stopped at Hatfield. He was at Windsor on the 1st of July, and, the headquarters of the Army being now at Reading, he lay for some days at Caversham in the house of Lord Craven.

It was the policy of the Army leaders – that is of Cromwell – to let the King have far more freedom than he had enjoyed in the hands of the Parliamentarians at Holmby; for they wished him, for the moment, to support them against the Parliament in a conflict which daily drew nearer; though all the while Cromwell was designing the King's destruction.

They allowed him to see his children, who came out to Maidenhead to meet him, and whom he kept with him at Caversham for two days; they allowed him to hunt and ride round about, and – what was for him a strong solace – he was allowed once more, after so many months, the ministrations of the Church of England. On the 27th of June, a Sunday, at Hatfield, and again on the Sunday after, when he had reached Caversham, he had heard the services of the Established Church in the chapel for the first time since he had left Oxford, fourteen months before.

The miserable Parliament, in its alarm, voted £10,000 more to be paid off the arrears owing to the Army, but it had no effect in soothing the soldiers. Their anger against the civilians increased.

The end of all this moving about did not come till the last days of August, on the 29th of which month the King was at Hampton Court, where he was to remain until that disastrous flight which was to be engineered by Cromwell for his destruction.

Throughout all this time, I say, it had been the policy of Cromwell to give the King all the freedom possible compatible with the fact that he was in reality a prisoner. He was to be made to feel that the Army was his friend, contrasted with what still called itself the Government at Westminster. The question therefore arises – it is the capital question at this stage of the tragedy – *when did Cromwell decide that the King should be put to death?* We must carefully distinguish between this question and another, to wit, when did Cromwell decide that the King *could* be killed?

The second question demands a different answer from the first. Cromwell's decision to aim at the death of Charles would obviously come earlier than his decision that the time had come when active preparations could be made for putting that decision into effect. The policy of Death would need support; it would need a previous groundwork: others would have to be demanding the King's trial before he himself should show his hand.

Now the answer to the first, and most important, question may be suggested not only by inference but by a certain amount of posi-

THE HOSTAGE

tive proof: and the answer is that Cromwell's decision to have Charles killed at last came early in the business, probably about the time when Cromwell made his speech to dupe the Parliament and when he first felt himself in peril.

Hugh Peters, the fanatical minister who was to preach in favour of that policy so violently, told Younge two years later, at the end of 1649, after the King's death, that, as early as the moment when he and Cromwell had left London in order to avoid arrest, the two had resolved "to bring the King to justice and to cut off his head." We may further note the action of one Marten, a Member of Parliament who was among the first to clamour openly for the same course. Now Marten was a creature of Cromwell's. He was one of the Puritan debauchees, that special type which arose at this time, men fanatical enough in Calvinistic religion, and probably sincerely so, but in their private lives dissolute. It was this looseness which had put him into Cromwell's power; he remained one of Cromwell's closest servants, and how closely he stood with the man who was to be master of England we shall see on a later page.

During all this time, while the King was thus with the Army, better treated, and deceived into thinking that his opportunities of final success were rising, the quarrel between the Army and the Parliament was getting steadily more open and defined. Less than a fortnight after Joyce's raid the Army had petitioned for the removal of eleven Members whom they accused of openly fomenting trouble between themselves and the politicians. The Commons hesitated, but ended by refusing, and therefore, within yet another fortnight, the Speaker, and fifty-eight members who sympathised with the Army, against their own body, left the House and took refuge with the soldiers. On the 6th of August the Army took them back to London, the eleven threatened members fled a few days later to France, and it was clear that the remnant of political authority at Westminster was tottering.

So far it must have seemed to Charles, by the time he reached Hampton Court at the end of August, that he was still securely advancing towards a solution which he might accept – the restoration of his throne on some basis of compromise with the Revolutionary demands. But Charles was wrong. The Army, as it became more and more master, would of course insist, just as much as the politicians had done, upon the main part of the Revolutionary programme; they were as much opposed as the Revolutionaries were to the main feeling of the English people in favour of a restoration, and no one dared to move against them.

With the King thus duped and in this mood Cromwell played the second stroke in his game. With the approach of autumn a demand breaking out in various places for the King's trial – which could only mean his death – began to be heard more loudly: it had been suggested first to fanatics, it is true, and mainly to men having no responsibility – but it was sufficient to bewilder the victim.

On the 1st of October, 1647, Hugh Peters, who worked in and in with Cromwell and whose violent sermons were the precursors of the final act, published a pamphlet hinting more openly at the King's death.

Charles's alarm increased. At the end of October he sent to Whalley, Cromwell's cousin and right-hand man, and said that he must "withdraw his Parole," that is, his word of honour not to attempt an escape; for Charles had by now become convinced, through these voices raised on various sides, that if he remained at Hampton Court he was in danger of assassination. He did not understand who they were who really plotted against his life; he did not yet sufficiently suspect Cromwell. He rather feared death at the hand of some assassin among the creatures who had been arranged to raise such a clamour. He had already during October been offered a chance by the Scottish Commissioners, who were in London at that moment intriguing with the Parliament against the Army, to escape by their aid; he had then refused to break his Parole; but now at the end of this month of October he refused to renew it. His sense of honour led him to his death. Later, when he might have saved his life by neglecting honour and breaking his Parole he would not save it.

The King having thus refused to promise that he would not attempt to escape, Whalley ostentatiously doubled the guards on the last day of the month, the 31st of October. But Whalley was playing a double game. He was serving a plan of Cromwell's. We shall see how, on the critical day, he took care that there should be no sentry at the critical point.

Charles was to be given every chance of escape, in order that he might be lured into a situation from which further escape should not

THE HOSTAGE

be possible, and therefore be got into the hands of those whom Cromwell intended should hold him until he should be ripe for the axe.

The craft of Cromwell in all this long business of eighteen months or more, indeed nearly two years, is admirable. At every stage you may see the action not of mere courage, which rarely has, alone, any effect, but of clear thinking and exact planning. Cromwell having seen earlier than any other man that, so long as Charles remained alive his own life was in jeopardy, having said months earlier, while the war was still lingering on and the final defeat of the King seemed indefinitely delayed, that though Charles were beaten ninety-nine times he still remained King, and that if ever Charles won "assuredly they would all be hanged," was now drawing in his net.

There is an old and well-worn saying imported from Asia that those who conduct a revolution ride on a tiger: in all the revolutions of European history this determination to avoid the consequences of treason or rebellion has necessarily appeared, and commonly the victorious party puts to death that man who, by his mere continued life, threatens their own security. Charles must not survive to be, even in close prison, let alone in exile, a possible rallying-point. For Cromwell, clear-sighted in this as in all things, also saw better than did any of his contemporaries how strong a national feeling was growing in favour of a Restoration of the old National Monarchy, and how the crushing taxation of the Revolution was fostering it.

On the 9th of November all was ready for the carefully shepherded evasion of the duped King. The gentlemen in his service, Ashburnham and Berkeley, had been sent away from his side, but they had prepared for a flight. Horses were ready at Bishop's Sutton, in Hampshire, and thither Charles was to repair.

That Whalley gave every opportunity for the King to get away is certain; there was but one obvious way the King could take, it was the way towards the river bank from the garden, and the backstairs into the garden from the King's apartments formed the obvious exit which anyone desiring to ensure the King's close captivity would have first seen to. Whalley deliberately left them unguarded on that night, Thursday, the 11th of November, dark, and stormy with rain.

On that day or the day before, quite probably even earlier – for we only have Whalley's word for so late a date as the 10th – Charles, perhaps already preparing his flight, had been given the final spur by the receipt of two letters. One was written by Cromwell himself to Whalley, saying that he feared the King was in danger; the other was anonymous, and pretended to give Charles information of his immediate peril from assassination. This last anonymous letter, signed E.R., and professing to be from some citizen in Broad Street, was believed to be of Cromwell's own concoction. It is noticeable that Whalley's own Chaplain tells us most men said it was contrived by Cromwell. In that letter two names were mentioned, the fanatical preachers Dell and Hugh Peters, as willing to bear company with the assassins.

No one was with the King when he got away but Legge. The two other gentlemen who were to further the flight, Ashburnham and Berkeley, were waiting at Thames Ditton on the further shore of the Thames – and Whalley was careful not to go and see whether anything had happened until after the King had got away.

The four men, the King and his three companions, rode all night missing their way in the darkness, they only came to Sutton, where the relays of horses were, by daybreak of Friday the 12th. It is after the arrival at Sutton on this day that the irreparable step was taken which is impossible of explanation unless we regard it as due to suggestions already made, through the agency of Cromwell, to those whom he knew would accompany the King. For what happened was this:—

It being now daylight, and therefore dangerous for the King to travel too far lest he should be recognised, it was decided that he should make for Tichfield House, the big place belonging to the Southamptons close to the shores of Southampton Water over against the Isle of Wight. From that place there would be a better opportunity for getting a ship, sooner or later; but more important still, Hammond, the new Governor of the Isle of Wight, was said, or believed, to be loyal.

The accounts of what happened after become contradictory, because, the event proving fatal to the King, the two men chiefly concerned, Ashburnham and Berkeley, would each be suspected of treason. But indeed there was no treason in either. They were both loyal men, and John Ashburnham in particular was devoted to his King.

Clearly someone had given the idea to those who were thus responsible for Charles's next movements that a ship would be waiting for him; and someone also must have put the idea into the heads of

THE HOSTAGE

the King's companions that if he could not get away overseas his best chance would be to make for the Isle of Wight, where the recently appointed Governor, young Colonel Hammond, was a nephew of one of the King's own loyal friends, Dr. Hammond, who had been Chaplain in the Royal Chapel. All the traditions of the family were Royalist. What had not been suggested – and what was really the key to the whole affair – was the fact that young Colonel Hammond was in the heart of the Cromwell clique. Charles had clearly been lured into a trap.

For who was this young Colonel Hammond, now Governor of the Isle of Wight? He was the son-in-law of Hampden. He was therefore a cousin by marriage of Cromwell and of Whalley. He was but twenty-six years old and had been given a regiment when he was but twenty-four through the influence of Cromwell and the Hampden connection.

We may marvel, looking back upon it and seeing it as clearly as we now can, that Charles should have trusted himself to a young man of such a character. Perhaps we should marvel more at those who cannot see the simple clue to the whole business: unless Charles were shepherded according to a pre-conceived plan, unless the suggestions had been conveyed with art by someone familiar with Ashburnham or Berkeley or both, the thing is inconceivable. If we see it as Marvell saw it and put it in his famous poem, as most contemporaries saw it and as common sense must see it, if we see it as a triumph of Cromwell's genius for combination and intrigue, the thing becomes simple enough.

While Charles went down the east side of Southampton Water towards Tichfield House, Berkeley and Ashburnham went down the west side to cross to the island from Lymington and see what they could do with the Governor. They found Hammond the next morning and put before him the proposal of the King that he, Hammond, should receive Charles no longer as a hostage but as a guest; should protect him and guarantee his liberty. That was the understanding. They proposed it in good faith; they thought they had found a friend.

Young Hammond seemed overwhelmed by the news of the proposal. He could not have heard of the hour of the King's flight;

CHARLES I

perhaps he thought that Charles was already on the island and that he would beheld responsible should successful escape be made.

Meanwhile, had he received instructions? Had he been coached in the part he was to play, supposing the King did fall into his hands? It is probable, but not certain. It is probable because it is unlikely that a man of his character (he was vacillating and hated responsibility) and so young should have acted as he now did without some previously fixed rôle. And it is doubly probable through his close connection with Cromwell. At any rate he procured from his visitors, or was perhaps spontaneously offered by them, a proposal to go over the water and see the King. On his way he took with him the officer in command of Cowes Castle, so that there might be two of them. This annoyed Berkeley; but Ashburnham pointed out that he and Berkeley could deal with the other two between them if it were necessary. Still, it would have been better to be two to one.

When they had all come over the water again to Tichfield, Ashburnham announced who it was he had brought; and the King saw at once what had happened. He cried out that he was undone! Ashburnham offered to kill the two servants of the Army there and then, Colonel Hammond and the Governor of Cowes, but the King would not have it done, characteristically refusing on a point of honour. If they were killed, he said, people would say that he had lured them over only to procure their death; and by this refusal he sealed his own fate. Charles consented to go back to the island with Hammond and from that moment, we, who can look back on all that happened, know that his enemy had won and that the end was certain. He was now more securely held, here, in Cromwell's hands than he would have been anywhere else in England; here, in the Island, quite cut off.

He was treated well at first, and given the full dignity of a King, save that of course he was watched and could not get away; but after just a month of this Cromwell himself came over to the Isle of Wight and saw his young cousin Hammond in private.

What passed between them as to the future we do not know, but this we do know, that all the complicated negotiations, all the efforts which Charles was still to make for more than eleven months – still attempting to play the Parliament against the Army, the Scotch against the Parliament, etc. – though they make a lengthy and compli-

THE HOSTAGE

cated story are not significant compared with the now clearly defined process whereby the King was to be led to his death.

Cromwell had landed in the Isle of Wight on the 16th of December, 1647, he left it a week later on the 23rd. During Christmas Week, Charles having received to his advance on the side of the Army a refusal, to his advance on the side of the Parliament a proposal called "The Four Points" reducing him still further, and such that he could not accept them because they involved that upon which he was fixed – the saving of the Episcopacy – fell back upon his third chance, the Scotch. To the Scottish Commissioners who came and negotiated with him he offered what history has called "The Engagement," much what he had accepted before; but the Scotch were now more amenable because their quarrel with the English had gone so far that they were willing to use the King as a card to be played against their opponents.

The whole thing was futile; negotiations whether with Parliament or the Scotch might as well not have been made; the Army, of which Cromwell was the necessary and admitted leader, would certainly master both, and the Army being Cromwell would achieve its end and destroy the King.

At the end of these negotiations from the 29th of December, 1647, onwards, the imprisonment of Charles grew rigorous. There was even a scene of violence between Hammond and the King; how grievous we do not know, for rumour may have exaggerated it, but there is no doubt that grave disrespect was shown – and for the first time since he had begun his wanderings Charles was treated with indignity.

As the months went by, the matter of moment was that every effort at rescue and escape failed. A ship had waited for the captive and had had to sail without him; a loyal man of good family and good courage had at one moment attempted to raise a small riot in Charles's favour in the town of Newport, but the reward of his effort was that he was hanged, drawn and quartered in the town of Winchester. Charles failed in an effort to get away through the narrow window of his room. He was but treated with greater rigour.

To the advancing plans for the destruction of the King there was one major obstacle, which, unlike all the other obstacles Crom-

CHARLES I

well had to overcome, loomed larger and larger before him as time went on; in everything else it was his power which was growing, his ultimate opportunity for having the King killed which became more and more secure; but in this one major point it was the other way about. Side by side with the growth of Cromwell's chance went the growth of this impediment – and this growing impediment was the royalist reaction throughout England. It was just possible that it would prove too strong for the full project to be carried out and for Cromwell to feel himself able to breathe freely at last.

Consider the situation. To begin with, even at the very start of the struggle between the Crown and the Houses of Parliament, the nation was divided. It is always dangerous to talk of majorities, because opinion on almost any disputed political matter is composed of an active right-wing, an active opposing left-wing, and a large central part, most of which is neutral. But anyhow, at the very beginning of the struggle, when it was a question of paying out as little as possible, or of Puritan enthusiasm in another and partly overlapping group, or of hatred of Catholicism, which accounted for a very much larger group, or of hatred of the foreigner, which is an emotion common to nearly the whole of every nation, opinion was divided.

And as the struggle proceeded opinion became more and more divided. By the time things came to open war the mass of the English people certainly disapproved of a rebellion against their hereditary King. There was a very large body which approved, but it was a minority; better led and better organised and with more permanent resources than their opponents – but a minority. As the war proceeded the opinion opposed to that which still called itself the Parliament got stronger. The Rebels were levying a ruthless taxation to maintain their cause, the general chaos was felt to be intolerable and it was clear that the initiative in provoking war had been with the rebellion. As the fighting died down the number of those who objected to the revolutionary claim, and the intensity of their objection, naturally increased. Since the fighting was over why could they not go back to the old light imposts and the old ordinary way of life? When it came to the virtual imprisonment of the King, to the baiting and badgering of him and the holding of him by force, a spirit of active loyalty was awakened and joined all the rest. And now that he was removed from

THE HOSTAGE

them, a prisoner in an island remote from all the rest of the country and clearly a victim, the feeling was so strong that it might become overwhelming.

The people were disarmed, they were held down by a well-organised and well-led permanent force, much larger than, indeed of a kind different from, and more efficient as an instrument of tyranny than, anything England had ever seen. But even so, things came to such a point that the new regime was imperilled. There were local revolts in the south, there was active fighting in Kent, and at last a considerable regular military force raised by Goring and prepared to stand a siege in Colchester.

All this might have found a sufficient ally in a Scottish army which was prepared to invade in aid of the King under Hamilton. Hamilton got as far as mid-Lancashire, but his doom was certain for two reasons. First of all he had not enough men, secondly he was opposed to a cavalry commander of genius, in that day when cavalry counted for so much; for Cromwell came up in person and by the middle of the summer, in August, 1648, Hamilton's force was destroyed and Hamilton himself taken prisoner. Following on that Colchester could no longer hold out, and it surrendered at the end of the month.

The result, therefore, was that Cromwell and the Army was stronger than ever, as a force is always stronger after the failure of an attempt at overthrowing it. By land, then, Cromwell and the Army were again supreme, but there was grave news now of reaction at sea. Eight ships of that Navy which Charles had created and Northumberland betrayed to the Revolutionaries mutinied. They sailed over the North Sea and gave themselves up to the Royalist Command. Had the Prince of Wales, who took them over, made for the Isle of Wight, he might have rescued his father; as it was he was advised to threaten London and the Parliament and its trade by way of the mouth of the Thames – and thus effected nothing. He had to return from lack of provisions just after the failure of Hamilton's invasion and of the revolts by land.

Not yet, however, were things ripe for mere force; the very fact that the Army had triumphed and had now no further resistance to meet emboldened the Parliament and led it into illusions of power which it did not really possess. They had passed resolutions that they would no longer negotiate with Charles; they now changed their minds and proposed negotiation, and even while the cry for Charles's blood grew louder and louder in the Army and more and more pleasing to the ears of Cromwell, down in the Isle of Wight were being laboriously hammered out the futile debates as to what Charles would or would not yield to the Politicians by way of a final compromise. He himself said in his private letters that all this would come to nothing, and he was right. The Politicians were ceasing to count. The Army would decide all.

Yet the futile episode was of a certain service to the King, it gave him a certain partial liberty; for he was allowed to leave Carisbrooke Castle and went to live in Newport, giving his Parole that he would not attempt to escape. There he remained until nearly the end of November, 1648.

For the negotiations of Charles with the Parliamentary Commissioners lasted longer than the time originally allowed for; they had been prolonged by order; they did not end until the 27th of November – and the King, in the peril which was now so great, abandoned nearly everything. He consented that seven of those who had supported him should not benefit by pardon (they included Newcastle and Digby) he allowed the incomes of the Bishops to go to the Crown until religion should be settled, reserving the point that Episcopacy should not be abolished by him nor its endowments permanently alienated, but still it would lie with Parliament (had there been any reality in all this) whether they should be returned or not. And there was as a fact no reality in all this talk: Cromwell was even now prepared to strike.

On the 28th of November, Charles, who had already distinguished between the reality of the situation and these empty negotiations, said good-bye to the Envoys of the Parliament (at the head of whom were Northumberland and Pembroke) and told them that he felt he should never see them again. The very next day after the departure of the peers who had been negotiating for Parliament, Cromwell's movement began; for it was upon Wednesday, the 29th of November, that the King and his companions in Newport (where he was allowed to associate freely with his cousin Lennox, Duke of Richmond, Lord Lindsey and others; he had a sort of little Court) heard that an armed force was on its way to take him captive.

THE HOSTAGE

The night was wet and it blew a gale, it was pitch dark for it was the very last of the old moon. The King's friends urged him to fly; he made that reply incomprehensible to his enemies (but his friends understood him well enough) that honour forbade because he had given his word. Escape would have been easy, the password was known, and on such a night the little cloaked figure would not have been recognised in the constant coming to and fro – it was of Charles's own choice that the thing was not done.

Early the next morning, Thursday, the last day of the month, at the first of the light, came Cobbett, one of Cromwell's colonels, with a troop of horse, and with that mounted guard was a coach. They bore Charles off to the coach, wherein he sat alone, to the little harbour of Yarmouth twelve miles off, and thence over the Solent to Hurst Castle.

Hurst Castle, standing at the end of a long narrow spit of sand and shingle which runs out for something like two miles from the Hampshire coast into the waters of the Solent, is a prison indeed. A fierce tide runs back and forth along the steep beach beneath its walls. It was then a dungeon so dark under the narrow windows in the thick walls in those mid-winter days that candles were lit at noon, and he who was gaoler of the King was consonant to the place – a dark, surly, bushy-bearded man, Ewer by name, swaggering with a great sword.

Therein lay Charles for nineteen days, quite cut off from all the world: and meanwhile outside those things were toward which introduced the last scene.

THE KILLING OF THE KING

THE LAST TWO MONTHS OF THE KING'S LIFE ON EARTH ARE AN episode separate from all the rest. The decision had been taken. He was openly marked for death.

Cromwell had been at work for long and now the time had come when the thing could be done, subject, of course, to his continued skill in the handling of the forces in action. From the beginning of December, 1648, to the last moments on the scaffold at the end of January, 1649, what goes on is tragically new. Negotiations lose their meaning; the hopes still entertained – even by Charles himself – lose all their substance; they become shadows. The succession of days is a direct procession to the scaffold. Those two months are in their entirety the killing of the King and the flowering of Cromwell's long-matured plan.

The story has been told a thousand times. Its smallest physical details have been examined and re-examined. Every site, every recorded word, has passed through three centuries of criticism. Nothing can be told on these that is not known and even a commonplace. Yet there is here, as in all the tragedy of Charles's life, the element of a problem to be solved, and if we do not solve it aright we misunderstand even those clear-cut sixty days of doom.

In the first place we must understand that the Army was now not only supreme, but stood alone. There was now no other power. There remained to the simulacrum of a Parliament the prestige of its name and (what is always important in political affairs) the momentum of the past. Men had thought in terms of Parliamentary authority as opposed to Royal authority for a quarter of a century; those two terms had been the antagonists of the war; the Royal authority having been destroyed under arms, only the term of Parliamentary authority remained. But its exercise in practice had ceased. It retained the name of ruler but had already lost the power thereof. It had really lost that

THE KILLING OF THE KING

power as early as that day, eighteen months before, when Cromwell had sent Joyce to seize the person of the King; but the open admitted loss of it had come by various stages – when the Parliament had failed to disband the troops, when its orders had been repeatedly disobeyed, when it had been roughly handled without any punishment for the assault being possible and – the last blow – when its orders against the removal of the King from the Isle of Wight were openly disobeyed.

But so much remained to the ghost of Parliamentary authority as was necessary for those who would act, that is, for the soldiers, to use the mere name of Parliament as a sanction for what they did.

Now when we say that the Army by this time, December, 1648, completely controlled and that all real authority had passed to it, that is equivalent to saying that all real authority had passed to Cromwell. Men in the plural, especially men in great numbers, even men corporate, cannot carry out a plan from stage to stage with precision; such action is not possible to acephalous mankind – and that is why Cabinets bungle war.

Here, in the killing of Charles Stuart, was a plan carried out most carefully over many months, step after step after step: first the capture of the person of the King, then the granting of relaxation to him, even of some honour, in the hope that he might be used for the plotter's purpose; then, on the failure of this, and on the determination to kill him, an accurate series of measures leading on to a pre-conceived conclusion. He was spurred on to escape, secret facilities were given him for doing so, he was shepherded to a place where he could be under a particular control and inaccessible to all save by permission of that control; the cry for his death was next raised, it grows louder, it spreads among the troops and falls from the pens of pamphleteers; the time is not yet quite ripe, there is still insurrection and invasion designed to save the King. The invasion and insurrection are easily mastered – and then indeed the carefully fostered clamour for a victim can be taken up and an official thing made of it.

To be able to wait for the precise moment after which a policy long matured can be openly declared is the very mark of a genius for intrigue. See how all this process has behind it the will and intelligence of Cromwell, from the day when (he remaining in the background) his agent seizes the King's person to the day when (he not presiding nor putting himself forward as the chief) he makes sure of the verdict and compels the signature of the Warrant.

There is not one man acting *throughout* that is not his; one of his creatures originates the cry for the King's death; another creature and close relative is the King's gaoler at Hampton Court, the man who delivered the menacing letter and facilitated the King's false escape; yet another creature and relative has Charles in bond during all those months in the Isle of Wight; it is Cromwell himself who comes there to give orders; to Cromwell are reported by his secret intelligence service the further attempts at evasion; it is Cromwell who sets the last warders to their task. Yes, there is one will and one plan behind it all, and they belittle Oliver Cromwell who think to do his memory a favour by pleading his reluctance or his ignorance. If such action were evil (and it was not evil to men with the code of Cromwell's religion, which knew nothing of, or rather was opposed to, the code of honour) it is nonetheless great. To wait so patiently, to grasp so many factors in their right proportion, to note the exact time for action and to obtain a final decision is Generalship. And of all his contemporaries no other showed Generalship but Cromwell alone in this matter of compassing the death of the King.

In the dead of the long night between Monday, the 18th of December, and Tuesday, the 19th, at the very turn of the winter darkness, the King heard the noise of horse approaching Hurst Castle drawbridge and the words of command. He waked in alarm and bade Herbert find out what was this stir, who returned and told him that Colonel Harrison had come. At that name "Harrison" the King was too much moved; it was a name which he associated with sudden death, for he had been awfully told that Harrison himself would do the deed. Yet Harrison did not come to act the murder with his own hand, he came with his mounted men to take the King away, upon that long and interrupted road to London which was to end as we know.

Let us here understand by its dates the secret plan which was so thoroughly carried out by its author.

The first thing we note is the connection between the actions of the Army (that is, of him who was moving all) and the events which were being watched by the plotters with such anxiety, lest their plans should miscarry. On the very day that Charles had suddenly been taken by force from the Island a Council of Officers had denounced

THE KILLING OF THE KING

the Parliamentary majority and warned "all good people" to put themselves under the protection of the soldiers.

The very day after Charles's first settlement in Hurst Castle several regiments were marched on to London. The first two were chosen for the violence of feeling among the men, and especially the regiment of Hewson — himself the most fanatical of the commanders. The idea of the whole proceeding was to strike terror, and in this it thoroughly succeeded. Hewson was given for quarters the Royal Palace of Whitehall. Pride, a singular character, commanded the other regiment, which was quartered in St. James's; he was an illiterate man, risen through some military aptitude and also strength of will and lack of scruple. He had begun life by driving a cart for a brewer. "Character," as it is called today, he had in plenty, and it is remarkable how much he was hated even among his colleagues.

So far the threat was to Westminster only and not directly to the City, though the City was overawed, knowing that its turn would come next. Then began that military occupation of London which was to be so much increased, until the soldiers openly ruled. That military occupation of the City lasted without interruption for eleven years.

What was left of the Parliament rallied, oddly enough, in spite of the military threat surrounding it; by its authority the Commissioners of the Commons had gone down to treat with the King at Newport; to it had those Commissioners reported the terms which Charles would accept; in a sort of desperation they made their last effort to affirm bravely that supremacy which they had long lost. In their numbers (under half the full complement of the House, less than 250 men) there was an opposition which sided in varying degrees with the military party. Therefore there was fierce debate all through Monday, the 4th of December, and on, right through the night; it was not until the morning of Tuesday, the 5th, that the wrangle ended from exhaustion and that a vote was taken. Then solemnly, as though they were still in the days of their power, the maimed Commons registered a decision in favour of accepting the King's terms. It was a sufficient majority: one of 44 in a House of 244 members: sufficient — but also without any effect. For on the next day, Wednesday, the 6th of December, Colonel Pride came down with his batch of soldiers to the doors of the House, turned away all those who had been suspected of resisting the Army, even in intention (and among those thus

CHARLES I

turned away were included not a few even of the members who had voted in the minority for refusing the King's terms). Altogether less than fifty men were allowed to enter the House and were bidden, or permitted, to call themselves the House of Commons still. Yet such was the force of the mere name "Parliament" that this petty fragment was retained with that name attached to it, in order that it might do the work required of it by Cromwell, one of its members.

That soldier was on his way back from the north, where, after his victory over the Scottish invasion, he had visited Edinburgh. He had many days since turned him homeward. It is to be remarked again that he was deliberately slow in his progress; he actually halted well outside London on the critical day when his work was being done for him by Pride, and the House of Commons reduced to the jest it had now become. He did not enter London until the next day, Thursday, the 7th of December. Further regiments were marched in as the week ended. The nave of old St. Paul's was turned into a barracks and the church fearfully desecrated, the treasure of the Parliament (£35,000 in gold, what we should today call a quarter of a million) was seized by the command of the Army and taken off in five carts. Then, all during that week-end, to enslave the City and keep it thoroughly in hand, regiments of foot and troops of horse paraded up and down through the streets.

Note the next coincidence, or rather the next exact timing of a military plan conducted as though it were a campaign, for there was behind it all the brain of a man now trained in the conduct of campaigns. The moment when proceedings against the King were first discussed by the remaining fragment of the House of Commons was also that moment in which Charles was beginning his long imprisonment in Windsor. This was because he must now be kept close at hand, within a day of London, to be moved up at the right moment. Cromwell reached St. James's on the night of the 19th of December, on the same day as Charles was taken from Hurst Castle. On the morrow, the 20th, was made the first suggestion of the trial which was to come. It was made in a House of only 43 members.

While this was proceeding in London the King rode up through the New Forest and on to Winchester, where the Mayor and authorities of the town paid loyal service. On the next day, Wednesday, the

THE KILLING OF THE KING

20th, to Farnham, and so up the road. Upon the noon of Saturday, the 23rd of December, there had been planned yet another attempt at escape, which failed as all had done. It was luck; the fast horse that was ready fell lame. But would any trickery have evaded the guard? He dined at Bagshot Park; he lay that night in the Castle at Windsor, sleeping in the old room which he had used in the better times at the end of the Castle ward, and the gentleman who served him lying in the dressing-room attached, the window of which looks out over Eton.

There he remained a full four weeks; it was not till Friday, the 19th of January, 1649, that he was to be taken on the last stage to London. He still hoped. Wherever he had passed he had noted the attitude of the people, in Windsor itself there had been on his arrival quite a throng, not only of the townspeople, but of men of his party, loyal men who had ridden in from outside, and that same evening there were brawls between them and the soldiers – ten troops of horse which formed the escort of Harrison's command.

His Christmas Day, a Monday, he had passed in state; and as they would not allow him the ministrations of the Church of England he read the service himself with solemnity. On the Wednesday came the order that he was no longer to be treated with the ceremonial of kingship. The cup was not to be offered to him with a genuflection, nor his dishes brought covered to table, nor the trumpets sounded at his meals. Therefore, for what he could save of his dignity, he determined to dine alone, and it was the easier for him because the greater part of his attendants had also been withdrawn. Move from his prison he could not; his exercise was pacing up and down the long terrace, and for his solace he would pass hours in what Milton so curiously condemned in him, the reading of Shakespeare's plays.

During that month of silence and segregation alone, all was moving at Westminster for the setting up of the final scene. On that same Saturday before Christmas, the 23rd of December, on which Charles had reached Windsor, the remnant of the House of Commons, the little group who still worked there as the servants of the Army, and therefore of its only true commander, proceeded obediently to demand the life of the King. Even among them there was some opposition, perhaps for the sake of form and to give some pretence of reality to the proceedings. But the bulk of those present,

38 members, were formed into a committee to arrange the affair and once again we find on that committee (and the leading manager of it) a creature of Cromwell's, Marten.

Even as it was, from that committee not a few slunk away, for the responsibility was heavy. But those who remained proposed that a declaration should be made as of law, and they solemnly voted that it was High Treason in the King of England to levy war against the Parliament. The vote was taken on New Year's Day, a week after the committee had formed, and on that same Monday the House passed an "Ordinance" setting up a High Court of Justice. The legal pedantry which runs through the whole of that time – for the lawyers had been half the spirit of it – was not absent. This High Court of Justice was to try a "question of fact," and the "question of fact" they were to try was whether Charles Stuart, King of England, had been guilty of such treason as they had defined.

Of the House of Lords at that time, seven would at the most assemble to carry on the figment of continuity; but now that there was an opportunity of saving skins, fifteen appeared and these unanimously refused the Ordinance. Which meant nothing. Nothing did mean anything at this moment but the will of the Army and its real chief. For within the week, on Twelfth Day, the 6th of January, the "House of Commons" (that is, the 46 men present) voted that in future they would make Acts of Parliament without Lords or King. They proceeded to set up a sort of Jury of Commission to try their Sovereign. They filled the list with 150 names, drawn from among themselves and from such in the City, the Inns of Court and the Officers of the Army as they thought they could count upon; yet in the event but a fraction of these consented to serve.

Three days later, Cromwell himself speaking in their midst upon the question of a new Great Seal to be used in the new regime, gave a last and interesting example of his caution in avoiding the first place, though he was the strength of all. "If any man whatsoever have carried on this design of deposing the King and disinheriting his posterity he must be the greatest traitor and rebel in the world." So he spoke. And then balanced it with further words, "but since the Providence of God has cast this upon us, we cannot but submit to Providence."

THE KILLING OF THE KING

On Wednesday, the 10th of January, the Commissioners who were to form the Court gathered in the Painted Chamber: there were 45 of them only. They had to choose a man for the perilous post of Chief Judge, or president. An obscure lawyer who had acted in a lesser judicial capacity in Chester, one John Bradshaw, was pitched upon, but only after more wary candidates had refused. Bradshaw also tried to be excused when he learnt the news, but he was lured by a sounding title, "Lord President," and promised a great reward – which indeed he got, for he was given the confiscated estates of Lord Cottington as well as permanent official salaries.

On Monday, the 15th of January, the charge against the King was drafted, and when the date of trial was finally fixed for the end of the week, Charles was sent for from Windsor. He was taken there on Friday, the 19th. It was a noisy cavalcade with a strong mounted guard, Hugh Peters, the frenzied Puritan preacher, riding in front of it, the King in the midst, alone, in a coach drawn by six horses. They lodged him that night in St. James's, and on the next day, Saturday, the 20th of January, the trial opened in Westminster Hall.

Only a part of the Hall was used, rather more than one-third of it to the southern end. There a raised platform had been set up with galleries above it where privileged spectators could have place. The King's Judges had benches set for them draped in scarlet, John Bradshaw on a higher chair in the midst. There were six such ranks; a space in front about 25 feet wide where the clerks sat at a table with the Mace and Sword thereon, and then, at the further edge of the platform, just in front of some steps that led up to it from the main hall, was a sort of dock wherein they all waited to see appearing the King.

He had been brought that morning from St James's in a fashion designed to avoid what Cromwell and his supporters most dreaded – the Royalist cries and perhaps the tumult of the populace. Bradshaw had provided himself with a bullet-proof hat. They brought him through the Park, hustled him through Whitehall Palace and on to a barge at the landing stage by the riverside. But even there, on the water, there was a demonstration, those present cheering for the King; and the men who rowed refused to be covered; they worked bareheaded – in despite of the Army. The King was landed at the stairs of that now ruinous old house which had been built for Cotton

277

CHARLES I

in Elizabeth's reign (it stood on the site now covered by the Houses of Parliament and about on a level with the modern statue of Richard I, only further east of course and nearer the river).

The little figure of the King in his black clothes and great hat going up this garden path was seen by his Judges, who were waiting in the Painted Chamber before going into Westminster Hall. They saw him through a window giving on to the garden. Cromwell, who watched it with the others, showed, what was rare with him, some doubt.

"What shall we say," he asked, "if he shall deny the authority of the Court?" And again as always, though he knows the answer, it is not he, but one of his, who replies. For it was Marten who said, "By the authority of the Commons and good people of England."

This being settled, and certain small details (such as that the King might wear his hat) they filed into Westminster Hall and took up their places on the red benches. Hewson was among them, but his regiment, which was on guard that day – a mass of soldiery grouped round the further end of the platform – was commanded by his Lieutenant-Colonel, Axtell.

The roll of the Judges was called; it was found that exactly half were present – 68 – and the name of "Fairfax" being called first, a woman from the gallery on the east side above the Judges called out, "He has more wit than to be here!" It was his wife.

Bradshaw ordered the King to be sent for; he came in wearing the Garter and his George and in his right hand a white cane with a silver handle. He did not recognise the Court in any way, nor bow to its President, nor use any such forms, but sat him in the chair provided facing Bradshaw with that open space in between. As yet the populace had not been admitted into the Hall; there was only the mass of the soldiery beyond the platform and the few privileged spectators in the gallery

The charge was read. When the word "treason" was used the King broke silence for the first time and cried out, "By your favour – hold!" He was told that he could not speak until the charge had been read, and it was read accordingly by the prosecutor, Cook. It was a long, tedious legal rigmarole, using, as such documents do, ten words where one would suffice;† and to those words Charles, though he did

---

† For instance, in the operative words, "by all which it appears that he, the said Charles

THE KILLING OF THE KING

not yet speak, again listened. There followed a disgusting episode,† so typical of the spirit in which all this was done that the reader must bear with it. There was in the hall, among the few and privileged spectators there, a Scottish woman, the widow of one of Charles's first captains at the beginning of the war, a daughter to the man who had been Secretary to Anne of Denmark, the King's mother. When the words were read in the charge "that it proceeded from the King's subjects" she cried that it did not, but only from "traitors and rebels." Hewson, with whose name we are now becoming familiar and whom we shall meet again, branded her with hot irons on the shoulder and head in the sight of the King, who "seeing her flesh smoke and her hair all of a fire for him by their hot irons, commiserated her." Things like this should be noted and remembered; for an understanding of the time they are worth much more than rhetoric about "Stern Puritans."

When the charge was finished Bradshaw told the King that he might speak, and at the same moment the gates at the north end of the hall were opened and the people flocked in. The King's answer was brief; he said what he continued to say during the whole of his ordeal; he took up at once the position on which he was steadfast and in which he died. He denied the authority of the Court.

He told them he was taken by mere force from the Isle of Wight where he had been making treaty with what was still the recognised authority of the Houses of Parliament; he told them that when he found himself before a lawful authority he would answer – but not before: not to an illegal body.

There followed that day, and after, a ding-dong of assertion and counter-assertion; Bradshaw could do no more than affirm, without precedent, the right of this Court (which was no Court) to sit as it did; the King continued to reply that he would only deal with lawful authority and that for him unlawful authority did not exist. When Bradshaw commanded the Guard to withdraw the prisoner, the King hearing the word "prisoner" at once said, "The King!"

When the Court met again on the Monday, the 22nd of January, the King looked weary and haggard enough. He had not slept in a

---

Stuart, had been and was the originator, author and continuer of the said unnatural, cruel and bloody wars, and therefore guilty of all the treasons, murders, rapines, burnings, spoils, desolations, damages, mischiefs," etc.

† I take it wholly from Mr. Muddiman, who is I believe, the first to have recorded it.

bed for those two nights, for the officers had insisted upon putting soldiers as guards into his very room and he would not suffer the indignity. So he sat up. His air of weariness was accentuated by the greyness of his beard, which was in some disorder, and of a thicker growth than he had allowed it in better days. But he was careful of his dress, as of all things pertaining to his dignity.

On that Monday the affirmation and reply went on again. At one moment there were shouts from the people in the Hall cheering the King – it was when he said that he had been forbidden to give his reasons for defending the liberty and freedom of his subjects. It is strange indeed to read how during all these days the attempt at the expression of loyalty, violent repression and insult, went on side by side.

But that which most lingered in the general mind was the repeated truth, from which Charles never swerved, that he had been brought there, and was subject to what he suffered in defence of the liberties of the English people. For if *his* rights could be arbitrarily disposed of by brute force, and he brought before a tribunal which had no legal standing, what security had any man? His contempt for the tribunal goaded one of its members out of his control. It was again Hewson. He came forward from the red benches close up to the King and spat in his face, calling to the men of his Regiment at the same time that "there should be justice for him!" and bidding them also cry for justice – which mean death. The King took out his handkerchief, wiped his face, and replied without heat that "God had justice in keeping for both of them."

On the third day of the trial, Tuesday, the 23rd of January, there was a somewhat larger attendance, and the Judges came to a complement of seventy-one. Though the King had rested that night he looked graver than ever: it is often so after a strain, the first repose is followed by a reaction. All that day was the same: question and answer; the steady refusal of the King to admit that Bradshaw and those about him had any status. The fear of a popular reaction becoming too strong for them made them do all they could to prevent the King's speaking at all; as he went out at the end of that day's fruitless session he was heard saying "that he cared not a straw for them all!"

The Wednesday, Thursday and Friday – all the middle of the week – Westminster Hall was abandoned, the Commissioners met in the Painted Chamber. They made arrangements for the sentence, they had it engrossed, and on the Saturday the King was brought in to hear his sentence.

The soldiery had orders to cry, "Execution! Execution!" and it was to the echoes of these shouts, when silence had been ordered, that Bradshaw rose. Again the King demanded to speak; he was told he should be heard before judgment was given. When Bradshaw brought into his remarks "the People of England" as accusers of the King, Lady Fairfax made her second and most famous interruption which almost led to a riot; she cried out loudly, "Not a quarter of them!" She might well have said not one-tenth. What is more, she named the captain of the whole business, Cromwell himself, and called him a traitor. Axtell, Hewson's second in-command, shouted at her and the women about her in the galleries the vilest term he could find, threatened to shoot, and already had the muskets prepared, when, in the confusion, the women went away.

Then Charles was allowed to speak freely for the last time: he bade them remember that a sentence once passed might not be remedied and demanded to be heard before what was even now by his own admission Parliament, that is, by the Lords and Commons. He adjured Bradshaw solemnly, for the sake of the peace of the kingdom – but at this moment there was an interruption of the most significant sort; it was yet another of those incidents which enable us to understand the time and must be dwelt upon particularly because it illuminates all the long and well-known tale of those days, and in the light of it we may see how close the issue was and how right was the judgment of Cromwell in dreading lest the victim should escape him.

On the bench behind that occupied by Cromwell, and therefore a rank or two from the Chair, a certain member of the Commissioners, sat one John Downes. He had already begun to murmur while Bradshaw was speaking, and the interruption was resented by his colleagues. They told him in low tones to cease – *"He would ruin them all and himself as well!"* To which he answered, perhaps a little louder, "If I die for it, I must do it!" Then Cromwell snarled at him, as he tells us in his own narrative of what passed, asking him what ailed him, was he mad? "Canst thou not sit still and be quiet?" But Downes stood up and was heard by all, saying he would not consent to the sentence. Now it is typical of the moment and of the men that this capital matter, formal dissention in this jury, was not allowed to appear in the official record.

CHARLES I

Allow me a digression to point out how excellent an example this is of the value of tradition in history and the danger of the scientific and documentary method. Had there been only a tradition of Downes action, how the academic historian would have ridiculed that tradition! "Why," he would say, "Downes? Downes would have been the last man in the world to have done such a thing! The only evidence we have about him is the undoubted fact that he signed the Warrant for the King's being put to death!" That is true. Downes did sign the Warrant; for he was like scores of men, brave under excitement, cowardly under prolonged pressure. But what he did then was spontaneous; what he did when he signed was not. And the spontaneity of his action flashes a light upon what men were thinking at the time. For Downes later testified of how many there were who were with him, but who were afraid to speak as he had spoken.

The Court adjourned upon the incident; they were all gravely disturbed, and Cromwell most of all. The spirit of protest might spread. They withdrew to the Court of Wards; Downes gave his reasons; Cromwell sneered at him, and bullied him back to his way, called the interrupter peevish and tenacious, begged the Court not to waver, and used the strange word "duty." But, and this is characteristic of the man, Cromwell also whispered into Downes's ear familiarly while they were thus together, away from the sight of the populace during the adjournment. He told him that such pleading would only lead to a mutiny in the Army; it was no longer in the power of any man to save Charles's life, for if they (the Commissioners) faltered, the soldiers alone would murder the King.

This critical and most illuminating adjournment lasted only half an hour; Bradshaw and the judges returned (Downes was no longer with them) and the dialogue continued; the King still demanding to be heard. He required Bradshaw to give him leave as he would answer for it on the Day of Judgment, but Bradshaw said he must proceed to sentence.

"Then," said the King, "I have no more to say." But he told them that what he *had* said should of right be put on record.

Bradshaw then spoke at great length with much legal quotation of Latin, interrupted only by one short phrase or two, and after having wound up his long harangue with yet another of those wearisome

THE KILLING OF THE KING

repetitions which legal documents use to spin out expenses, he gave sentence. "The Court doth adjudge that the said Charles Stuart, as a tyrant, traitor, murderer and public enemy to the good people of this nation should be put to death by the severing of his head from his body." Three times the King demanded yet again to be heard, but they had privately decided not to run the risk of it after they had condemned him to death, and as he rose to go out at the end of the strain he was heard saying, "I am not suffered to speak – expect what justice other people will have!"

As he passed through the soldiery they cried as they had been ordered, "Justice!—Justice!" and "Execution!—Execution!" They blew tobacco smoke in the King's face while he was hurrying past them to a hackney closed chair in which he was to be carried back. In the street without, great crowds of the common people gave different cries, but the soldiers the same noise always, "shouting in triumph," of whom Charles said truly enough to those who heard him that "The poor men for sixpence would cry out in the same way against their own commanders!"

*****

They took the King to Whitehall. There he was given some respite, the guards were not thrust into his sleeping room. On the Sunday he was allowed to sit under his friend, the man who had been more than once his spiritual adviser, and who might almost be called his Confessor, Juxon, whom he had made Bishop of London. In the City certain ministers also preached against the Army, but it was of no effect. Peters, however, ran true to form, and in his sermon called loudly for the King's blood; and when he had done so, said that he had intended to say all those things before the King himself but that "the poor wretch would not hear him."

On Monday, the 29th, Charles was carried back again to St. James's, for they had begun setting up the scaffold, and it was not right that the King should hear that hammering. And to St. James's they brought him the two children who remained, for Charles, the heir, was safely overseas and so was the younger brother, the Duke of York, who was later to be James II. The two children now in the hands of the Army were Elizabeth and Henry, the girl thirteen years

CHARLES I

old, the little boy (whose title was Duke of Gloucester) ten. The sister had but a year to live, the brother survived to his majority at the Restoration, when he too died.

Charles told them to forgive his enemies, to obey their elder brother as their King; he tried to console the elder one, the Princess, by telling her that she would forget, meaning that the violence of the moment would soften with time. But in a passion of weeping she said she would never forget till she died – and that was to be soon. To the little boy, whom he had taken upon his knee, he explained carefully what he most dreaded from his enemies, that they would take the child and make him King. He must refuse, for they had no mercy and would kill his brother and him too, "therefore I charge you, do not be made King by them!" And the King's last moment of pleasure on earth was when the little boy answered, "I will be torn in pieces first!"

On that Monday at Westminster the Commissioners had before them the Death Warrant. Some had already signed, others had delayed as long as possible; it seems that some of those who had signed got leave to have their writing scratched out again, for fear and disgust were moving in many of them – but not in Cromwell. One of them did Cromwell seize by force, and, with some others helping him, held him down in the midst of hearty laughter and compelled him to sign. At last, what with bullying and intimidation for the hesitant, what with the concurrence of the bolder or the more sincere, they nearly got to sixty names – they got fifty-nine signatures. But after that, no more. Harvey, hardly pressed, refused. Wayte refused. But he heard Cromwell saying, "They shall set their hands! I will have their hands now!" There were other protests, other refusals; but at last, when they had got all they thought possible they called it sufficient and, the thing being over, Cromwell and Marten had a little horse-play together, dabbing each other's faces with ink from their pens.

So passed that last day.

*****

On the morning of Tuesday, the 30th of January, great crowds began to pour in by way of the fields and from the Strand into the open market-place of Charing Cross, and down through the funnel-shaped wide street which slightly narrowed at its southern end

THE KILLING OF THE KING

in front of the Banqueting Hall – all that now remains to us of the Palace.

At that southern end in those days stood a towered gateway with a broad arch for carriages to pass, and a lower arch at the side for people on foot; through this also up from Westminster came the crowds. They increased with the morning. Somewhat before ten o'clock the distant roll of drums was heard, and those on the roof tops looking back over the Park could see two long files of soldiery stretching all the way from St. James's Palace, and between them the little figure of the King walking briskly in the midst of the armed men who guarded him. Indeed, he had bade these walk more quickly. The weather was exceedingly cold, the sky grey with intervals of sunshine, and the frost so sharp that great blocks of ice floating on the Thames had jammed in the narrow arches of old London Bridge. But there was no storm, the air was still. The guard marched through by the space kept open, where a double regiment of horse stood in rank all round the scaffold several lines deep to overawe the people. As Charles passed by he passed in silence, save for the continuous roll of the drums.

Those dense crowds had long to wait in the bitter weather, nearly four hours. From roof tops and the higher windows it was possible to look down on the scaffold, but the thousands in the streets could not see it, for it was surrounded by a breast-high railing hung with black which concealed the block and the boards of the flooring. The mounted men around could not quite see over the railing, and to the crowds only the heads and shoulders of those upon it were visible.

At two o'clock there was a break in the clouds and a brilliant sun shone down upon all those uplifted faces, and upon the stage whereon Charles Stuart was to die. The populace could see figures passing rapidly behind the windows of the Banqueting Hall. They came the whole length of it, and out through a door which had been made by lowering a window at the extreme northern end. From that door it was a step round the corner pilaster of the building on to the scaffold itself, and thither, on this scaffold, rapidly gathered somewhat more than a dozen men. Among whom the King. In his hand was a paper, from which he read. Standing by among the rest, but near the block, were two masked men, dressed as sailors, and grotesque in huge false wigs. None save those close around could hear the words which

CHARLES I

Charles read from the writing in his hand, and when the reading was over he himself was no longer seen, when he knelt down, save by those on the higher parts of the houses opposite. For the black hangings hid from the onlookers in the street half the figures of those on the high scaffold floor.

For one second they saw the great axe lifted high in the sight of all, then flashing down, and the thud of the blow. One of those masked figures held up the severed head, and immediately there rose from the vast multitude an awful groan such as those who heard it had never thought to hear; and one of them prayed to God that he might never hear such a human sound again.

But the soldiery, having orders from those who feared so acutely the anger of the people, charged at once with vigour up towards Charing Cross market-place and down towards Westminster, clearing the streets of people, rushing and crushing men and women one against another, trampling them down with horses, and putting all into great fear of the Army.

*****

In a room of the Louvre in Paris the Queen of England still waited for news, and was given none. All those about her knew. It had come through at first as a rumour, then with precision and confirmed: but she had not been told. Paris was beleaguered, for the nobles were in revolt against the King (who was still but a child) and the Court was some miles off at St. Germains. She sent one of her gentlemen thither and bade that messenger go through the lines as best he could and return with whatever was certainly known among those at Court. She waited hour after hour, but the messenger did not return.

At last one of the Priests present, who knew all, said "Surely the news cannot be good or he would have returned," so preparing her. Then he told her all.

She sat mute, gazing before her at nothingness hour after hour, and none of her ladies dared invade that silence. So the better part of the day stretched on: fixed, and, as it were, timeless; with this woman still staring. Until one whom she loved, the Duchess of Vendôme entered full of tears, knelt at Henrietta Maria's feet and clasped her knees. The strain snapped, and the Queen wept loudly in the breaking of a storm.

Execution of Charles I at Whitehall
A PAINTING BY ERNEST CROFTS CA. 1900